£11.99
6c96

Trinity & All Saints

ACCREDITED BY THE UNIVERSITY OF LEEDS

LIS LIBRARY

This book is due for return on or before the last date
stamped below

ON DECONSTRUCTION

Theory and Criticism after Structuralism

JONATHAN CULLER

LONDON

First published in Great Britain in 1983

Reprinted in 1985 and 1987
by Routledge & Kegan Paul Ltd

Reprinted 1989, 1993, 1994
by Routledge
11 New Fetter Lane, London EC4P 4EE

Set in Linotron 202 Baskerville
and printed in Great Britain by
St Edmundsbury Press Ltd,
Bury St Edmunds, Suffolk

ISBN 0–415–04555–X

CONTENTS

PREFACE   7

INTRODUCTION   17

Chapter One. READERS AND READING   31
   1. New Fortunes   31
   2. Reading as a Woman   43
   3. Stories of Reading   64

Chapter Two. DECONSTRUCTION   85
   1. Writing and Logocentrism   89
   2. Meaning and Iterability   110
   3. Grafts and Graft   134
   4. Institutions and Inversions   156
   5. Critical Consequences   180

Chapter Three. DECONSTRUCTIVE CRITICISM   227

BIBLIOGRAPHY   281

INDEX   303

Author's Note

PORTIONS of Chapter Two, section 1, appeared in *Structuralism and Since*, ed. John Sturrock (Oxford: Oxford University Press, 1979), and a shorter version of Chapter Two, section 2, was published in *New Literary History*, 13 (1982).

References are given parenthetically in the text. Where two page numbers are separated by a slash, the first is the reference to the French text and the second to the English translation. Details of works cited are given in the bibliography. I have silently modified translations where it seemed appropriate.

PREFACE

THIS BOOK is a sequel to my *Structuralist Poetics*, though both the method and conclusions are different. *Structuralist Poetics* set out to survey comprehensively a body of critical and theoretical writings, to identify their most valuable proposals and achievements, and to introduce them to an English and American audience that had little interest in continental criticism. Today the situation has changed. Introductions have been performed and quarrels have broken out. To write about critical theory at the beginning of the 1980s is no longer to introduce unfamiliar questions, methods, and principles, but to intervene in a lively and confusing debate. The pages that follow provide an account of what I have found most vital and significant in recent theoretical writing and undertake an exposition of issues that often seem poorly understood.

One of these issues is the status of theoretical debate and of the genre of writing to which this book belongs. English and American critics often assume that literary theory is the servant to a servant: its purpose is to assist the critic, whose task is to serve literature by elucidating its masterpieces. The test of critical writing is its success in enhancing our appreciation of literary works, and the test of theoretical discussion is its success in providing instruments to help the critic provide better interpretations. "Criticism of criticism," as it is sometimes called, is placed at two removes from the object of concern and is thought useful when it helps to keep criticism on the proper track. This view is widespread. Wayne Booth, a man of considerable achievement in the realm of literary theory, finds it appropriate to apologize for what he does. "Who would really want to write a long book of what current jargon might well call meta-meta-meta-criticism?" he asks in the preface to a long work of literary theory. "But I see myself as having been forced into deeper and deeper waters simply by trying to face the situation of literature and criticism at the present time" (*Critical Understanding*, p. xii).

If critical theory is often seen as an attempt to establish the validity or invalidity of particular interpretive procedures, this view is doubtless the legacy of the New Criticism, which not only instilled the assumption that the purpose of literary study is the interpretation of literary works but also implied by its most memorable theoretical project—the effort to define and combat the intentional fallacy—that literary theory is the attempt to eliminate methodological errors so as to set interpretation on its proper course. Recently, though, there has been increasing evidence that literary theory should be conceived differently. Whatever their effects on interpretation, works of literary theory are closely and vitally related to other writings within a domain as yet unnamed but often called "theory" for short. This domain is not "literary theory," since many of its most interesting works do not explicitly address literature. It is not "philosophy" in the current sense of the term, since it includes Saussure, Marx, Freud, Erving Goffman, and Jacques Lacan, as well as Hegel, Nietzsche, and Hans-Georg Gadamer. It might be called "textual theory," if *text* is understood as "whatever is articulated by language," but the most convenient designation is simply the nickname "theory." The writings to which this term alludes do not find their justification in the improvement of interpretations, and they are a puzzling mixture. "Beginning in the days of Goethe and Macaulay and Carlyle and Emerson," writes Richard Rorty, "a kind of writing has developed which is neither the evaluation of the relative merits of literary productions, nor intellectual history, nor moral philosophy, nor epistemology, nor social prophecy, but all of these mingled together in a new genre" ("Professionalized Philosophy and Transcendentalist Culture," pp. 763–64).

This new genre is certainly heterogeneous. Its individual works are tied to other distinctive activities and discourses:

Gadamer to a particular strand of German philosophy, Goffman to empirical sociological research, Lacan to the practice of psychoanalysis. "Theory" is a genre because of the way its works function. The practitioners of particular disciplines complain that works claimed by the genre are studied outside the proper disciplinary matrix: students of theory read Freud without enquiring whether later psychological research may have disputed his formulations; they read Derrida without having mastered the philosophical tradition; they read Marx without studying alternative descriptions of political and economic situations. As instances of the genre of "theory," these works exceed the disciplinary framework within which they would normally be evaluated and which would help to identify their solid contributions to knowledge. To put it another way, what distinguishes the members of this genre is their ability to function not as demonstrations within the parameters of a discipline but as redescriptions that challenge disciplinary boundaries. The works we allude to as "theory" are those that have had the power to make strange the familiar and to make readers conceive of their own thinking, behavior, and institutions in new ways. Though they may rely on familiar techniques of demonstration and argument, their force comes—and this is what places them in the genre I am identifying—not from the accepted procedures of a particular discipline but from the persuasive novelty of their redescriptions.

In the development of this genre in recent years, Hegel, Marx, and Freud have eclipsed Macaulay and Carlyle, though Emerson and Goethe from time to time play honorable roles. There are no obvious limits to the subjects works of theory may treat. Recent books whose theoretical power may bring them into the genre include Michael Thompson's *Rubbish Theory*, Douglas Hofstader's *Gödel, Escher, Bach,* and Dean MacCannell's *The Tourist.* If this domain, which takes up the most original thinking of what the French call *les sciences humaines*, is sometimes called "critical theory," or even "literary theory," rather than "philosophy," this is owing to the recent historical roles of philosophy and literary criticism in England and America. Richard Rorty, himself an eminent analytical philosopher, writes, "I think that in England and America philosophy has already been displaced by literary criticism in its principal cultural function—as a source for youth's self-description of its own difference from the past. . . . This is roughly because of the Kantian and anti-historicist tenor of Anglo-Saxon philosophy. The cultural function of teachers of philosophy in countries where Hegel was not forgotten is quite different and closer to the position of literary critics in America" (*Philosophy and the Mirror of Nature*, p. 168).

Literary critics, who are more accustomed to accusations of irrelevance and parasitism than to the admiration of youths clamoring for descriptions of their difference from the past, may well be skeptical of this claim, and doubtless Rorty would be less swift to assert that criticism has displaced philosophy if he were a critic rather than a philosopher. One might suspect, for example, that for descriptions of its difference from the past youth turns to advertising and popular culture rather than to literary theory. There are, though, two indications that might support Rorty's claims. First, the frequency with which attacks on theoretically-oriented criticism condemn graduate students for mechanically imitating certain models, for taking on ideas they are too ignorant and immature to handle, and for rushing to adopt a spurious or faddish novelty, suggests that the threat of recent critical theory is linked to its specific appeal to the young. For its opponents, theory may be dangerous precisely because it threatens to play the role Rorty ascribes to it, as the source of intellectual youth's attempt to differentiate itself from the past. Second, it does seem true that recent European philosophy—Heidegger, the Frankfurt School, Sartre, Foucault, Derrida, Serres, Lyotard, Deleuze—has been imported to England and America by literary theorists rather than philosophers. In this sense, it is literary theorists who have done most to constitute the genre of "theory."

Moreover, whether or not the claims Rorty makes for criticism are justified, there are several reasons why it would not be inappropriate for literary theory to play a central role in the emerging genre of "theory." First, since literature takes as its subject all human experience, and particularly the ordering, interpreting, and articulating of experience, it is no accident that the most varied theoretical projects find instruction in literature and that their results are relevant to thinking about literature. Since literature analyzes the relations between men and women, or the most puzzling manifestations of the human psyche, or the effects of material conditions on individual experience, the theories that most powerfully and insightfully explore such matters will be of interest to literary critics and theorists. The comprehensiveness of literature makes it possible for any extraordinary or compelling theory to be drawn into literary theory.

Second, because of its exploration of the limits of intelligibility, literature invites or provokes theoretical discussions that draw in or draw upon the most general questions of rationality, of self-reflexivity, and of signification. The social and political theorist Alvin Gouldner defines rationality as "the capacity to make problematic what had hitherto been treated as given; to bring to reflection what before had only been used; to transform resource into topic; to examine critically the life we lead. This view of rationality situates it in the capacity to think *about* our thinking. Rationality as reflexivity about our groundings premises an ability to speak about our speech and the factors that ground it. Rationality is thus located in metacommunication" (*The Dialectic of Ideology and Technology*, p. 49). Given the ability of literary works to foreground what might previously have been taken for granted, including the language and categories through which we articulate our world, literary theory is inexorably caught up in problems of reflexivity and metacommunication, trying to theorize the exemplary self-reflexiveness of literature. Literary theory thus tends to bring into its orbit diverse speculations on the problems of framing, communication about communication, and other forms of *mise en abyme* or infinite regress.

Third, literary theorists may be particularly receptive to new theoretical developments in other fields because they lack the particular disciplinary commitments of workers in those fields. Though they have commitments of their own that will produce resistance to certain types of unusual thinking, they are able to welcome theories that challenge the assumptions of orthodox contemporary psychology, anthropology, psychoanalysis, philosophy, sociology, or historiography, and this makes theory— or literary theory—an arena of lively debate.

In these circumstances, the discussion of a decade's literary theory cannot be comprehensive—the range of theoretical writings drawn into literary theory is too vast. In taking deconstruction as my focus, I am suggesting not only that it has been the leading source of energy and innovation in recent theory but that it bears on the most important issues of literary theory. I devote much space to Jacques Derrida because I have found that many of his writings require and sustain exposition, which I hope readers will find valuable. These writings are not, of course, literary criticism or literary theory; but I might justify my focus by appealing to a self-styled historian of the critical scene, Frank Lentricchia, who writes:

> Sometime in the early 1970s we awoke from the dogmatic slumber of our phenomenological sleep to find that a new presence had taken absolute hold over our avant-garde critical imagination: Jacques Derrida. Somewhat startlingly, we learned that, despite a number of loose characterizations to the contrary, he brought not structuralism but something that would be called "post-structuralism." The shift to post-structuralist direction and polemic in the intellectual careers of Paul de Man, J. Hillis Miller, Geoffrey Hartman, Edward Said, and Joseph Riddel—all of whom were fascinated in the 1960s by strains of phenomenology—tells the whole story. [*After the New Criticism*, p. 159]

This is not, of course, the whole story—the straining prose is a symptom of the desire to make a history at all costs—but this mythification of Derrida as a new absolute presence suggests that one might use deconstruction to focus a number of problems: about structuralism and post-structuralism, poetics and interpretation, readers and critical metalanguages. Though writing about theory in the past decade, I have neglected many important figures—Roland Barthes, for example. In his case I can cite in mitigation an extensive discussion in another book, but for others I have no excuse and can only note that critics within the orbit of deconstruction may suffer the same neglect as those without.

Any discussion of contemporary critical theory must, however, confront the confusing and confused notion of post-structuralism, or more specifically, the relation of deconstruction to other critical movements. The Introduction approaches this question in one way, Chapter One in another. Structuralist, phenomenological, feminist, and psychoanalytic critics have concurred recently in emphasizing readers and reading, and analysis of problems that arise in these accounts of reading sets the stage for the discussion of deconstruction that occupies Chapter Two. I have not attempted a chronological or systematic survey of Derrida's writings but have drawn upon them in discussing a range of topics and their bearing on literary criticism and theory. In the course of this extended exposition, I have risked repetition for the sake of clarity and apologize to readers if I have miscalculated. Chapter Three analyzes a range of studies from the growing store of deconstructive literary criticism in order to identify its major features and axes of variation.

I am grateful to all those who have discussed these matters with me over the years or answered my questions about their writings. The issue of responsibility in situations of this sort is highly problematical, and readers will see that there can be no question of holding one Jacques Derrida responsible for the implications I draw from works he has signed. I would insist, however, that this book owes much to the advice of several Cornell colleagues, Laura Brown, Neil Hertz, Mary Jacobus, Richard Klein, Philip Lewis, and Mark Seltzer, but most of all Cynthia Chase, whose writings stimulated this work and whose readings corrected it. I thank the John Simon Guggenheim Foundation for a Fellowship during which this work was begun but not, alas, completed.

JONATHAN CULLER

Ithaca, New York

ON DECONSTRUCTION

INTRODUCTION

IF THE observers and belligerents of recent critical debates could agree on anything, it would be that contemporary critical theory is confusing and confused. Once upon a time it might have been possible to think of criticism as a single activity practiced with different emphases. The acrimony of recent debate suggests the contrary: the field of criticism is contentiously constituted by apparently incompatible activities. Even to attempt a list—structuralism, reader-response criticism, deconstruction, Marxist criticism, pluralism, feminist criticism, semiotics, psychoanalytic criticism, hermeneutics, antithetical criticism, *Rezeptionsästhetik* . . . —is to flirt with an unsettling glimpse of the infinite that Kant calls the "mathematical sublime." Contemplation of a chaos that threatens to overwhelm one's sensible powers may produce, as Kant suggests, a certain exultation, but most readers are only baffled or thwarted, not filled with awe.

Though it does not promise awe, this book seeks to contend with bafflement. Critical debate should stimulate, not stupefy, as it has often done of late. When even those well read in contemporary theory have difficulty determining what is important or where and how competing theories compete, one is challenged to attempt explanation, especially if explanation can also benefit the many students and teachers of literature who have neither the time nor the inclination to keep up with theoretical debate and who, without reliable guides, find themselves at a modern Bartholomew Fair, contemplating what seems to them a "blank confusion," of "differences / That have no law, no meaning, and no end."[1] This book attempts to dispel confusion, to furnish meanings and ends, by discussing what is at stake in today's critical debates and analyzing the most interesting and valuable projects of recent theory.

An initial source of confusion is the instability of key terms, whose scope varies with the level of specificity of critical discussion and the contrasts or differences at work at that level. The term *structuralism* is an instructive example. A commentator analyzing an essay by Roland Barthes might distinguish its specifically structuralist moves from its other procedures, thus drawing upon and contributing to a highly restricted notion of structuralism. A critic of broader ambitions, trying to describe the fundamental procedures of modern thought, might, on the other hand, contrast the "structuralism" of twentieth-century thinking with an earlier "essentialism," making us all structuralists today, whatever our claims. A plausible defense of each use of the term could be mounted, since the distinctions that are crucial at one level fade away at another; but if the functioning of *structuralism* aptly illustrates the structural determination of meaning that structuralism purports to describe, the results are still confusing for anyone who hopes that the term will serve as a convenient and reliable label. Vincent Descombes's *Le Même et l'autre*, a powerful account of French philosophy from 1933 to 1978, scrupulously explores distinctions until it makes Michel Serres the only real structuralist (pp. 96–111). For other commentators structuralism includes not just recent French thought but all theoretically-inclined criticism: William Phillips, in a discussion of contemporary criticism organized for his journal, the *Partisan Review*, designates by the term *structuralism* the panoply of recent critical and theoretical writings that refuse to espouse the traditional project of elucidating an author's message and evaluating his achievement ("The State of Criticism," p. 374). What are we to make of this shift in terminology?

It would be easy to dismiss such broad usage as uninformed

---

[1] William Wordsworth, *The Prelude* (1850), Book vii, lines 722 & 727–28. For a shrewd discussion of the relation of chaos and blockage to the critic's situation, see Neil Hertz, "The Notion of Blockage in the Literature of the Sublime." Full bibliographical information for this and subsequent references is given in the bibliography. Henceforth references will be given parenthetically in the text.

lumping together of what should be distinguished. When someone speaks of critics such as Roland Barthes, Harold Bloom, John Brenkman, Shoshana Felman, Stanley Fish, Geoffrey Hartman, Julia Kristeva, and Wolfgang Iser as structuralists all, one can respond by showing that they use diverse methods, work from opposing assumptions, announce different goals, and emerge from incompatible traditions. The more we know of critical theory the more interest we are likely to take in accurate discriminations, and the more we will smile with disdain at the ignorance of those who, in reducing criticism to a simple moral scenario, abandon all pretense of discernment. The restaurateur who tells us that he has two kinds of wine, red and white, does not impress us as a connoisseur.

To describe all theoretically-oriented critics as structuralists is generally a sign of ignorance, yet in this use of *structuralism* there is an implicit assertion that might be defended—defended at this first level of generality. The claim would be that the articulation of literary study upon various theoretical enterprises produces a change of greater moment than do the displacements of one theory by another, and that the nature of this change is related to central aspects of structuralism. Those who use *structuralism* in this broad way do not actually argue for this claim; they generally contrast structuralism with a humanistic criticism—a generalized version of the New Criticism—that relies on common sense and shared values in interpreting literary works as aesthetic achievements which speak to us about familiar human concerns. The most common complaints about structuralism seem to be, first, that it uses concepts from other disciplines—linguistics, philosophy, anthropology, psychoanalysis, Marxism—to dominate literature, and, second, that it threatens the very *raison d'être* of literary studies by forgoing the attempt to discover the true meaning of a work and by deeming all interpretations equally valid.

The relation between these two objections to structuralism is not clear; they might even be thought contradictory, since one would expect a critic attempting to dominate literature—say, through psychoanalysis—to assert the priority of psychoanalytic interpretations. The very difficulty of reconciling these complaints suggests that we need to look beyond our assumptions about literature and criticism to understand the forces at work here and to grasp the connection between the use of various theoretical discourses and an undercutting of criticism's traditional interpretive project. The distinctiveness of an inclusive "structuralism" does not in fact lie in its cosmopolitan theoretical interests. The New Criticism, with which it is often contrasted, was by no means antitheoretical or provincial, as the discussions in René Wellek and Austin Warren's *Theory of Literature* show. What distinguishes this inclusive structuralism may perhaps emerge in the connection, often concealed in critical discussion, between the deployment of theoretical categories and the threat to the traditional program of elucidating the meaning of an aesthetic object. The interpretive projects of the New Criticism were linked to the preservation of aesthetic autonomy and the defense of literary studies against encroachment by various sciences. If, in attempting to describe the literary work, "structuralist" criticism deploys various theoretical discourses, encouraging a kind of scientific encroachment, then critical attention comes to focus not on a thematic content that the work aesthetically presents but on the conditions of signification, the different sorts of structures and processes involved in the production of meaning. Even when structuralists engage in interpretation, their attempt to analyze the structure of the work and the forces on which it depends leads to concentration on the relation between the work and its enabling conditions and undermines, as the opponents of structuralism seem to sense, the traditional interpretive project.

This happens in two ways, apparently quite different but, in the eyes of structuralism's opponents, similarly misguided. On the one hand, a structuralism like Barthes's, Todorov's, or Genette's, that remains preeminently literary in its references, is accused of formalism: of neglecting the thematic content of a work in order to concentrate on its playful, parodic, or disruptive relation to literary forms, codes, and conventions. On the other hand, critics who employ categories from psychoanalytic, Marxist, philosophical, or anthropological theory are accused not of formalism but of preemptive or biased reading: of neglecting the distinctive themes of a work in order to find in it manifestations of a structure or system prescribed by their discipline. Both sorts of structuralists are engaged, for similar reasons, in something other than traditional humanistic interpretation.

If *structuralism* seems an appropriate cover term for a range of critical activities that draw upon theoretical discourses and neglect to pursue the "true" meaning of the works they study, it is doubtless because structuralism in a more narrow sense, with its deployment of the linguistic model, is the most decisive instance of this critical reorientation. The categories and methods of linguistics, whether applied directly to the language of literature or used as the model for a poetics, enable critics to focus not on the meaning of a work and its implications or value but on the structures that produce meaning. Even when linguistics is explicitly enlisted in the service of interpretation, the fundamental orientation of the discipline, which does not devise new interpretations for sentences but attempts to describe the system of norms that determine the form and meaning of linguistic sequences, works to focus attention on structures and to identify meaning and reference not as the source or truth of a work but as effects of the play of language. The plausibility of treating, say, Barthes, Bloom, Girard, Deleuze, Felman, and Serres as structuralists lies in the sense that their writings turn aside in different ways from the explication and appreciation of an achieved meaning to an investigation of a text's relation to particular structures and processes, be they linguistic, psychoanalytic, metaphysical, logical, sociological, or rhetorical. Languages and structures, rather than authorial self or consciousness, become the major source of explanation.

The division of literary studies into an old but persistent New Criticism and a new structuralism could be defended by arguments such as these, but those who make this distinction— generally the opponents of a broad, menacing structuralism— are not well served by it, for they find it hard to mount a consistent and pertinent critique at this level of generality. Their charges are varied and specific. Some fault structuralism for its scientific pretensions: its diagrams, taxonomies, or neologisms, and its general claim to master and account for elusive products of the human spirit. Others charge it with irrationalism: a self-indulgent love of paradox and bizarre interpretations, a taste for linguistic play, and a narcissistic relation to its own rhetoric. To some, structuralism means rigidity: a mechanical extraction of certain patterns or themes, a method that makes every work mean the same thing. To others it seems to allow the work to mean anything whatsoever, either by asserting the indeterminacy of meaning or by defining meaning as the experience of the reader. Some see structuralism as the destruction of criticism as a discipline; others find that it abusively glorifies the critic, setting critic above author and suggesting that mastery of a body of difficult theory is the precondition of any serious engagement with literature.

Science or irrationalism, rigidity or permissiveness, destruction of criticism or inflation of criticism—the possibility of such contradictory charges might suggest that the primary quality of "structuralism" is an indeterminate radical force: it is perceived as extreme, as violating previous assumptions about literature and criticism, though there is disagreement about precisely how it does so. But these contradictory charges also indicate that the opponents of structuralism have different works in mind and that to clarify these issues we must move to another level of specificity.

At this second level, perhaps more important in critical debate than the first, the crucial distinction is not between an inclusive structuralism and traditional criticism but between structuralism and "post-structuralism," as it is often called. Derrida, in Lentricchia's words, brought not structuralism but post-structuralism (see above, p. 12). By this contrast, structuralism becomes a series of systematic, scientific projects—semiotics, the successor to structuralism in this sense, is generally defined as the "science" of signs—and structuralism's opponents are various post-structuralist critiques of these projects or explorations of their ultimate impossibility. In simplest terms, structuralists take linguistics as a model and attempt to develop "grammars" —systematic inventories of elements and their possibilities of combination—that would account for the form and meaning of literary works; post-structuralists investigate the way in which this project is subverted by the workings of the texts themselves. Structuralists are convinced that systematic knowledge is possible; post-structuralists claim to know only the impossibility of this knowledge.

A detailed version of this distinction, interesting for the complex issues it introduces, was proposed in 1976 by J. Hillis Miller, champion of a version of American post-structuralism. "A distinctive feature of English and American literary criticism today," he begins, "is its progressive naturalization, ap-

propriation, or accommodation of recent continental criticism."
To speak of all such criticism as "structuralism," however, is to
neglect a major division.

> Already a clear distinction can be drawn, among critics influ-
> enced by these new developments, between what might be called
> . . . Socratic, theoretical, or canny critics, on the one hand, and
> Apollonian/Dionysian, tragic, or uncanny critics, on the other.
> Socratic critics are those who are lulled by the promise of a ra-
> tional ordering of literary study on the basis of solid advances in
> scientific knowledge about language. They are likely to speak of
> themselves as "scientists" and to group their collective enterprise
> under some term like "the human sciences." . . . Such an enter-
> prise is represented by the discipline called "semiotics," or by
> new work in the exploration and exploitation of rhetorical terms.
> Included would be aspects of the work of Gérard Genette, Roland
> Barthes, and Roman Jakobson. . . .
> For the most part these critics share the Socratic penchant, what
> Nietzsche defined as "the unshakable faith that thought, using the
> thread of logic, can penetrate the deepest abysses of being." . . .
> The inheritors today of the Socratic faith would believe in the
> possibility of a structuralist-inspired criticism as a rational and
> rationalizable activity, with agreed-upon rules of procedure, given
> facts, and measurable results. This would be a discipline bringing
> literature out into the sunlight in a "happy positivism.". . .
> Opposed to these are the critics who might be called "uncanny."
> Though they have been inspired by the same climate of thought
> as the Socratic critics and though their work would also be impos-
> sible without modern linguistics, the "feel" or atmosphere of their
> writing is quite different. . . .
> These critics are not tragic or Dionysian in the sense that their
> work is wildly orgiastic or irrational. No critic could be more rig-
> orously sane and rational, Apollonian, in his procedure, for ex-
> ample, than Paul de Man. One feature of Derrida's criticism is a
> patient and minutely philological "explication de texte." Never-
> theless, the thread of logic leads in both cases into regions which
> are alogical, absurd. . . . Sooner or later there is the encounter
> with an "aporia" or impasse. . . . In fact the moment when logic
> fails in their work is the moment of their deepest penetration into
> the actual nature of literary language, or of language as such.
> ["Stevens' Rock and Criticism as Cure, II," pp. 335–38]

To distinguish structuralism from post-structuralism in these
terms suggests a complicated relationship, for the canny and

the uncanny are not simple opposites. A successful uncanny critic may well be as shrewd as her canny counterpart, and though the uncanny is a violation of order, the unsettling mystery of an uncanny moment in literature or in criticism is the manifestation of a hidden order. "The uncanny," writes Freud, "is that class of the frightening which leads back to what is known of old and long familiar"; "the frightening element can be shown to be something repressed which *recurs*" ("The Uncanny," vol. 17, pp. 220, 241). The uncanny is not simply weird or bizarre but suggests deeper laws, and Miller's formulations certainly imply the superiority of the uncanny to the canny: uncanny post-structuralism arrives to waken canny structuralism from the dogmatic slumbers into which it was lulled by its "unshakable faith" in thought and "the promise of a rational ordering." Is deconstruction in fact an undoing of delusion? What is the relationship between a deconstruction and what it deconstructs? Is post-structuralism a refutation of structuralism? Observers often assume that if post-structuralism has succeeded structuralism it must have refuted it, or at least transcended it: *post hoc ergo ultra hoc*. Miller's account moves toward this view, but the opposition between the *canny* and the *uncanny* resists it, for the uncanny is neither a refutation of nor a replacement for the canny.

Nevertheless, structuralism and post-structuralism are clearly distinguished for Miller by the test of faith. Both canny and uncanny critics rigorously pursue a logical enquiry, but the uncanny, who have no faith in logic, are rewarded with "deep penetration" into the nature of language and literature, while the canny critics with their unshakable faith in thought are rebuffed. Without raising the novel questions this perspective invites—does Roland Barthes have more faith in reason than Paul de Man?—one can note that the canny insights achieved by the uncanny of little faith make this story above all a parable of pride. Theorists swollen with scientific ambition are outstripped by patient explicators, who are alert to the perverse, aporetical moments of the texts they are studying. Though Miller's terms do not claim that either side has a monopoly on truth, order, or shrewdness, they enable him to divide recent criticism into two camps on the basis of confidence in systematic thought: structuralists and semioticians optimistically elaborate theoretical metalanguages to account for textual phenomena; post-structuralists skeptically explore the paradoxes that arise in the pursuit of such projects and stress that their own work is not science but more text.

The issues raised by this division figure prominently in discussions of literary theory today, but a number of problems arise when one tries to map contemporary theory according to this scheme. First, as one might expect, one has some difficulty deciding which theorists belong to which camp. A recent anthology of post-structuralist criticism, edited by Josué Harari, a young critic who cannot be convicted of ignorance, is composed primarily of writings by thinkers who had been featured in the editor's earlier bibliography of structuralism: Roland Barthes, Gilles Deleuze, Eugenio Donato, Michel Foucault, Gérard Genette, René Girard, Louis Marin, Michael Riffaterre, and Michel Serres. Harari's articulation of the field makes Claude Lévi-Strauss and Tzvetan Todorov the only true structuralists, since everyone else has become post-structuralist. Of course, radical transformations and conversions do occur, but when so many of yesterday's structuralists are today's post-structuralists, doubts arise about the distinction, especially since it is so dubiously defined. If post-structuralism is supposed to be the vigilant critique of prior delusions of mastery, it is difficult to find writings by structuralists that are sufficiently unself-conscious to fit this pattern. As Philip Lewis writes in the best study of this problem, "reading the work of pioneer structuralists such as Lévi-Strauss and Barthes does not really show us that structuralism, as it aged, gradually became aware of its own limitations and problems, but rather that an acute self-critical awareness was there from the start and reinforced the scientific spirit of the structuralist enterprise" ("The Post-Structuralist Condition," p. 8). Enterprises now deemed post-structuralist, such as critiques of the sign, of representation, and of the subject, were manifestly already under way in the structuralist writings of the 1960s.

Nor are our doubts about the distinction allayed when we look at individual cases. Is Roland Barthes a structuralist or a post-structuralist? Is he a structuralist who recanted and became a post-structuralist? If so, where does the change occur? Barthes's 1967 semiological study of fashion, *Système de la mode*, and his 1966 program for a structural analysis of narrative, "Introduction à l'analyse structurale des récits," are the works which would most clearly identify him as an orthodox structuralist; but writings that precede these by several years, such as the important preface to his 1964 collection, *Essais critiques,* prevent one from locating a radical change after 1967. And Barthes's best-known work in the field of criticism, *S/Z,* is very difficult to classify, not because it avoids the issues on which a distinction between structuralism and post-structuralism is generally based but because it seems to adopt both modes with a vengeance, as though unaware that they are supposed to be radically different movements. *S/Z* displays a powerful metalinguistic drive: it seeks to break the literary work down into its constituents, naming and classifying in a rationalist or scientific spirit; it identifies and describes the various codes on which the classical, readable text is based and explores at length the conventions of this mode of writing. It tries to elucidate the operations by which readers make sense of novels, making astute and pertinent contributions to a poetics of fiction. Yet at the same time, *S/Z* opens with what Barthes and others have regarded as a renunciation of the structuralist project: Barthes insists that rather than treat the text as the product or manifestation of an underlying system, he will explore its difference from itself, the way in which it outplays the codes on which it seems to rely. The fact that *S/Z* owes its power and interest to the combination of modes which supposedly belong to opposing schools suggests that we treat this opposition with caution and may serve to remind us that from the very beginning structuralist attempts to describe the conventions of literary discourse were linked to an exploration of the ways in which the most interesting works foreground, parody, and violate those conventions. In Barthes's *Essais critiques,* for example, the most powerful impulse toward a poetics is provided by the radical innovations of the *nouveau roman.* "Post-structuralist" interests seem intertwined with Barthes's structuralism from the start.

Similar problems arise when we turn to Jacques Lacan. Proclaimed a structuralist in the heyday of structuralism, explicit in his use of Saussure and Jakobson and in his claim that the unconscious is structured like a language, Lacan nevertheless became a post-structuralist eminence, undermining through his style the certainties to which he lays claim, rejecting the canny critic's "unshakable faith" in reason, but nevertheless presuming to "penetrate the deepest abysses of being."[2] The opposition between structuralism and post-structuralism merely complicates the attempt to understand such major figures.

Although the conflict between the rational and the irrational, between the attempt to establish distinctions and the attempt to subvert them, or between the quest for knowledge and the questioning of knowledge is a powerful factor in contemporary critical theory, these oppositions do not, finally, provide reliable distinctions between critical schools. One notes, for example, that Miller praises his uncanny critics for a canny achievement: their penetrating insight into the nature of literary language or textuality. Not only is the moment when logic fails

---

[2]For an incisive discussion, see Jacques Derrida's "Le Facteur de la vérité" in *La Carte postale*. Lacan's attraction for many critics and theorists lies in the fact that, beyond the complexities and uncertainties of his prose, his assertions promise a truth, the truth of the subject, a truth that is not simply a true reading of a text but the truth of the human psyche and human desire: in short, a penetration of the deepest abysses of being. Barbara Johnson, in a subtle response that places Derrida and Lacan in a complex transferential relation, argues that Derrida's critique applies decisively to Lacan *as he is read*—the Lacan who is read as the sibylline source of truth—but that the evasiveness of Lacan's writing makes Derrida's critique (with its transferral of guilt from a certain reading of Lacan onto Lacan's text) something of a frame-up (*The Critical Difference*, pp. 125–26). We find here, in the relation between a text and a reading of that text that Johnson analyzes, a pattern of considerable importance and generality which leads some interpreters to speak of all readings as misreadings (see pp. 175–79). For the moment we might simply note by way of illustration that Hillis Miller's critique of structuralism seems to be based not so much on the texts of Barthes and his colleagues as on a *reading* or interpretation of structuralism: specifically the systematizing presentation of structuralism in my *Structuralist Poetics*. At the moment when Miller first draws the contrast between the uncanny critics and the canny critics previously described, he writes, in a sentence of which a portion was quoted above, "though they have been inspired by the same climate of thought as the Socratic critics and though their work would also be impossible without modern linguistics, the 'feel' or atmosphere of their writing is quite different from that of a critic like Culler, with his brisk common sense and his reassuring notions of 'literary competence' and the acquisition of 'conventions,' his hope that all right-thinking people might agree on the meaning of a lyric or a novel, or at any rate share a 'universe of discourse' in which they could talk about it" ("Stevens' Rock and Criticism as Cure, II," p. 336). Whether or not this is an apt characterization of the mode of *Structuralist Poetics*, it helps to illustrate the way in which critiques rely on a reading of what is criticized, just as a critique of uncanny criticism might rely on Miller's own systematizing and hence canny presentation of it.

in their work "the moment of their deepest penetration into the actual nature of literary language, or of language as such," but "it is also the place where Socratic procedures will ultimately lead, if they are carried far enough" ("Stevens' Rock and Criticism as Cure, II," p. 338). Both approaches can produce the same insights. Derrida's reading of Saussure, to be discussed in Chapter Two, achieves insights into the nature of language, but they are also insights produced by Saussure's canny investigation of language. Derrida, it could be said, is pursuing with the greatest possible rigor the structuralist principle that in the linguistic system there are only differences, without positive terms. Derrida reads this insight in Saussure, as de Man reads insights in Proust, Rilke, Nietzsche, and Rousseau, or as Miller finds his uncanny knowledge already elaborated in Stevens, George Eliot, or Shakespeare. As Miller notes at the conclusion of his essay, "the most uncanny moment of all, however, in this developing polarity among critics today, is the moment when the apparent opposites reverse themselves, the Socratic becoming uncanny, the uncanny canny, sometimes all too shrewdly rational" (p. 343). This possibility of reversal, which we shall find to be more common than we might have expected, preserves a distinction between the canny and the uncanny, or between confident rationality and skepticism, but prevents it from serving as a test of critical affiliation or a basis of classification.

The continual reference in critical debate to a distinction between structuralism and post-structuralism has several unfortunate effects. First, the terms of the opposition assimilate all interest in what resists intelligibility or outplays convention to post-structuralism, leaving us with a blind and programmatic structuralism. By the same token, to define deconstruction and other versions of post-structuralism by contrasting them with the systematic projects of structuralism is to treat them as celebrations of the irrational and the unsystematic. If defined in opposition to "scientific" structuralism, deconstruction can be labeled "Derridadaism"—a witty gesture by which Geoffrey Hartman blots out Derridean argument (*Saving the Text*, p. 33). In another framework, deconstruction would have other contours.

Third, the opposition between structuralism and post-structuralism works to suggest that the diverse writings of recent
theory constitute a post-structuralist movement. Thus, theo-
retically-minded critics such as Harold Bloom and René Girard
are treated as post-structuralists since they seem not to be structuralists. Bloom is celebrated by Miller and others as a member
of the "Yale School" and was the moving spirit behind its collection of essays, *Deconstruction and Criticism,* yet his work explicitly attempts that most nondeconstructive of tasks, the development of a psychological model for describing the genesis
of poems, and he explicitly takes issue with deconstruction by
insisting on the primacy of the will: the will of strong poets
locked in battle with their titanic precursors. Though a skilled
interpreter might reveal important affinities between Bloom
and Derrida or de Man, Bloom strives mightily to set his work
against theirs, insisting that the human subject is a ground or
source rather than an effect of textuality: "the human writes,
the human thinks, and always following after and defending
against another human" (*A Map of Misreading,* p. 60). To define
recent criticism as post-structuralist is to obscure issues such as
this.

René Girard is associated with post-structuralism partly because of his French background and partly because of the tex-
tualism of his early account of mimetic desire. His important
book on the novel, *Deceit, Desire, and the Novel,* analyzes desire
as imitation of another's represented desire. But it is difficult to
imagine a theorist more at odds with post-structuralism than
the Girard of later years, who defines himself as a scientist
seeking to demonstrate that culture and institutions originate
in real, specific acts of violence against arbitrarily chosen scapegoats. Literary works are ritual repetitions of original events
of victimization that culture conceals but whose traces can be
studied in its writings. In developing and extending his powerful anthropological hypothesis, Girard has become a religious
thinker, for whom the Christian revelation, with its authentic,
divine sacrificial victim, offers the only escape from the violence of mimetic desire. The hostility to numerous post-structuralist concerns, quite marked in Girard's own account of his
work, is obscured by a framework that urges one to deem him

either a structuralist or a post-structuralist.[3] A scrupulous discussion of criticism focusing on the difference between structuralism and post-structuralism would have to conclude that structuralists generally resemble post-structuralists more closely than many post-structuralists resemble one another.

Finally, attention to this distinction hampers one's investigation of other issues and movements. In mapping contemporary criticism as a struggle between New Critics, structuralists, and then post-structuralists, one would find it hard to do justice to feminist criticism, which has had a greater effect on the literary canon than any other critical movement and which has arguably been one of the most powerful forces of renovation in contemporary criticism. Though numerous post-structuralists are feminists (and vice versa), feminist criticism is not post-structuralist, especially if post-structuralism is defined by its opposition to structuralism. To discuss feminist criticism adequately, one would need a different framework where the notion of post-structuralism was a product rather than a given.

In short, though the most common articulations of recent criticism raise a number of important problems—about the relationship between literature and the theoretical languages of other disciplines, about the possibility and status of a systematic theory of language or of texts—the distinction between structuralism and post-structuralism is highly unreliable, and instead of mounting a discussion of post-structuralism within which deconstruction would be identified as a major force, it seems preferable to try another approach, which may permit a richer and more pertinent array of connections. Since most contemporary criticism has something to say about reading, this topic may offer a better way of establishing a context for a discussion of deconstruction.

[3]For discussion of Girard's work, see Philippe Lacoue-Labarthe, "Typographie."

Chapter One

READERS AND READING

1. NEW FORTUNES

ROLAND BARTHES opens *Le Plaisir du texte* by asking us to imagine a bizarre creature who has rid himself of the fear of self-contradiction, who mixes reputedly incompatible languages and patiently endures charges of illogicality. The rules of our institutions, Barthes writes, would make such a person an outcast. Who, after all, can live in contradiction without shame? "Yet this anti-hero exists: he is the reader of texts at the moment when he takes his pleasure" (p. 10/3). Other critics and theorists have disagreed about the character of the reader, celebrating her freedom or his consistency, making her a hero rather than anti-hero, but they have concurred in casting the reader in a central role, both in theoretical discussion of literature and criticism and in interpretations of literary works. If, as Barthes claims, "the birth of the reader must be at the cost of the death of the author," many have been willing to pay that price (*Image, Music, Text*, p. 148).

Even critics who find the price exorbitant and resist what they consider dangerous trends in contemporary criticism seem inclined to join in the study of readers and reading. Witness some recent titles: Wayne Booth's *Critical Understanding*, Walter Davis's *The Act of Interpretation*. E. D. Hirsch's *The Aims of Interpretation*, John Reichert's *Making Sense of Literature*, Geoffrey Strickland's *Structuralism or Criticism: Some Thoughts on How We Read*. These theorists for whom criticism is essentially an elucidation of an author's purposes have felt compelled to provide their own accounts of reading so as to challenge those that make the reader an anti-hero, a fall guy, an unabashed hedonist, a prisoner of an identity theme or of an unconscious, or a willful inventor of meanings. Seeking to eliminate such nonsense with, as Reichert puts it, a criticism that "cuts through the plethora of competing critical languages to recover and re-dignify the simple procedures of reading, understanding, and assessing," they have thrown themselves into the critical competition for the rights to "the reader" (*Making Sense of Literature*, p. x). If, as Barthes says, the reader can live in contradiction without shame, this is doubtless a good thing, for on this disputed figure converge the contradictory claims and descriptions of current critical debate. "*Reader* and *audience*," writes Susan Suleiman, introducing a reader-centered anthology, "once relegated to the status of the unproblematic and the obvious, have acceded to a starring role" (*The Reader in the Text*, p. 3). Why should this be?

One reason for interest in readers and reading is the orientation encouraged by structuralism and semiotics. The attempt to describe structures and codes responsible for the production of meaning focuses attention on the reading process and its conditions of possibility. A structuralist poetics or *science de la littérature*, Barthes writes, "will not teach us what meaning must definitively be attributed to a work; it will not provide or even discover a meaning but will describe the logic according to which meanings are engendered" (*Critique et vérité*, p. 63). Taking the intelligibility of the work as its point of departure, a poetics would try to account for the ways in which the work has been understood by readers, and basic concepts of this poetics, such as Barthes's distinction between the *lisible* and the *scriptible*, would refer to reading: the *lisible* is that which accords with the codes and which we know how to read, the *scriptible* that which resists reading and can only be written.

A structuralist pursuit of codes leads critics to treat the work as an intertextual construct—a product of various cultural discourses on which it relies for its intelligibility—and thus consolidates the central role of the reader as a centering role. "We now know," writes Barthes with that assurance that comes upon some writers in Paris, "that the text is not a line of words releasing a single 'theological' meaning (the 'message' of an Author-God) but a multi-dimensional space in which a variety of writings, none of them original, blend and clash. The text is a tissue of quotations drawn from the innumerable centers of culture." But, he continues, "there is one place where this multiplicity is focused and that place is the reader, not, as was hitherto said, the author. The reader is the space on which all the quotations that make up a writing are inscribed. . . . A text's unity lies not in its origin but in its destination" (*Image, Music, Text*, pp. 146, 148). To be sure, emphasis falls on the reader as a function rather than as a person, as the *destinataire* or place where the codes on which the unity and intelligibility of the text depends are said to be inscribed. This dissolution of the reader into codes is a critique of the phenomenological account of reading; but even if the reader is conceived as the product of codes—a product whose subjectivity, Barthes writes, is an assemblage of stereotypes—this would still make possible a differentiation of stereotypes, as in Barthes's typology of "pleasures of reading or readers of pleasure," which "links the reading neurosis to the hallucinated form of the text" and distinguishes four readers or reading pleasures: the fetishist, the obsessional, the paranoiac, and the hysteric (*Le Plaisir du texte*, p. 99/63).

Discrimination of readers might be a fruitful line of research —or speculation—but is seldom pursued by structuralists themselves, who focus on the codes and conventions responsible for the work's *lisibilité* or intelligibility. In *S/Z* Barthes describes reading as a process of relating elements of the text to five codes, each of which is a series of stereotyped models and "perspective of citations," "the wake of what has always already been read, seen, done, lived" (pp. 27–28/20). In a later essay, "Analyse textuelle d'un conte d'Edgar Poe," he increases the number of codes by dividing what he had previously called "the cultural code"; and doubtless further additions are necessary. Michael Riffaterre argues in his *Semiotics of Poetry* that codes of poetic stereotypes serve as the basis for the production of poetic texts and that recognizing the transformations of these codes is a decisive moment in reading. One must also add to the list a code generally neglected in *S/Z* but extensively studied in other contributions to poetics: the code of narration, which enables readers to construe the text as the communication of a narrator to a narrative audience or *narratee*.

Work on the audience of narration, an important branch of the poetics of reading, investigates what discriminations are necessary to account for narrative effects. The narratee, defined by Gerald Prince as someone a narrator addresses, must be distinguished from the ideal reader an author might imagine (who would appreciate and admire every word and device of the work) and from what Wolfgang Iser calls "the implied reader," a textual structure incorporating "those predispositions necessary for the literary work to exercise its effect" (Prince, "Introduction à l'étude du narrataire," p. 178/7; Iser, *The Act of Reading*, p. 34). Peter Rabinowitz, in a series of excellent discussions, distinguishes four audiences: the actual audience, the authorial audience (which takes the work as a fictional communication from an author), the narrative audience (which takes the work as a communication from the narrator), and an ideal narrative audience (which interprets the narrator's communication as the narrator appears to wish). "Thus, in John Barth's *End of the Road* the authorial audience knows that Jacob Horner [the narrator and principal character] has never existed; the narrative audience believes he has existed but does not entirely accept his analyses; and the ideal narrative audience accepts uncritically what he has to say" ("Truth in Fiction: A Reexamination of Audiences," p. 134).

Two things should be emphasized here. First, one proposes these distinctions in order to account for what happens in reading: Rabinowitz is particularly interested in radical disagreements about Nabokov's *Pale Fire*, which can be traced to disagreements about what the narrative audience and authorial audience are supposed to believe. Second, these "audiences" are in fact roles that readers posit and partially assume in reading. Someone who reads Swift's "A Modest Proposal" as a masterpiece of irony first postulates an audience that the narrator appears to think he is addressing: an audience entertaining specific assumptions, inclined to formulate certain objections, but likely to find the narrator's arguments cogent and compelling. The second role the reader postulates is that of an audience attending to a serious proposal for relieving famine in Ireland but finding the values and assumptions of the proposal (and of the "ideal narrative audience") singularly skewed. Finally, the reader participates in an audience that reads the work not as a narrator's proposal but as an author's ingenious construction, and appreciates its power and skill. Actual readers will combine the roles of authorial, narrative, and even ideal narrative audiences in varying proportions—without embarrassment living in contradiction. One ought perhaps to avoid speaking of "the implied reader" as a single role that the reader is called upon to play, since the reader's pleasure may well come, as Barthes says, from the interaction of contradictory engagements.

Focus on the conventions and operations of reading leads critics to treat literary works as a succession of actions on the understanding of the reader. An interpretation of a work thus comes to be an account of what happens to the reader: how various conventions and expectations are brought in to play, where particular connections or hypotheses are posited, how expectations are defeated or confirmed. To speak of the meaning of the work is to tell a story of reading. This is to some extent the mode of Barthes's *S/Z* but is more pronounced in works such as Stanley Fish's *Surprised by Sin: The Reader in Paradise Lost*, Wolfgang Iser's *The Implied Reader*, Stephen Booth's *An Essay on Shakespeare's Sonnets*, Michael Riffaterre's *Semiotics of Poetry*, and my *Flaubert: The Uses of Uncertainty*.[1] Each of these critical accounts describes the reader's attempt to bring to bear on the text the codes and conventions deemed relevant and the text's resistance to or compliance with particular interpretive operations. The structure and meaning of the work emerge through an account of the reader's activity.

This use of the reader and reading is not, of course, new. Long before Barthes, the response of the reader was often essential to accounts of literary structure. In Aristotle's *Poetics* the reader's or spectator's experience of pity and terror, at

---

[1]Though some of these works are treated briefly in this chapter, the problems they raise are discussed at greater length in my book *The Pursuit of Signs: Semiotics, Literature, Deconstruction*. See chapter 3 for a general account of "Semiotics as a Theory of Reading," chapter 4 for Riffaterre, and chapter 6 for Fish. Structuralist accounts of reading are discussed in part II of my *Structuralist Poetics* and Roland Barthes's contribution is assessed in my *Barthes*.

certain moments and under certain conditions, is what makes possible an account of tragic plots: the types of tragic plot are correlated with differences in effects on the reader. In Renaissance criticism too, as Bernard Weinberg notes, the qualities of a poem were to be sought through a study of its effects upon an audience.[2]

Even the New Critics of our own day, now reviled for banning talk of readers as an instance of the affective fallacy ("confusion of what a poem *is* with what it *does*"), often show considerable interest in what a poem does when they describe its dramatic structure or praise the complex balance of attitudes it produces. The moments when New Critics do specifically acknowledge the role of the reader suggest a connection between reader-oriented criticism and modernism. In "Poetry since *The Waste Land*" Cleanth Brooks argues that a basic technique of modernist poetry is the deployment of unanalyzed juxtapositions, where "the interconnections are left to the reader's imagination." In *The Waste Land* Eliot declines to develop the implications of a juxtaposition of scenes but "has thrown this burden upon the reader himself, demanding that he relate the two scenes in his own imagination." Once this modernist technique is identified, the critic can recognize its importance in earlier poems: Wordsworth's Lucy poems, Brooks notes, "reveal gaps in logic that the reader is forced to cross with a leap of the imagination—they hint at analogies that cry out to be completed—and yet which can only be completed by the reader himself" (*A Shaping Joy*, p. 58).

Criticism must acknowledge the role of the reader when literary works, in Henry James's phrase, "once more and yet once more glory in a gap" (*Selected Literary Criticism*, p. 332). But such acknowledgment does not basically alter the role that notions of reader and audience have played in descriptions of literary structure. When discussing many modernist works, one can stress the activity of the reader while treating it as the accomplishment of a determinate task: the reader must "work out for

---

[2]*A History of Literary Criticism in the Italian Renaissance* (Chicago: University of Chicago Press, 1961), vol. 2, p. 806, quoted by Jane Tompkins in her valuable essay, "The Reader in History: The Changing Shape of Literary Response," p. 207. Tompkins points out that classical and Renaissance criticism was interested in the impact on an audience rather than meaning for an audience.

himself" the relation between two images, must complete analogies that "cry out to be completed," or must piece together from disparate clues what must "really" have happened, bringing to the surface a pattern or design that the work conceals. This is the general role that Roman Ingarden and Wolfgang Iser have assigned the reader: to fill in gaps, to render concrete and determinate the *Unbestimmtheitsstellen* or places of indeterminacy of a work.[5]

If the activity of the reader has recently become decisive for criticism, it may be because some works—those Umberto Eco describes in *L'Opera aperta* as "open works"—provoke a general revaluation of the status of reading by inviting the reader or performer to play a more fundamental role as constructor of the work. Music provides striking examples, such as Pierre Boulez's *Third Sonata for Piano*, whose first section consists of ten different pieces on ten sheets of music paper that can be arranged in various sequences (Eco, *The Role of the Reader*, p. 48). Works presented as a series of components that readers or performers put together in different ways often seem rather obvious experiments, whose primary interest may well lie in their impact on notions of art and of reading. By foregrounding reading as writing—as construction of the text—they provide a new model of reading that can describe the reading of other texts as well. One can maintain, for example, that to read *Finnegans Wake* is not so much to recognize or work out for oneself connections inscribed in the text as to produce a text: through the associations followed up and the connections established, each reader constructs a different text. In the case of more traditional works, this model invites one to account for resemblances among readers' productions by investigating the productive influence of textual codes and institutionalized conventions. In this perspective, other accounts of reading—reading as recognizing a meaning or a pattern—are not eliminated but become particular and limited cases of reading as production. Although, as we shall see later, there are disadvantages to

---

[5]See Ingarden, *The Cognition of the Literary Work of Art* and *The Literary Work of Art*, and Iser's "The Reading Process: A Phenomenological Approach," in *The Implied Reader*, or his full-length study, *The Act of Reading*. For discussion see Henryk Markiewicz, "Places of Indeterminacy in a Literary Work," Stanley Fish, "Why No One's Afraid of Wolfgang Iser," and Iser's "Interview."

the view of reader as producer, theorists such as Booth, Hirsch, and Reichert, who combat this view of reading, in fact offer proposals that can be inscribed within it, as rules for particular, restricted sorts of rewriting.

In this perspective where, as Barthes says, "the stakes of literary work (of literature as work) are to make the reader no longer the consumer but the producer of the text," variations in readers' construction are no longer regarded as accidents but treated as normal effects of the activity of reading (*S/Z*, p. 10/4). This has implications even for critics who reject notions of readers constructing texts, for emphasis on the variability of reading and its dependence on conventional procedures makes it easier to raise political and ideological issues. If the reader always rewrites the text and if the attempt to reconstruct an author's intentions is only a particular, highly restricted case of rewriting, then a Marxist reading, for example, is not an illegitimate distortion, but one species of production. This revised conception of the status of reading may thus subtend criticism that takes no interest in the avant-garde texts that provide the leverage for the change in perspective.

Contemporary literature also encourages concentration on the reader because many of the difficulties and discontinuities of recent works become amenable to critical discussion only when the reader serves as protagonist. To analyze one of John Ashbery's poems is first of all to describe the reader's difficulties in making sense. In France interest in the reader seems to have arisen at the moment when it became impossible to discuss the *nouveau roman* as a purely objective, nonanthropocentric presentation of reality. The problematizing of plot and character in works such as Robbe-Grillet's *Le Voyeur* and *Dans le labyrinthe* encouraged critics to locate the force and interest of these novels in their violent engagement with the conventional novelistic expectations of readers and their disruption of habitual processes of sense-making. Outside the French tradition we find further evidence that analysis of difficult modern works requires reference to readers and reading. To take just one example, Veronica Forrest-Thomson's energetic and inventive *Poetic Artifice: A Theory of Twentieth-Century Poetry* displays no interest in the behavior of individual readers. Concerned with poems as artifice or artifact, and with what they mean, Forrest-

Thomson describes two processes, "external expansion and limitation" and "internal expansion and limitation," by which difficult modern poems produce effects of pastoral and parody. But to explain these effects and to show how formal features block certain kinds of thematic synthesis, one has to describe reading: readers, accustomed by novels to interpreting details by expanding them into an external world (and thus limiting the formal features that can be deemed functional) find this process checked by formal patterns—the only apparent forces of cohesion in many of these poems—and in exploiting these formal patterns they establish internal relationships that limit movement toward an external world and produce a critique of language. Such poetry works, as Barthes puts it in *Essais critiques*, "to unexpress the expressible" (p. 15/xvii). Its significance lies in the reader's struggle with the disordering orders of language.

The structuralist emphasis on literary codes, the constructive role forced upon readers by certain experimental fictions, and the need to find ways to talk about the most refractory contemporary works have all contributed to a change in the reader's role, but one should not overlook an aspect of that change that is easily ignored. For the rhetoricians of antiquity and the Renaissance, and for many critics of other times, a poem is a composition designed to produce an effect on readers, to move them in certain ways; and one's judgment of a poem depends on one's sense of the quality and intensity of its effect. To describe this impact is not, though, to give what we would today regard as an interpretation, as Jane Tompkins points out ("The Reader in History," pp. 202–9). The experiences or responses that modern reader-oriented critics invoke are generally cognitive rather than affective: not feeling shivers along the spine, weeping in sympathy, or being transported with awe, but having one's expectations proved false, struggling with an irresolvable ambiguity, or questioning the assumptions on which one had relied. In attacking the affective fallacy, Stanley Fish insists that "in the category of response I include not only 'tears, prickles,' and 'other psychological symptoms'" that Wimsatt and Beardsley's fallacy sets aside, "but all the precise mental operations involved in reading, including the formulation of complete thoughts, the performing (and regretting) of acts of judgment, the following and making of logical sequences" (*Is There a Text in This Class?*, pp. 42–43). In fact, Fish never mentions tears or prickles; his reader-response criticism treats the reader's encounter with literature as an experience of interpretation.

If the reader's experience is an experience of interpretation, then one is better placed to make the further claim that the experience *is* the meaning. "It is the experience of an utterance," Fish writes,"—*all* of it and not anything that could be said about it, including anything I could say—that is its meaning" (p. 32). The temporal experience of reading is not simply a way of coming to know a work, as someone studying Notre Dame cathedral inspects first one part and then another, but a series of events that are as important as the conclusions the reader may achieve. To interpret a work you must ask what it does and to answer that question, says Fish, you must analyze "the developing responses of the reader in relation to the words as they succeed one another in time" (p. 27). Even in his seventeenth-century examples Fish stresses the experience, familiar to the reader of modernist literature, of being checked and thwarted in the quest for meaning. When the reader encounters Milton's line "Nor did they not perceive the evil plight," the experience the syntax momentarily offers, of being suspended between alternatives, is as important to the meaning of the line as the conclusion that they did perhaps perceive their plight (pp. 25–26). Nor are conjectures that prove mistaken to be eliminated: "they have been experienced; they have existed in the mental life of the reader; they *mean*" (p. 48).

Other critics are less forthright in their appeal to what is present in the reader's mental life, but reader-oriented criticism relies heavily on notions of the reader's experience, referring to what *the* or *a* reader finds, feels, wonders, conjectures, or concludes to justify its accounts of the meaning and structure of literary works. A question therefore arises about the nature of the reader and of this experience.

Fish answers that "the reader of whose responses I speak" is a complex figure, an "informed reader, neither an abstraction, nor an actual living reader, but a hybrid—a real reader (me) who does everything within his power to make himself informed," including "the attendant suppressing, in so far as that is possible, of what is personal and idiosyncratic and 1970ish in my response." "Each of us," he continues democratically, "if we are sufficiently responsible and self-conscious, can, in the course of applying the method, become the informed reader" (p. 49).

This passage reveals a curious structure: a doubling of the notion of experience or a division within the notion. On the one hand, experience is a given to which one appeals; on the other hand, the experience one proposes to use is to be produced by particular operations—here the acquisition of knowledge and the suppression of idiosyncrasies. The relations between the knowledge, beliefs, and experiences of persons and those of the informed reader is somewhat unclear, but to the question of whether an informed Catholic or atheist could be as "fit" a reader of Milton as a Protestant believer, Fish answers, "No. There are some beliefs that cannot be momentarily suspended or assumed" (p. 50). More extensive consideration of how readers might relate to persons can be found in Walter Slatoff's *With Respect to Readers*. Urging us to remember that literature requires the active, personal involvement of readers, Slatoff objects to

> the tendency of most aestheticians and critics to speak as though there were only two sorts of readers: the absolutely particular, individual human being with all his prejudices, idiosyncrasies, personal history, knowledge, needs, and anxieties, who experiences the work of art in solely "personal" terms, and the ideal or universal reader whose response is impersonal and aesthetic. Most actual readers, except for the most naive, I think, transform themselves as they read into beings somewhere between these extremes. They learn, that is, to set aside many of the particular conditions, concerns and idiosyncrasies which help to define them in everyday affairs. [P. 54]

They learn, that is to say, to have a certain kind of experience, to become, as they read, a reader who can have that experience. In his own case, for example, "the reading self is by no means an ideal or impersonal entity. He is mostly over 35 and under 50, has experienced war, marriage, and the responsibility of children, belongs in part to some kind of minority group, is male and not female, and shares most of Slatoff's general ways of thinking and feeling" (p. 55). If the experience of literature depends upon the qualities of a reading self, one can ask what difference it would make to the experience of literature and thus to the meaning of literature if this self were, for example, female rather than male. If the meaning of a work is the experience of a reader, what difference does it make if the reader is a woman?

This question proves an excellent way of addressing the problems raised by criticism's emphasis on the reading experience, first because the question of the woman reader poses concretely and politically the problem of the relation of the experience of the reader when reading to other sorts of experiences, and second because issues often swept under the carpet by male stories of reading are brought into the open in the debates and divisions of feminist criticism.

Though one of the most significant and broadly-based critical movements of recent years, feminist criticism is often ignored by self-styled historians of criticism and critical theory.[4] Whether or not it displays striking philosophical affiliations, feminist criticism addresses theoretical questions in concrete and pertinent ways. Its impact on the reading and teaching of literature and on the composition of the literary canon is in part due to its emphasis on the notion of the reader and her experience. It has a considerable stake in the question of the relation of the reading self and the experience of the reader to other moments of the self and other aspects of experience, for

[1]Frank Lentricchia's *After the New Criticism* claims to be, among other things, "a historical account of what has happened here since the American New Critics passed out of favor," specifically of the period 1957–77, but does not so much as mention feminist criticism. One speculates that this is because feminist criticism, in its specifically political orientations, does what Lentricchia condemns others for failing to do and would thus expose, if he addressed it, the dubiousness of his own critical ideal: a Foucauldian literary criticism that would advance the proletarian revolution and provide solid historical knowledge while avoiding all the problems and paradoxes analyzed by deconstruction. The example of feminist criticism suggests that politically successful criticism may be immensely heterogeneous and epistemologically problematical. Whatever the explanation, Lentricchia's decision to ignore feminist criticism while devoting an entire chapter to "Versions of Phenomenology" (Georges Poulet and J. Hillis Miller) casts doubt upon his claim to historical understanding and his authority to criticize others for their lack of it. For a judicious critique of other aspects of *After the New Criticism*, see Andrew Parker's telling discussion, "Taking Sides (On History): Derrida Re-Marx."

the arguments that are advanced about the significance being a woman has or could have in reading bear also on analogous questions about its significance in other activities. If feminist criticism has no single or simple answer to the question of the nature of the reading experience and its relation to other experience, it is because it takes it seriously and explores it in ways that bring out the complexity of the question and of the notion of "experience." We can follow these explorations at three levels or moments of feminist criticism.

2. READING AS A WOMAN

Suppose the informed reader of a work of literature is a woman. Might this not make a difference, for example, to "the reader's experience" of the opening chapter of *The Mayor of Casterbridge*, where the drunken Michael Henchard sells his wife and infant daughter to a sailor for five guineas at a country fair? Citing this example, Elaine Showalter quotes Irving Howe's celebration of Hardy's opening:

> To shake loose from one's wife; to discard that drooping rag of a woman, with her mute complaints and maddening passivity; to escape not by slinking abandonment but through the public sale of her body to a stranger, as horses are sold at a fair; and thus to wrest, through sheer amoral wilfulness, a second chance out of life—it is with this stroke, so insidiously attractive to male fantasy, that *The Mayor of Casterbridge* begins.

The male fantasy that finds this scene attractive may also be at work transforming Susan Henchard into a "drooping rag," passive and complaining—a portrait scarcely sustained by the text. Howe goes on to argue that in appealing to "the depths of common fantasy," the scene draws us into complicity with Henchard. Showalter comments:

> In speaking of "our common fantasies," he quietly transforms the novel into a male document. A woman's experience of this scene must be very different; indeed, there were many sensation novels of the 1870s and 1880s which presented the sale of women into marriage from the point of view of the bought wife. In Howe's

reading, Hardy's novel becomes a kind of sensation-fiction, playing on the suppressed longings of its male audience, evoking sympathy for Henchard because of his crime, not in spite of it. ["The Unmanning of the Mayor of Casterbridge," pp. 102–3]

Howe is certainly not alone in assuming that "the reader" is male. "Much reading," writes Geoffrey Hartman in *The Fate of Reading*, "is indeed like girl-watching, a simple expense of spirit" (p. 248). The experience of reading seems to be that of a man (a heart-man?) for whom girl-watching is the model of an expense of spirit in a waste of shame.[5] When we posit a woman reader, the result is an analogous appeal to experience: not to the experience of girl-watching but to the experience of being watched, seen as a "girl," restricted, marginalized. A recent anthology that stresses the continuity between women's experience and the experience of women reading is appropriately entitled *The Authority of Experience: Essays in Feminist Criticism.* One contributor, Maurianne Adams, explains:

> Now that the burden of trying to pretend to a totally objective and value-free perspective has finally been lifted from our shoulders, we can all admit, in the simplest possible terms, that our literary insights and perceptions come, in part at least, from our sensitivity to the nuances of our own lives and our observations of other people's lives. Every time we rethink and reassimilate *Jane Eyre*, we bring to it a new orientation. For women critics, this orientation is likely not to focus particular attention upon the dilemmas of the male, to whom male critics have already shown themselves understandably sensitive, but rather on Jane herself and her particular circumstances. ["*Jane Eyre*: Woman's Estate," pp. 140–41]

"Rereading *Jane Eyre*," she notes, "I am led inevitably to feminist issues, by which I mean the status and economics of female dependence in marriage, the limited options available to Jane as an outlet for her education and energies, her need to love and to be loved, to be of service and to be needed. These

[5]This alerts one to the remarkable scenario of Hartman's recent criticism. *The Fate of Reading* offers this prognostic: most reading is like girl-watching, doubtless "perjur'd, murderous, bloody, full of blame." The cure is a period of *Criticism in the Wilderness*, after which, chastened and purified, criticism can turn to *Saving the Text*—saving it, it turns out, from a frivolous, seductive, and "self-involved" deconstruction that ignores the sacred.

aspirations, the ambivalence expressed by the narrator toward them, and the conflicts among them, are all issues raised by the novel itself" (p. 140).

An unusual version of this appeal to women's experience is an essay in the same collection by Dawn Lander that explores the literary commonplace that "the frontier is no place for a woman," that women hate the primitive conditions, the absence of civilization, but must stoically endure them. Lander reports that her own experience as a woman living in the desert made her question this cliché and seek out what frontier women had written about their lives, only to discover that her "own feelings about the wilderness were duplicated in the experience of historic and contemporary women" ("Eve among the Indians," p. 197). Appealing to the authority first of her own experience and then of others' experiences, she reads the myth of women's hatred of the frontier as an attempt by men to make the frontier an escape from everything women represent to them: an escape from renunciation to a paradise of male camaraderie where sexuality can be an aggressive, forbidden commerce with nonwhite women. Here the experience of women provides leverage for exposing this literary topos as a self-serving male view of the female view.

Women's experience, many feminist critics claim, will lead them to value works differently from their male counterparts, who may regard the problems women characteristically encounter as of limited interest. An eminent male critic, commenting on *The Bostonians*, observes that "the doctrinaire demand for equality of the sexes may well seem to promise but a wry and constricted story, a tale of mere eccentricity" (Lionel Trilling, *The Opposing Self*, p. 109). This is no doubt what Virginia Woolf calls "the difference of view, the difference of standard" (*Collected Essays*, vol. 1, p. 204). Responding to a male critic who had patronizingly reproached her for trying to "aggrandize [Charlotte] Gilman's interesting but minor story" of incarceration and madness, "The Yellow Wallpaper," by comparing it with Poe's "The Pit and the Pendulum," Annette Kolodny notes that while she finds it as skillfully crafted and tightly composed as anything in Poe, other considerations doubtless take precedence when judging whether it is "minor" or not: "what may be entering into *my* responses is the fact that, as

a female reader, I find the story a chillingly symbolic evoca-
tion of realities which women daily encounter even in our own
time" ("Reply to Commentaries," p. 589). Conviction that their
experience as women is a source of authority for their responses as readers has encouraged feminist critics in their revaluation of celebrated and neglected works.

In this first moment of feminist criticism, the concept of a
woman reader leads to the assertion of continuity between
women's experience of social and familial structures and their
experience as readers. Criticism founded on this postulate of
continuity takes considerable interest in the situations and psychology of female characters, investigating attitudes to women
or the "images of women" in the works of an author, a genre,
or a period. In attending to female characters in Shakespeare,
the editors of a critical anthology observe, feminist critics are
"compensating for the bias in a critical tradition that has tended
to emphasize male characters, male themes, and male fantasies"
and drawing attention instead to the complexity of women
characters and their place in the order of male values represented in the plays (Lenz et al., *The Woman's Part*, p. 4). Such
criticism is resolutely thematic—focused on woman as a theme
in literary works—and resolute too in its appeal to the literary
and nonliterary experience of readers.

> Feminist criticism of Shakespeare begins with an individual reader,
> usually, although not necessarily, a female reader—a student,
> teacher, actor—who brings to the plays her own experience, con-
> cerns, questions. Such readers trust their responses to Shake-
> speare even when they raise questions that challenge prevailing
> critical assumptions. Conclusions derived from these questions are
> then tested rigorously against the text, its myriad contexts, and
> the explorations of other critics. [P. 3]

Criticism based on the presumption of continuity between the
reader's experience and a woman's experience and on a concern with images of women is likely to become most forceful as
a critique of the phallocentric assumptions that govern literary
works. This feminist critique is by now a familiar genre, authoritatively established by such works as Simone de Beauvoir's
The Second Sex, which, while indicting familiar ways of thinking

about women, provides readings of the myths of women in Montherlant, Lawrence, Claudel, Breton, and Stendhal. A similar enterprise, in which a woman reader responds critically to the visions embodied in the literature celebrated by her culture, is Kate Millett's *Sexual Politics*, which analyzes the sexual visions or ideologies of Lawrence, Miller, Mailer, and Genet. If these discussions seem exaggerated or crude, as they have seemed to male critics who find it hard to defend the sexual politics of the writers they may have admired, it is because by posing the question of the relation between sex and power and assembling relevant passages from Lawrence, Miller, and Mailer, one displays in all their crudity the aggressive phallic visions of three "counterrevolutionary sexual politicians" (p. 233). (Genet, by contrast, subjects the code of male and female roles to withering scrutiny.)

Millett's strategy in reading as a woman is "to take an author's ideas seriously when, like the novelists covered in this study, they wish to be taken seriously," and to confront them directly. "Critics who disagree with Lawrence, for example, about any issue are fond of saying that his prose is awkward. . . . It strikes me as better to make a radical investigation which can demonstrate why Lawrence's analysis of a situation is inadequate, or biased, or his influence pernicious, without ever needing to imply that he is less than a great and original artist" (p. xii).

Instead of playing down, as critics are wont to do, those works whose sexual vision is most elaborately developed, Millett pursues Lawrence's sexual religion to an apotheosis where sexuality is separated from sex: the priests of "The Women Who Rode Away" are "supernatural males, who are 'beyond sex' in a pious fervor of male supremacy that disdains any genital contact with woman, preferring instead to deal with her by means of a knife." This pure or ultimate maleness is, Lawrence says, "something primevally male and cruel" (p. 290). Miller's sexual ethos is much more conventional: "his most original contribution to sexual attitudes is confined to giving the first full expression to an ancient sentiment of contempt": he has "given voice to certain sentiments which masculine culture had long experienced but always rather carefully suppressed" (pp. 309, 313). As for Mailer, his defense of Miller against Millett's cri-

tique confirms Millett's analysis of Mailer himself, as "a prisoner of the virility cult" "whose powerful intellectual compre-
hension of what is most dangerous in the masculine sensibility
is exceeded only by his attachment to the malaise" (p. 314).
Here is Mailer restating, in Miller's defense, their male ideology:

> For he captured something in the sexuality of men as it had never
> been seen before, precisely that it was man's sense of awe before
> woman, his dread of her position one step closer to eternity (for
> in that step were her powers) which made men detest women,
> revile them, humiliate them, defecate symbolically on them, do
> everything to reduce them so one might dare to enter them and
> take pleasure of them. . . . Men look to destroy every quality in a
> woman which will give her the powers of a male, for she is in their
> eyes already armed with the power that she brought them forth,
> and that is a power beyond measure—the earliest etchings of
> memory go back to that woman between whose legs they were
> conceived, nurtured, and near strangled in the hours of birth.
> [*The Prisoner of Sex*, p. 116]

How does a woman read such authors? A feminist criticism
confronts the problem of women as the consumer of male-
produced literature.

Millett also offers, in an earlier chapter, brief discussions of
other works: *Jude the Obscure, The Egoist, Villette,* and Wilde's
Salomé. Analyzing these reactions to the sexual revolution of
the nineteenth century, she establishes a feminist response that
has served as a point of departure for debates within feminist
criticism—disagreements about whether, for example, despite
his sensitive portrait of Sue Bridehead, Hardy is ultimately
"troubled and confused" when it comes to the sexual revolution.[6] But the possibility of quarreling with Millett to develop
more subtle feminist readings should not obscure the main
point. As Carolyn Heilbrun puts it,

> Millett has undertaken a task which I find particularly worth-
> while: the consideration of certain events or works of literature

[6]See, for example, an early rejoinder by Mary Jacobus, who argues that what
Millett calls Hardy's "confusion" is in fact "careful non-alignment": "through
Sue's obscurity he probes the relationship between character and idea in such a
way as to leave one's mind engaged with her as it is engaged with few women in
fiction" ("Sue the Obscure," pp. 305, 325).

from an unexpected, even startling point of view. . . . Her aim is
to wrench the reader from the vantage point he has long oc-
cupied, and force him to look at life and letters from a new coign.
Hers is not meant to be the last word on any writer, but a wholly
new word, little heard before and strange. For the first time we
have been asked to look at literature as women; we, men, women
and Ph.D's, have always read it as men. Who cannot point to a
certain overemphasis in the way Millett reads Lawrence or Stalin
or Euripides. What matter? We are rooted in our vantage point
and require transplanting. ["Millett's *Sexual Politics*: A Year Later,"
p. 39]

As Heilbrun suggests, reading as a woman is not necessarily
what occurs when a woman reads: women can read, and have
read, as men. Feminist readings are not produced by recording
what happens in the mental life of a female reader as she
encounters the words of *The Mayor of Casterbridge*, though they
do rely heavily on the notion of the experience of the woman
reader. Shoshana Felman asks, "Is it enough to be a woman in
order to speak as a woman? Is 'speaking as a woman' determined by some biological condition or by a strategic, theoretical
position, by anatomy or by culture?" ("Women and Madness:
The Critical Phallacy," p. 3). The same question applies to
"reading as a woman."

To ask a woman to read as a woman is in fact a double or
divided request. It appeals to the condition of being a woman
as if it were a given and simultaneously urges that this condition be created or achieved. Reading as a woman is not simply,
as Felman's disjunctions might seem to imply, a theoretical position, for it appeals to a sexual identity defined as essential and
privileges experiences associated with that identity. Even the
most sophisticated theorists make this appeal—to a condition or
experience deemed more basic than the theoretical position
it is used to justify. "As a female reader, I am haunted rather
by another question," writes Gayatri Spivak, adducing her sex
as the ground for a question ("Finding Feminist Readings," p.
82). Even the most radical French theorists, who would deny
any positive or distinctive identity to woman and see *le feminin*
as any force that disrupts the symbolic structures of Western
thought, always have moments, in developing a theoretical position, when they speak as women, when they rely on the fact

that they *are* women. Feminist critics are fond of quoting Virginia Woolf's remark that women's "inheritance," what they are given, is "the difference of view, the difference of standard"; but the question then becomes, what is the difference? It is never given as such but must be produced. Difference is produced by differing. Despite the decisive and necessary appeal to the authority of women's experience and of a female reader's experience, feminist criticism is in fact concerned, as Elaine Showalter astutely puts it, "with the way in which the *hypothesis* of a female reader changes our apprehension of a given text, awakening us to the significance of its sexual codes" ("Towards a Feminist Poetics," p. 25, my italics).[7]

Showalter's notion of the *hypothesis* of a female reader marks the double or divided structure of "experience" in reader-oriented criticism. Much male response criticism conceals this structure—in which experience is posited as a given yet deferred as something to be achieved—by asserting that readers simply do in fact have a certain experience. This structure emerges explicitly in a good deal of feminist criticism which takes up the problem that women do not always read or have not always read as women: they have been alienated from an experience appropriate to their condition as women.[8] With the shift to the

[7]Feminist criticism is, of course, concerned with other issues as well, particularly the distinctiveness of women's writing and the achievements of women writers. The problems of reading as a woman and of writing as a woman are in many respects similar, but concentration on the latter leads feminist criticism into areas that do not concern me here, such as the establishment of a criticism focused on women writers that parallels criticism focused on male writers. Gynocriticism, says Showalter, who has been one of the principal advocates of this activity, is concerned "with woman as the producer of textual meaning, with the history, themes, genres, and structures of literature by women. Its subjects include the psychodynamics of female creativity; linguistics and the problem of a female language; the trajectory of the individual or collective female literary career; literary history; and, of course, studies of particular writers and works" ("Towards a Feminist Poetics," p. 25). For work of this kind, see Sandra Gilbert and Susan Gubar, *The Madwoman in the Attic*, and the collection edited by Sally McConnell-Ginet, Ruth Borker, and Nelly Furman, *Women and Language in Literature and Society* (New York: Praeger, 1980).

[8]The analogy with social class is instructive: progressive political writing appeals to the proletariat's experience of oppression, but usually the problem for a political movement is precisely that the members of a class do not have the experience their situation would warrant. The most insidious oppression alienates a group from its own interests as a group and encourages it to identify with the interests of the oppressors, so that political struggles must first awaken a group to its interests and its "experience."

hypothesis of a female reader, we move to a second moment or level of feminist criticism's dealings with the reader. In the first moment, criticism appeals to experience as a given that can ground or justify a reading. At the second level the problem is precisely that women have not been reading as women. "What is crucial here," writes Kolodny, "is that reading is a *learned* activity which, like many other learned interpretive strategies in our society, is inevitably sex-coded and gender-inflected" ("Reply to Commentaries," p. 588). Women "are expected to identify," writes Showalter, "with a masculine experience and perspective, which is presented as the human one" ("Women and the Literary Curriculum," p. 856). They have been constituted as subjects by discourses that have not identified or promoted the possibility of reading "as a woman." In its second moment, feminist criticism undertakes, through the postulate of a woman reader, to bring about a new experience of reading and to make readers—men and women—question the literary and political assumptions on which their reading has been based.

In feminist criticism of the first sort, women readers identify with the concerns of women characters; in the second case, the problem is precisely that women are led to identify with male characters, against their own interests as women. Judith Fetterly, in a book on the woman reader and American fiction, argues that "the major works of American fiction constitute a series of designs upon the female reader." Most of this literature "insists on its universality at the same time that it defines that universality in specifically male terms" (*The Resisting Reader*, p. xii). One of the founding works of American literature, for instance, is "The Legend of Sleepy Hollow." The figure of Rip Van Winkle, writes Leslie Fiedler, "presides over the birth of the American imagination; and it is fitting that our first successful homegrown legend should memorialize, however playfully, the flight of the dreamer from the shrew" (*Love and Death in the American Novel*, p. xx). It is fitting because, ever since then, novels seen as archetypally American—investigating or articulating a distinctively American experience—have rung the changes on this basic schema, in which the protagonist struggles against constricting, civilizing, oppressive forces embodied by woman. The typical protagonist, continues Fiedler, the protagonist seen as embodying the universal American dream, has been "a man on the run, harried into the forest and out to sea, down the river or into combat—anywhere to avoid 'civilization,' which is to say, the confrontation of a man and a woman which leads to the fall to sex, marriage, and responsibility."

Confronting such plots, the woman reader, like other readers, is powerfully impelled by the structure of the novel to identify with a hero who makes woman the enemy. In "The Legend of Sleepy Hollow," where Dame Van Winkle represents everything one might wish to escape and Rip the success of a fantasy, Fetterly argues that "what is essentially a simple act of identification when the reader of the story is male becomes a tangle of contradictions when the reader is female" (*The Resisting Reader*, p. 9). "In such fictions the female reader is co-opted into participation in an experience from which she is explicitly excluded; she is asked to identify with a selfhood that defines itself in opposition to her; she is required to identify against herself" (p. xii).

One should emphasize that Fetterly is not objecting to unflattering literary representations of women but to the way in which the dramatic structure of these stories induces women to participate in a vision of woman as the obstacle to freedom. Catherine in *A Farewell to Arms* is an appealing character, but her role is clear: her death prevents Frederic Henry from coming to feel the burdens she fears she imposes, while consolidating his investment in an idyllic love and in his vision of himself as a "victim of cosmic antagonism" (p. xvi). "If we weep at the end of the book," Fetterly concludes, "it is not for Catherine but for Frederic Henry. All our tears are ultimately for men, because in the world of *A Farewell to Arms* male life is what counts. And the message to women reading this classic love story and experiencing its image of the female ideal is clear and simple: the only good woman is a dead one, and even then there are questions" (p. 71). Whether or not the message is quite this simple, it is certainly true that the reader must adopt the perspective of Frederic Henry to enjoy the pathos of the ending.

Fetterly's account of the predicament of the woman reader—seduced and betrayed by devious male texts—is an attempt to change reading: "Feminist criticism is a political act whose aim is not simply to interpret the world but to change it by changing the consciousness of those who read and their relation to what they read" (p. viii). The first act of a feminist critic is "to become a resisting rather than an assenting reader and, by this refusal to assent, to begin the process of exorcizing the male mind that has been implanted in us" (p. xxii).

This is part of a broader struggle. Fetterly's account of the woman reader's predicament is powerfully confirmed by Dorothy Dinnerstein's analysis of the effects, on women as well as men, of human nurturing arrangements. "Woman, who introduced us to the human situation and who at the beginning seemed to us responsible for every drawback of that situation, carries for all of us a pre-rational onus of ultimately culpable responsibility forever after" (*The Mermaid and the Minotaur*, p. 234). Babies of both sexes are generally nurtured at first by the mother, on whom they are completely dependent. "The initial experience of dependence on a largely uncontrollable outside source of good is focused on a woman, and so is the earliest experience of vulnerability to disappointment and pain" (p. 28). The result is a powerful resentment of this dependency and a compensatory tendency to identify with male figures, who are perceived as distinct and independent. "Even to the daughter, the mother may never come to seem so completely an 'I' as the father, who was an 'I' when first encountered" (p. 107). This perception of the mother affects her perception of all women, including herself, and encourages her "to preserve her 'I' ness by thinking of men, not women, as her real fellow creatures"—and to become engaged as a reader in plots of escape from women and domination of women (p. 107). What feminists ignore or deny at their peril, warns Dinnerstein, "is that women share men's anti-female feelings—usually in a mitigated form, but deeply nevertheless. This fact stems partly, to be sure, from causes that other writers have already quite adequately spelled out: that we have been steeped in self-derogatory societal stereotypes, pitted against each other for the favors of the reigning sex, and so on. But it stems largely from another cause, whose effects are much harder to undo: that we, like men, had female mothers" (p. 90). Without a change in nurturing arrangements, fear and loathing of women will not disappear, but some measure of progress might come with an understanding of what women want: "What women want is to stop serving as scapegoats (their own scapegoats as well as men's and children's scapegoats) for human resentment of the human condition. They want this so painfully, and so pervasively, and until quite recently it was such a hopeless thing to want, that they have not yet been able to say out loud that they want it" (p. 234).

This passage illustrates the structure at work in the second moment of feminist criticism and shows something of its power and necessity. This persuasive writing appeals to a fundamental desire or experience of women—what women want, what women feel—but an experience posited to displace the self-mutilating experiences Dinnerstein has described. The experience appealed to is nowhere present as indubitable evidence or *point d'appui*, but the appeal to it is not factitious: what more fundamental appeal could there be than to such a possibility? This postulate empowers an attempt to alter conditions so that women will not be led to cooperate in making women scapegoats for the problems of the human condition.

The most impressive works in this struggle are doubtless books like Dinnerstein's, which analyzes our predicament in terms that make comprehensible a whole range of phenomena, from the self-estrangement of women readers to the particular cast of Mailer's sexism. In literary criticism, a powerful strategy is to produce readings that identify and situate male misreadings. Though it is difficult to work out in positive, independent terms what it might mean to read as a woman, one may confidently propose a purely differential definition: to read as a woman is to avoid reading as a man, to identify the specific defenses and distortions of male readings and provide correctives.

By these lights, feminist criticism is a critique of what Mary Ellmann, in her witty and erudite *Thinking about Women*, calls "phallic criticism." Fetterly's most impressive and effective chapter, for example, may well be her discussion of *The Bostonians*, where she documents the striking tendency of male critics to band together and take the part of Basil Ransom in his determination to win Verena away from her feminist friend, Olive Chancellor. Treating the relation between the women as perverse and unnatural, critics identify with Ransom's fear that female solidarity threatens male dominance and the male character: "The whole generation is womanized; the masculine tone is passing out of the world; . . . The masculine character . . . that is what I want to preserve, or rather, as I may say, to recover; and I must tell you that I don't in the least care what becomes of you ladies while I make the attempt."

Rescuing Verena from Olive is part of this project, for which the critics show considerable enthusiasm. Some recognize Ransom's failings and James's precise delineation of them (others regard this complexity as an artistic error on James's part), but all seem to agree that when Ransom carries Verena off, this is a consummation devoutly to be wished. The narrator tells us in the concluding sentence of the book that Verena will have cause to shed more tears: "It is to be feared that with the union, so far from brilliant, into which she was about to enter, these were not to be the last she was destined to shed." But critics generally regard this, as one of them observes, as "a small price to pay for achieving a normal relationship." Faced with a threat to what they regard as normalcy, male critics become caught up in Ransom's crusade and outdo one another in finding reasons to disparage Olive, the character in whom James shows the greatest interest, as well as the feminist movements James criticizes. The result is a male chorus. "The criticism of *The Bostonians* is remarkable for its relentless sameness, its reliance on values outside the novel, and its cavalier dismissal of the need for textual support" (*The Resisting Reader*, p. 113).

The hypothesis of a female reader is an attempt to rectify this situation: by providing a different point of departure it brings into focus the identification of male critics with one character and permits the analysis of male misreadings. But what it does above all is to reverse the usual situation in which the perspective of a male critic is assumed to be sexually neutral, while a feminist reading is seen as a case of special pleading and an attempt to force the text into a predetermined mold. By confronting male readings with the elements of the text they neglect and showing them to be a continuation of Ransom's position rather than judicious commentary on the novel as a whole, feminist criticism puts itself in the position that phallic criticism usually attempts to occupy. The more convincing its critique of phallic criticism, the more feminist criticism comes to provide the broad and comprehensive vision, analyzing and situating the limited and interested interpretations of male critics. Indeed, at this level one can say that feminist criticism is the name that should be applied to all criticism alert to the critical ramifications of sexual oppression, just as in politics "women's issues" is the name now applied to many fundamental questions of personal freedom and social justice.

A different way of going beyond phallic criticism is Jane Tompkins's discussion of *Uncle Tom's Cabin*, a novel relegated to the trash heap of literary history by male critics and fellow travelers such as Ann Douglas, in her influential book *The Feminization of American Culture*. "The attitude Douglas expresses toward the vast quantity of literature written by women in this country between 1820 and 1870 is the one that the male-dominated scholarly tradition has always expressed—contempt. The query one hears behind every page of her indictment of feminization is: why can't a woman be more like a man?" ("*Sentimental Power*," p. 81). Though in some respects the most important book of the century, *Uncle Tom's Cabin* is placed in a genre—the sentimental novel—written by, about, and for women, and therefore seen as trash, or at least as unworthy of serious critical consideration. If one does take this book seriously, one discovers, Tompkins argues, that it displays in exemplary fashion the features of a major American genre defined by Sacvan Bercovitch, "the American Jeremiad": "a mode of public exhortation . . . designed to join social criticism to spiritual renewal, public to private identity, the shifting 'signs of the times' to certain traditional metaphors, themes, and symbols," especially those of typological narrative (p. 93). Bercovitch's book, notes Tompkins, "provides a striking instance of how totally academic criticism has foreclosed on sentimental fiction; since, even when a sentimental novel fulfills a man's theory to perfection, he cannot see it. For him the work doesn't even exist. Despite the fact that his study takes no note of the most obvious and compelling instance of the jeremiad since the Great Awakening, Bercovitch's description in fact provides an excellent account of the combination of elements that made Stowe's novel work" (p. 93). Rewriting the Bible as the story of a Negro slave, "*Uncle Tom's Cabin* retells the culture's central myth—the story of the crucifixion—in terms of the nation's greatest political conflict—slavery—and of its most cherished social beliefs—the sanctity of motherhood and the family" (p. 89).

Here the hypothesis of a woman reader helps to identify male exclusions that forestall serious analysis, but once that analysis is undertaken it becomes possible to argue

> that the popular domestic novel of the nineteenth century represents a monumental effort to reorganize culture from the woman's point of view, that this body of work is remarkable for its intellectual complexity, ambition, and resourcefulness, and that, in certain cases, it offers a critique of American society far more devastating than any delivered by better-known critics such as Hawthorne and Melville. . . . Out of the ideological materials they had at their disposal, the sentimental novelists elaborated a myth that gave women the central position of power and authority in the culture; and of these efforts *Uncle Tom's Cabin* is the most dazzling exemplar. [Pp. 81–82]

In addition to the devastating attack on slavery, reputed to have "changed the hearts" of many of its readers, the novel attempts to bring on, through the same sort of change of heart, a new social order. In the new society, envisioned in a chapter called "The Quaker Settlement," man-made institutions fade into irrelevance, and the home guided by the Christian woman becomes, not a refuge from the real order of the world, but the center of meaningful activity (p. 95). "The removal of the male from the center to the periphery of the human sphere is the most radical component of this millenarian scheme which is rooted so solidly in the most traditional values—religion, motherhood, home, and family. [In the details of this chapter,] Stowe reconceives the role of men in human history: while Negroes, children, mothers, and grandmothers do the world's primary work, men groom themselves contentedly in a corner" (p. 98).

In this sort of analysis, feminist criticism does not rely on the experience of the woman reader as it does at the first level but employs the hypothesis of a woman reader to provide leverage for displacing the dominant male critical vision and revealing its misprisions. "By 'feminist,'" suggests Peggy Kamuf, "one understands a way of reading texts that points to the masks of

57

truth with which phallocentrism hides its fictions" ("Writing like a Woman," p. 286). The task at this level is not to establish a woman's reading that would parallel a male reading but rather, through argument and an attempt to account for textual evidence, to produce a comprehensive perspective, a compelling reading. The conclusions reached in feminist criticism of this sort are not specific to women in the sense that one can sympathize, comprehend, and agree only if one has had certain experiences which are women's. On the contrary, these readings demonstrate the limitations of male critical interpretations in terms that male critics would purport to accept, and they seek, like all ambitious acts of criticism, to attain a generally convincing understanding—an understanding that is feminist because it is a critique of male chauvinism.

In this second moment of feminist criticism there is an appeal to the potential experience of a woman reader (which would escape the limitations of male readings) and then the attempt to make such an experience possible by developing questions and perspectives that would enable a woman to read as a woman—that is, not "as a man." Men have aligned the opposition male/female with rational/emotional, serious/frivolous, or reflective/spontaneous; and feminist criticism of the second moment works to prove itself more rational, serious, and reflective than male readings that omit and distort. But there is a third moment in which, instead of contesting the association of the male with the rational, feminist theory investigates the way our notions of the rational are tied to or in complicity with the interests of the male. One of the most striking analyses of this kind is Luce Irigaray's *Speculum, de l'autre femme*, which takes Plato's parable of the cave, with its contrast between a maternal womb and a divine paternal *logos*, as the point of departure for a demonstration that philosophical categories have been developed to relegate the feminine to a position of subordination and to reduce the radical Otherness of woman to a specular relation: woman is either ignored or seen as man's opposite. Rather than attempt to reproduce Irigaray's complex argument, one might take a single striking example adduced by Dorothy Dinnerstein, Peggy Kamuf, and others: the connection between patriarchy and the privileging of the rational, the abstract, or the intellectual.

In *Moses and Monotheism*, Freud establishes a relation between three "processes of the same character": the Mosaic prohibition against making a sensible image of God (thus, "the compulsion to worship a God whom one cannot see"), the development of speech ("the new realm of intellectuality was opened up, in which ideas, memories, and inferences became decisive in contrast to the lower psychical activity which had direct perceptions by the sense-organs as its content") and, finally, the replacement of a matriarchal social order by a patriarchal one. The last involves more than a change in juridical conventions. "This turning from the mother to the father points in addition to a victory of intellectuality over sensuality—that is, an advance of civilization, since maternity is proved by the evidence of the senses while paternity is a hypothesis, based on an inference and a premiss. Taking sides in this way with a thought-process in preference to a sense perception has proved to be a momentous step" (vol. 23, pp. 113–14). Several pages further on, Freud explains the common character of these processes:

> An advance in intellectuality consists in deciding against direct sense-perception in favour of what are known as the higher intellectual processes—that is, memories, reflections, and inferences. It consists, for instance, in deciding that paternity is more important than maternity, although it cannot, like the latter, be established by the evidence of the senses, and that for that reason the child should bear his father's name and be his heir. Or it declares that our God is the greatest and mightiest, although he is invisible like a gale of wind or like the soul. [Pp. 117–18]

Freud appears to suggest that the establishment of patriarchal power is merely an instance of the general advance of intellectuality and that the preference for an invisible God is another effect of the same cause. But when we consider that the invisible, omnipotent God is God the Father, not to say God of the Patriarchs, we may well wonder whether, on the contrary, the promotion of the invisible over the visible and of thought and inference over sense perception is not a consequence or effect of the establishment of paternal authority: a consequence of the fact that the paternal relation is invisible.

If one wished to argue that the promotion of the intelligible over the sensible, meaning over form, and the invisible over the visible was an elevation of the paternal principle and paternal power over the maternal, one could draw support from the character of Freud's arguments elsewhere, since he shows that numerous enterprises are determined by unconscious interests of a sexual character. Dorothy Dinnerstein's discussions would also support the view that the intangibility and uncertainty of the paternal relation have considerable consequences. She notes that fathers, because of their lack of direct physical connection with babies, have a powerful urge to assert a relation, giving the child their name to establish genealogical links, engaging in various "initiation rites through which they symbolically and passionately affirm that it is they who have themselves created human beings, as compared with the mere flesh spawned by woman. Think also of the anxious concern that men have so widely shown for immortality through heirs, and their efforts to control the sexual life of women to make sure that the children they sponsor really do come from their own seed: the tenuousness of their physical tie to the young clearly pains men in a way that it could not pain bulls or stallions" (*The Mermaid and the Minotaur*, p. 80).

Men's powerful "impulse to affirm and tighten by cultural inventions their unsatisfactorily loose mammalian connection with children" leads them to value highly cultural inventions of a symbolic nature (pp. 80–81). One might predict an inclination to value what are generally termed metaphorical relations—relations of resemblance between separate items that can be substituted for one another, such as obtain between the father and the miniature replica with the same name, the child—over metonymical, maternal relationships based on contiguity.

Indeed, if one tried to imagine the literary criticism of a patriarchal culture, one might predict several likely concerns: (1) that the role of the author would be conceived as a paternal one and any maternal functions deemed valuable would be assimilated to paternity;[9] (2) that much would be invested in

[9]See Gilbert and Gubar, *The Madwoman in the Attic*, pp. 3–92. Feminist critics have shown considerable interest in Harold Bloom's model of poetic creation because it makes explicit the sexual connotations of authorship and authority. This oedipal scenario, in which one becomes a poet by struggling with a poetic father for possession of the muse, indicates the problematical situation of a woman who would be a poet. What relation can she have to the tradition?

paternal authors, to whose credit everything in their textual progeny would redound; (3) that there would be great concern about which meanings were legitimate and which illegitimate (since the paternal author's role in the generation of meanings can only be inferred); and that criticism would expend great efforts to develop principles for, on the one hand, determining which meanings were truly the author's own progeny, and on the other hand, controlling intercourse with texts so as to prevent the proliferation of illegitimate interpretations. Numerous aspects of criticism, including the preference for metaphor over metonymy, the conception of the author, and the concern to distinguish legitimate from illegitimate meanings, can be seen as part of the promotion of the paternal. Phallogocentrism unites an interest in patriarchal authority, unity of meaning, and certainty of origin.

The task of feminist criticism in this third moment is to investigate whether the procedures, assumptions, and goals of current criticism are in complicity with the preservation of male authority, and to explore alternatives. It is not a question of rejecting the rational in favor of the irrational, of concentrating of metonymical relations to the exclusion of the metaphorical, or on the signifier to the exclusion of the signified, but of attempting to develop critical modes in which the concepts that are products of male authority are inscribed within a larger textual system. Feminists will try various strategies—in recent French writing "woman" has come to stand for any radical force that subverts the concepts, assumptions, and structures of traditional male discourse.[10] One might suspect, however, that attempts to produce a new feminine language will prove less effective at this stage than critiques of phallocentric criticism, which are by no means limited to the strategies of feminist criticism's second moment. There, feminist readings identify male bias by using concepts and categories that male critics purport to accept. In this third moment or mode, many of

[10]The articles in Elaine Marks and Isabelle de Courtivron's *New French Feminisms* provide an excellent conspectus of recent strategies. See also the discussions in *Yale French Studies* 62 (1981), "Feminist Readings: French Texts/American Contexts." The relation between feminism and deconstruction is a complicated question. For some brief indications, see Chapter Two, section 4, below. Derrida's *Eperons*, on Nietzsche and the concept of woman, is a relevant but in many ways unsatisfying document in this case.

these concepts and theoretical categories—notions of realism, of rationality, of mastery, of explanation—are themselves shown to belong to phallocentric criticism.

Consider, for instance, Shoshana Felman's discussion of the text and readings of Balzac's short story "Adieu," a tale of a woman's madness, its origin in an episode of the Napoleonic wars, and her former lover's attempt to cure it. Feminist perspectives of the first and second moment bring out what was previously ignored or taken for granted, as male critics set aside women and madness to praise the "realism" of Balzac's description of war. Felman shows that critics' dealings with the text repeat the male protagonist's dealings with his former mistress, Stéphanie. "It is quite striking to observe to what extent the logic of the unsuspecting 'realistic' critic can reproduce, one after the other, all of Philippe's delusions" ("Women and Madness: The Critical Phallacy," p. 10).

Philippe thinks he can cure Stéphanie by making her recognize and name him. To restore her reason is to obliterate her otherness, which he finds so unacceptable that he is willing to kill both her and himself if he should fail in his cure. She must recognize him and recognize herself as "his Stéphanie" again. When she finally does so, as a result of Philippe's elaborate realistic reconstruction of the scene of wartime suffering where she lost her reason, she dies. The drama played out in the story reflects back on the attempt by male critics to make the story a recognizable instance of realism, and thus questions their notions of "realism" or reality, of reason, and of interpretive mastery, as instances of a male passion analogous to Philippe's. "On the critical as well as on the literary stage, the same attempt is played out to appropriate the signifier and to reduce its differential repetition; we see the same endeavor to do away with difference, the same policing of identities, the same design of mastery, of *sense-control*. . . . Along with the illusions of Philippe, the realistic critic thus repeats, in turn, his allegorical act of murder, his obliteration of the Other: the critic also, in his own way, *kills the woman*, while killing, at the same time, the question of the text and the text as question" (p. 10).

Balzac's story helps to identify notions critics have employed with the male stratagems of its protagonist and thus to make possible a feminist reading that situates these concepts and describes their limitations. Insofar as the structure and details of Balzac's story provide a critical description of its male critics, exploration and exploitation of its textuality is a feminist way of reading, but a way of reading that poses rather than solves the question of how to get around or to go beyond the concepts and categories of male criticism. Felman concludes, "from this confrontation in which Balzac's text itself seems to be an ironic reading of its own future reading, the question arises: how *should* we read?" (p. 10).

This is also the question posed in feminist criticism's second moment—how should we read? what kind of reading experience can we imagine or produce? what would it be to read "as a woman"? Felman's critical mode thus leads back to the second level at which political choices are debated and where notions of what one wants animate critical practice. In this sense, the third level, which questions the framework of choice and the affiliations of critical and theoretical categories, is not more radical than the second; nor does it escape the question of "experience."

From these varied writings, a general structure emerges. In the first moment or mode, where woman's experience is treated as a firm ground for interpretation, one swiftly discovers that this experience is not the sequence of thoughts present to the reader's consciousness as she moves through the text but a reading or interpretation of "woman's experience"—her own and others'—which can be set in a vital and productive relation to the text. In the second mode, the problem is how to make it possible to read as a woman: the possibility of this fundamental experience induces an attempt to produce it. In the third mode, the appeal to experience is veiled but still there, as a reference to maternal rather than paternal relations or to woman's situation and experience of marginality, which may give rise to an altered mode of reading. The appeal to the experience of the reader provides leverage for displacing or undoing the system of concepts or procedures of male criticism, but "experience" always has this divided, duplicitous character: it has always already occurred and yet is still to be produced—an indispensable point of reference, yet never simply there.

63

Peggy Kamuf provides a vivid way of understanding this situation of deferral if we transpose what she says about writing as a woman to reading as a woman:

> —"a woman [reading] as a woman"—the repetition of the "identical" term splits that identity, making room for a slight shift, spacing out the differential meaning which has always been at work in the single term. And the repetition has no reason to stop there, no finite number of times it can be repeated until it closes itself off logically, with the original identity recuperated in a final term. Likewise, one can find only arbitrary beginnings for the series, and no term which is not already a repetition: ". . . a woman [reading] as a woman [reading] as a . . ." ["Writing like a Woman," p. 298]

For a woman to read as a woman is not to repeat an identity or an experience that is given but to play a role she constructs with reference to her identity as a woman, which is also a construct, so that the series can continue: a woman reading as a woman reading as a woman. The noncoincidence reveals an interval, a division within woman or within any reading subject and the "experience" of that subject.

3. STORIES OF READING

The division that emerges in the reader and reader's experience in feminist criticism also structures accounts of reading in male reader-response criticism. Norman Holland argues that the meaning of a work is the reader's experience of it and that each reader experiences it in terms of his or her own distinctive "identity theme." He reports, however, that in order to bring to light the sort of experience that interested him, "Over and over again, I would ask, 'How do you feel about' characters, events, situations, or phrasings," so as to elicit "free associations to the stories" (*5 Readers Reading*, p. 44). He hopes to recover what he calls the response to the work, but the experience he seeks is powerfully shaped, if not produced, by these tendentious questions. What is the relation between the experience readers are supposed to have had and the responses they give to Holland's queries? David Bleich, an eminent practitioner of what

he terms "subjective criticism," shares Holland's conviction that
the meaning of the work is the distinctive experience of each
reader, but he explains that he must train his students to produce their "response statements," instructing them in what to
include and what to leave out.

> A response statement aims to record the perception of a read-
> ing experience and its natural, spontaneous consequences, among
> which are feelings, or affects, and peremptory memories and
> thoughts, or free associations. While other forms of mentation
> may be considered "natural and spontaneous," they would not be
> so in this context. Recording a response requires the relaxation of
> cultivated analytical habits, especially the habit of automatic objec-
> tification of the work of literature. . . . Normally, the act of objec-
> tification inhibits awareness of response. [*Subjective Criticism*, p.
> 147]

The appeal to a natural response is coupled with attempts to
eliminate aspects of available responses, such as the "automatic
objectification" that forms part of the students' experiences.
The concept of experience is divided between what the students have already had and the possibility which their teacher
hopes to make accessible.

In *Surprised by Sin* and *Self-Consuming Artifacts*, Stanley Fish
claimed to report what readers actually experience when reading and argued that critics reach different conclusions because their erroneous theories (or, as Bleich might say, "menta-
tion") lead them to forget, distort, or misconstrue their actual
experience of the work. Many were skeptical of this claim, suggesting that Fish was merely reporting his own experience, and
at times Fish has conceded the point that he "was not revealing
what readers had always done but trying to persuade them to a
set of community assumptions so that when they read they
would do what I did" (*Is There a Text in This Class?*, p. 15). Yet
the situation is not so simple. There are good reasons to suspect that his so-called experience of reading is more complex
than the stories he tells. For one thing, Fish's reader never
learns anything from his experience. Time after time he is
discomfited to see the second half of a sentence take away what
the first half had seemed to assert. Time after time he is bewil-
dered to see the self-consuming artifact he is reading consume

itself. What distinguishes Fish's reader is this propensity to fall into the same traps over and over again. Each time it is possible to interpret the end of a line of verse as completing a thought, he does so, only to find, in numerous cases, that the beginning of the next line brings a change of sense. One would expect any real reader, especially one striving to be informed, to notice that premature guesses often prove wrong and to anticipate this possibility as he reads. Stanley E. Fish, after all, not only notices this possibility but writes books about it. We can confidently suppose that as Fish reads he is on the lookout for such cases and is pleased rather than dismayed when they occur. The conclusion seems inescapable: what Fish, reports is not Stanley Fish reading but Stanley Fish imagining reading as a Fishian reader. Or perhaps we ought to say, since a Fishian reader is a reader who resolutely holds himself to a particular role, that his accounts of the reading experience are reports of Fish reading as a Fishian reader reading as a Fishian reader.

Would Fish have fared otherwise if he had tried to transcribe his own experience? If the first problem in his account is the gap between his reported experiences and his presumed experience, the second problem is what sort of thing "his own experience" might be. What is Fish's experience when he reads these lines in *Lycidas*?

> He must not float upon his wat'ry bier
> Unwept . . .

He remarks that "I 'saw' what my interpretive principles permitted or directed me to see" (*Is There a Text in This Class?*, p. 163). His principles direct him to see, and thus lead him to expect, line endings which interrupt sentences so as to encourage readers to premature conclusions. He expects that sequences such as "He must not float upon his wat'ry bier" may not prove complete, and here "Unwept" confirms his view of poetic structure. Yet his experience must also involve, by virtue of this expectation, an imaginative experience of what he describes as the reader's experience: the experience of taking the first line "as a resolution bordering on a promise," anticipating "a call to action, perhaps even a program for the undertaking of a rescue mission," and then having that expectation and anticipation disappointed. "The reader, having resolved a sense, unresolves it" (pp. 164–65). Fish's experience of these lines from *Lycidas*, if there is such a thing, is most likely divided: an experience of expecting resolved senses to come unresolved, yet also of confidently resolving a sense as though it could not be unresolved. Like Barthes's anti-hero, Fish lives in contradiction without shame, playing a role with which he never coincides, reading as a Fishian reader reading as a Fishian reader. . . . The repetition reveals an interval or division that has always been at work in the single term.

To read is to play the role of a reader and to interpret is to posit an experience of reading. This is something that beginning literature students know quite well but have forgotten by the time they get to graduate school and begin teaching literature. When student papers refer to what "the reader feels here" or what "the reader then understands," teachers often take this as a spurious objectivity, a disguised form of "I feel" or "I understand," and urge their charges either to be honest or to omit such references. But students know better than their teachers here. They know it is not a matter of honesty. They have understood that to read and interpret literary works is precisely to imagine what "a reader" would feel and understand.[11] To read is to operate with the hypothesis of a reader, and there is always a gap or division within reading.

Our most familiar versions of this division are the notion of "suspension of disbelief," or our simultaneous interest in char-

[11]John Reichert notes that "critics often argue in behalf of a response that no reader ever had" and infers from this, in the most interesting discussion of *Making Sense of Literature*, that statements about response are in fact claims about how we ought to understand a passage or a work (p. 87). Statements such as "The reader pities Macbeth" do generally attempt to persuade to a certain understanding of the play, and I take this as further evidence of the divided and deferred character of response: "The reader pities Macbeth" attempts to produce the response to which it refers and on whose authority it relies. Reichert, however, with his deep conviction that things are unproblematical, dismisses such complications with the claim that "one *always* feels the emotion appropriate to one's understanding" (p. 85). But then the critic arguing for a certain understanding of a play necessarily feels the emotion and has had the response appropriate to that understanding; his claim that the reader feels pity would in fact be a report of his own feeling of pity. As we have seen, this is not the way response functions, and Reichert recognizes this when he notes, more astutely than his theory will allow, that critics may argue for a response that no one—including themselves—has ever had.

acters as people and in characters as devices of the novelist's art, or our appreciation of the suspense of a story whose ending, in fact, we already know. The apparently more problematical structures of women reading as women and Fish reading as a Fishian reader are versions of the same kind of division, which prevents there from being experiences that might simply be grasped and adduced as the truth of the text.

But we have a stake, it seems, in maintaining our belief in experience as foundation and thus in obscuring or displacing those divisions. A common way of dealing with them has been to draw upon the familiar and plausible notion that different readers or groups of readers read differently and to present divisions within reading as distinctions between readers. One might be tempted to argue, for example, that if some feminists claim to report the distinctive experience of women readers while others complain that women have not yet learned to read as women, it is doubtless because the two groups of critics are reporting on two different groups of readers. To argue thus would be to ignore the questions feminists debate—such as what it means for a woman to read as a woman—by assuming that the answer has been found by one group and not found by the other, instead of being problematically at stake in each reading.

When Stanley Fish's claim to report the experience of all readers was challenged, he had recourse to the notion of "interpretive communities": he was not, he admitted, reporting a universal experience but attempting to persuade others to join his interpretive community of like-minded readers (*Is There a Text in This Class?*, p. 15). Some have thought this an exceedingly weak descriptive move, which leaves us with a large number of independent communities unable to argue with one another: some readers read one way—say, Fishian readers—others read another way—say, Hirschian readers—and so on, for as many different reading strategies as we can identify. But however frustrating some may find this conception, which separates us into monadic communities, it is in one way quite reassuring: by taking the differences and problems *within* reading and projecting them into differences *between* interpretive communities, it assumes the unity and identity of each reader's and each community's procedures and experiences.

As we have seen, though, there are reasons to doubt whether

one can take for granted the unity and identity of one's reading strategies and experiences. If even Fish reading does not coincide with the Fishian reader, the problems are quite severe and suggest that reading is divided and heterogeneous, useful as a point of reference only when composed into a story, when construed or constructed as a narrative.

There are, of course, many different stories of reading. Wolfgang Iser tells of the reader actively filling in gaps, actualizing what the text leaves indeterminate, attempting to construct a unity, and modifying the construction as the text yields further information. Michael Riffaterre's *Semiotics of Poetry* tells a more dramatic story: thwarted in the attempt to read everything in a poem as representations of a state of affairs, the reader undertakes a second, retroactive reading in which the obstacles previously encountered become the clues to a single "matrix"—a minimal, literal sentence—of which everything in the poem can be seen as a periphrastic transformation. Suddenly, as one reads, "the puzzle is solved, everything falls into place" (p. 12). Stephen Booth tells a sadder tale of readers continually encountering patterns—phonological, syntactic, thematic—that suggest coherence, and repeatedly feeling poised on the threshold of understanding, without ever quite being able to get their bearings or resolve multiple patterns into an order. "The mind of the audience [of *Hamlet*] is in constant but gentle flux, always shifting but never completely leaving familiar ground," so that the play allows them to "hold on to" but not to resolve "all the contradictions it contains" ("On the Value of *Hamlet*," pp. 287, 310). Norman Holland, on the contrary, tells of readers merrily using the work "to replicate themselves." "The individual can accept the literary work only to the extent he exactly re-creates with it a verbal form of his particular pattern of defense mechanisms." After matching defenses, the reader derives from the work "fantasies of the particular kind that yield him pleasure," and finally justifies the fantasy by transforming it "into a total experience of esthetic, moral, intellectual, or social coherence and significance" ("Unity Identity Text Self," pp. 816–18).

What do such narrative constructs reveal about reading? What problems emerge when we consider a corpus of stories about reading? One prominent variable in stories of response is the issue of control. For Holland, of course, readers dominate the text as they construct works to match their own defenses. Other stories too celebrate the creative or productive role of the reader as a major insight of reader-oriented criticism and conclude, with Fish, that readers read the poem they have made (*Is There a Text in This Class?*, p. 169). But a curious feature of these narratives is how easily text and reader can switch places: a story of the reader structuring the text easily becomes a story of the text provoking certain responses and actively controlling the reader. This switch occurs when one moves from Bleich and Holland to Riffaterre and Booth, but it may also take place within a single critical article. In the entry on "Texte, théorie du" for the *Encyclopaedia Universalis*, Barthes writes that "the signifier belongs to everyone," but, he quickly continues, "it is the text which works untiringly, not the artist or the consumer" (p. 1015). On the next page, he reverts to the first position: "the theory of the text removes all limits to the freedom of reading (authorizing the reading of a past work from an entirely modern standpoint . . .) but it also insists greatly on the (productive) equivalence of reading and writing" (p. 1016). Elsewhere Barthes's celebrations of the reader as producer of the text are matched by accounts of the text's disruption of the reader's most basic conceptions: "The orgasmic text [*texte de jouissance*] dislocates the reader's historical, cultural, and psychological assumptions, the consistency of his tastes, values, memories, and brings to a crisis his relation with language" (*Le Plaisir du texte*, pp. 25–26/14).

Striking confirmation of the easy shift between freedom and constraint comes in Umberto Eco's discussions of "open works," which require readers to write the text through their reading. The tight structures of "closed works" seem to give readers no options, while the unrealized constructions of open works invite creativity, but, Eco notes, the very openness of the latter forces a particular role on the reader more imperiously than does the closed work. "An open text outlines a 'closed' project of its Model Reader as a component of its structural strategy" (*The Role of the Reader*, p. 9). The reader is required to play an organizing role: "You cannot use the text as you want but only as the text wants you to use it," while you can use closed works in numerous different ways. "The free interpretive choices elicited by a purposeful strategy of openness" (p. 40) can be considered or narrated as acts provoked by the manipulative strategy of a scheming author.

Fish's stories too switch back and forth between a reader who actively takes charge and a hapless reader buffeted by fierce sentences. Fish sets out to challenge the formalist notion of the text as a structure that determines meaning, contrasting his view of "human beings as at every moment creating the experiential spaces into which personal knowledge flows" with the opposing view of "human beings as passive and disinterested comprehenders of a knowledge external to them" (*Is There a Text in This Class?*, p. 94); but when he narrates specific acts of reading, something peculiar occurs. Here is what happens when the reader, creator of meaning, encounters Walter Pater's sentence "That clear perceptual outline of face and limb is but an image of ours."

> In terms of the reader's response, "that" generates an expectation that impels him forward, the expectation of finding out *what* "that" is. . . . The adjective "clear" works in two ways; it promises the reader that when "that" appears, he will be able to see it easily, and, conversely, that it can be easily seen. "Perceptual" stabilizes the visibility of "that" even *before* it is seen and "outline" gives it potential form, while at the same time raising a question. That question—outline of what?—is obligingly answered by the phrase "face and limb," which, in effect, fills the outline in. By the time the reader reaches the declarative verb "is" . . . he is fully and securely oriented in a world of perfectly discerned objects and perfectly discerning observers, of whom he is one. But then the sentence turns on the reader, and takes away the world it has itself created. . . . "image" resolves that uncertainty, but in the direction of insubstantiality; and the now blurred form disappears altogether when the phrase "of ours" collapses the distinction between the reader and that which is (or was) "without" (Pater's own word). Now you see it (that), now you don't. Pater giveth and Pater taketh away. [P. 31]

Despite the claims of Fish's theory, the reader becomes the victim of a diabolical author's strategy. In fact, the more active, projective, or creative the reader is, the more she is manipulated by the sentence or by the author.

Fish later noticed that this shift had undermined his ostensible program. "The argument in 'Literature in the Reader,'" he noted in the introduction to this collection of papers, "was mounted (or so it is announced) on behalf of the reader and against the self-sufficiency of the text, but in the course of it the text becomes more and more powerful, and rather than being liberated, the reader finds himself more constrained in his new prominence than he was before" (p. 7). Fish is mistaken only in thinking this an error he can put right by arguing, as he does in later papers, that the formal features by which the reader is manipulated are the products of interpretive principles brought to bear by the reader. The story of manipulation will always reassert itself, first because it is a much better story, full of dramatic encounters, moments of deception, and reversals of fortune, second, because it deals more easily and precisely with details of meaning, and third, because this sort of narrative confers value on the temporal experience of reading. A reader who creates everything learns nothing, but one who is continually encountering the unexpected can make momentous, unsettling findings. The more a theory stresses the reader's freedom, control, and constitutive activity, the more likely it is to lead to stories of dramatic encounters and surprises which portray reading as a process of discovery.

The reemergence of the text's control, in stories that sought to recount just the opposite, is a powerful illustration of the constraints discursive structures impose on theories that claim to master or describe them. Theories of reading stories and descriptions of reading stories seem themselves to be governed by aspects of story. But there is another structural necessity at work in the switches back and forth between the reader's dominance and the text's dominance. A study of reading would not permit one to decide between these alternatives, for the situation can be theorized from either perspective, and there are reasons why it must be theorized from both perspectives. The example of the joke elucidates very nicely the curious situation of reading. The listener is essential to the joke, for unless the listener laughs, the joke is not a joke. Here, as reader-response criticism would have it, the reader plays a decisive role in determining the structure and meaning of the utterance. As Samuel Weber writes, explicating Freud's theory of *Witz*, "The third person, as listener, decides whether or not the joke is success-ful—i.e. whether it is a joke or not—. . . And yet this decisive action of the third person lies beyond all volition—one cannot will to laugh—and outside of consciousness, insofar as one never knows, at the moment of laughter, what one is laughing at" ("The Divaricator," pp. 25–26). The listener does not control the outburst of laughter: the text provokes it (the joke, one says, *made me* laugh). But on the other hand, the unpredictable response determines the nature of the text that is supposed to have produced it. No compromise formulation, with the reader partly in control and the text partly in control, would accurately describe this situation, which is captured, rather, by juxtaposi-tion of two absolute perspectives. The shift back and forth in stories of reading between readers' decisive actions and read-ers' automatic responses is not a mistake that could be cor-rected but an essential structural feature of the situation.

A second, closely related question that arises from stories of reading is what is "in" the text. Is it so rich a plenitude that no reader can ever grasp it all? a determinate structure with some gaps the reader must fill in? a set of indeterminate marks on which the reader confers structure and meaning? Stanley Fish, for example, has adopted a series of positions in trying to cope with this problem. Each change of position attributes to the constitutive activity of the reader something that had pre-viously been located in the text. At first Fish argued that mean-ing does not lie in the text but in the experience of the reader. The text is a series of formal structures on which readers con-fer meaning, as in the Pater example cited above. Investigating stylistics, however, Fish decided that the reader's interpretive hypotheses determine which of many formal features and pat-terns count as facts of the text. At the third stage he claimed that formal patterns are not *in* the text at all. Discussing the lines from *Lycidas* cited earlier, he writes,

> I appropriate the notion of "line ending" and treat it as a fact of nature; one might conclude that as a fact it is responsible for the reading experience I describe. The truth I think is exactly the reverse: line endings exist by virtue of perceptual strategies rather than the other way around. Historically the strategy that we know

as "reading (or hearing) poetry" has included paying attention to
the line as a unit, but it is precisely that attention which has made
the line as a unit (either of print or of aural duration) available.
. . . In short, what is noticed is what has been made noticeable, not
by a clear and undistorting glass, but by an interpretive strategy.
[*Is There a Text in This Class?*, pp. 165–66]

The same argument can be repeated for the most basic phenomena: any repetition of the same sound or letter is a function of phonological or orthographic conventions and thus may
be regarded as the result of the interpretive strategies of particular communities. There is no rigorous way to distinguish
fact from interpretation, so nothing can be deemed to be definitively *in* the text prior to interpretive conventions.

Fish takes one further step: like the text and its meanings,
the reader too is a product of the strategies of an interpretive
community, constituted as reader by the mental operations it
makes available. "At a stroke," Fish writes, "the dilemma that
gave rise to the debate between the champions of the text and
the champions of the reader (of whom I had certainly been
one) is dissolved because the competing entities are no longer
perceived as independent. To put it another way, the claims of
objectivity can no longer be debated because the authorizing
agency, the center of interpretive authority, is at once both and
neither" (p. 14). "Many things look rather different," he claims,
"once the subject-object dichotomy is eliminated" (p. 336).

This radical monism, by which everything is the product of
interpretive strategies, is a logical result of analysis that shows
each entity to be a conventional construct; but the distinction
between subject and object is more resilient than Fish thinks
and will not be eliminated "at a stroke." It reappears as soon as
one attempts to talk about interpretation. To discuss an experience of reading one must adduce a reader and a text. For every
story of reading there must be something for the reader to
encounter, to be surprised by, to learn from. Interpretation is
always interpretation of something, and that something functions as the object in a subject-object relation, even though it
can be regarded as the product of prior interpretations.

What we see in Fish's turnings are the moments of a general
struggle between the monism of theory and the dualism of

narrative. Theories of reading demonstrate the impossibility of establishing well-grounded distinctions between fact and interpretation, between what can be read in the text and what is read into it, or between text and reader, and thus lead to a monism. Everything is constituted by interpretation—so much so that Fish admits he cannot answer the question, what are interpretive acts interpretations *of*? (p. 165). Stories of reading, however, will not let this question go unanswered. There must always be dualisms: an interpreter and something to interpret, a subject and an object, an actor and something he acts upon or that acts on him.

The relation between monism and dualism is particularly striking in the work of Wolfgang Iser. His account of reading is eminently sensible, designed to do justice to the creative, participatory activity of readers, while preserving determinate texts which require and induce a certain response. He attempts, that is, a dualistic theory, but his critics show that his dualism cannot be sustained: the distinction between text and reader, fact and interpretation, or determined and undetermined breaks down, and his theory becomes monistic. What kind of monism it becomes depends on which of his arguments and premises one takes most seriously. Samuel Weber argues in "The Struggle for Control" that in Iser's theory everything ultimately depends on the authority of the author, who has made the text what it is: the author guarantees the unity of the work, requires the reader's creative participation, and through his text "prestructures the shape of the aesthetic object to be produced by the reader," so that reading is an actualization of the author's intention (*The Act of Reading*, p. 96). But one can also argue convincingly, as Stanley Fish does in "Why No One's Afraid of Wolfgang Iser," that his theory is a monism of the other sort: the objective structures which Iser claims guide or determine the reader's response are structures only for a certain practice of reading. "Gaps are not built into the text but appear (or do not appear) as a consequence of particular interpretive strategies," and thus "there is no distinction between what the text gives and what the reader supplies; he supplies *everything*; the stars in a literary text are not fixed; they are just as variable as the lines that join them" (p. 7). Iser's mistake is to take the dualism necessary to stories of reading as theoretically sound, not realizing that the variable distinction between fact and interpretation or text's contribution and reader's contribution will break down under theoretical scrutiny.[12]

The possibility of demonstrating that Iser's theory leads to a monism in which reader or author supplies everything helps to show what is wrong with his eminently sensible notion that something is provided by the text and something else provided by the reader, or that there are some determinate structures and other places of indeterminacy. Jean-Paul Sartre provides one of the best correctives when discussing, in *Qu'est-ce que la littérature?*, the way in which readers "create and disclose at the same time, disclose by creating and create by disclosing" (p. 55/30). "Ainsi pour le lecteur," Sartre writes, "tout est à faire et tout est déjà fait" [Thus for the reader everything is to be done and everything is already done] (p. 58/32). For the reader the work is not partially created but, on the one hand, already complete and inexhaustible—one can read and reread without ever grasping completely what has already been made—and, on the other hand, still to be created in the process of reading, without which it is only black marks on paper. The attempt to produce compromise formulations fails to capture this essential, divided quality of reading.

Stories of reading, however, require that something be taken as given so that the reader can respond to it. E. D. Hirsch's arguments about meaning and significance are relevant here. "Meaning," which Hirsch identifies with the author's intended meaning, "refers to the whole verbal meaning of a text, and 'significance' to textual meaning in relation to a larger context, i.e. another mind, another era, a wider subject matter" (*The Aims of Interpretation*, pp. 2–3). Hirsch's opponents reject the distinction, arguing that there is no meaning in the text except

[12]In a response to Fish, "Talk like Whales," Iser claims that "the words of the text are given, the interpretation of the words is determinate, and the gaps between given elements and/or interpretations are the indeterminacies" (p. 83). This is clearly unsatisfactory, since in many cases the interpretation of certain words is quite indeterminate, and often the question of what word one is dealing with is a matter of interpretation, not a given. The hint of a more judicious reply, which makes the distinction between determinate and indeterminate a variable and operational contrast, comes in his *Diacritics* interview, where he speaks of "the distinction between a significance which is to be supplied and a significance which has been supplied." "Once the reader supplies the link it becomes determinate" (Interview, p. 72).

in a context of interpretation; but Hirsch claims that the activity of interpretation depends on a distinction between a meaning that is in the text (because the author put it there) and a significance that is supplied. "If an interpreter did not conceive a text's meaning to be *there* as an occasion for contemplation or application, he would have nothing to think or talk about. Its thereness, its self-identity from one moment to the next allows it to be contemplated. Thus, while meaning is a principle of stability in an interpretation, significance embraces a principle of change" (p. 80). The indispensability of this distinction is confirmed, for Hirsch, by his opponents' willingness to claim that he has misinterpreted them (and thus that their works do have stable meanings different from the significance interpreters might give them). But what Hirsch's arguments show is the need for dualisms of this kind in our dealings with texts and the world, not the epistemological authority of a distinction between the meaning of a text and the significance interpreters give it, or even the possibility of determining in a principled way what belongs to the meaning and what to the significance. We employ such distinctions all the time because our stories require them, but they are variable and ungrounded concepts.

This point is well made by Richard Rorty in a discussion of the problems raised by Thomas Kuhn's treatment of science as a series of interpretive paradigms. Are there properties *in* nature that scientists discover, or do their conceptual frameworks *produce* such entities as subatomic particles, light waves, etc.? Does science *make* or does it *find*? "In the view I want to recommend," writes Rorty,

> nothing deep turns on the choice between these two phrases—between the imagery of making and of finding. . . . It is less paradoxical, however, to stick to the classic notion of "better describing what was already there" for physics. This is not because of deep epistemological or metaphysical considerations, but simply because, when we tell our Whiggish stories about how our ancestors gradually crawled up the mountain on whose (possibly false) summit we stand, we need to keep some things constant throughout the story. The forces of nature and the small bits of matter, as conceived by current physical theory, are good choices for this role. Physics is the paradigm of "finding" simply because it is hard (at least in the West) to tell a story of changing physical

universes against the background of an unchanging Moral Law or poetic canon, but very easy to tell the reverse sort of story. Our tough-minded "naturalistic" sense that spirit is, if not reducible to nature, at least parasitic upon it, is no more than the insight that physics gives us a good background against which to tell our stories of historical change. It is not as if we had some deep insight into the nature of reality which told us that everything save atoms and the void was "by convention" (or "spiritual," or "made up"). Democritus's insight was that a story about the smallest bits of things forms a background for stories about changes among things made of these bits. The acceptance of this genre of world-story (fleshed out successively by Lucretius, Newton, and Bohr) may be definatory of the West, but it is not a choice which could obtain, or which requires, epistemological or metaphysical guarantees. [*Philosophy and the Mirror of Nature*, pp. 344–45]

In much the same way, the notion of a given text with unchanging, discoverable properties provides an excellent background for arguments about interpretation and accounts of changing interpretations. Reader-oriented critics have themselves found that it makes a better story to talk of texts inviting or provoking responses than to describe readers creating texts, but the distinctions that structure these stories are open to question and accounts that rely on them prove vulnerable to criticism. Theories that make the text the reader's construct play a vital role in preventing a solidification of these variable, pragmatic distinctions and in casting light on aspects of reading that might otherwise go unnoticed.

A third important feature of stories of reading is the ending. Adventures of reading generally turn out well. Riffaterre's stories climax in a triumphant recovery of the matrix which masters and unifies the poem. Iser's also end in discovery: "At the end of the seventeenth century discovery was a process offering reassurances as regards the *certitudo salutis*, thus relieving the distress caused by the Calvinist doctrine of predestination." In the eighteenth century, instead of discovering that they were saved, readers discovered "human nature." In the nineteenth century the reader "had to discover the fact that society imposed a part on him, the object being for him eventually to take up a critical attitude toward this imposition." In the twentieth century, "the discovery concerns the functioning of our own faculties of perception" (*The Implied Reader*, p. xiii). The outcome of reading, it seems, is always knowledge. Readers may be manipulated and misled, but when they finish the book their experience turns to knowledge—perhaps an understanding of the limitations imposed by familiar interpretive conventions—as though finishing the book took them outside the experience of reading and gave them mastery of it. Critics such as Fish, who speaks of "the experience of a prose that undermines certainty and moves away from clarity, complicating what has at first seemed perfectly simple, raising more problems than it solves," nonetheless construct *Bildungsromane* (*Self-Consuming Artifacts*, p. 378). Their stories follow an innocent reader, confident in traditional assumptions about structure and meaning, who encounters the deviousness of texts, falls into traps, is frustrated and dismayed, but emerges wiser for the loss of illusions.[13] It is as though what permits one to describe reading as misadventure is the happy ending that transforms a series of reactions into an understanding of the text and of the self that had engaged with the text. The text's manipulation of the reader makes a good story only if it turns out well.

Such optimistic conclusions are a questionable feature of stories of reading. Some critics, not surprisingly, have grown suspicious of the idealization by which reading is shown to lead to a morally productive self-consciousness. "Nothing is gained," Harold Bloom writes, "by continuing to idealize reading, as though reading were not an art of defensive warfare" (*Kabbalah and Criticism*, p. 126). Where idealizing stories describe readers' submission to the text in order to posit a triumphant understanding of what has occurred, Bloom sees no escape or transcendence. "Poetic language makes of the strong reader what it will, and it chooses to make him a liar." The best a reader

[13]This is a story I have myself told and by which I set some store. *Flaubert: The Uses of Uncertainty* posits a reader who expects the novel to obey the conventions of the Balzacian novel, and describes how Flaubert's texts undermine this reader's assumptions about the function of description, the signifying role of binary oppositions, the coherence of point of view, and the possibilities of thematic synthesis. The result for the reader of this unsettling experience is a self-conscious understanding of the processes by which we construct meaning. For further discussion of some stories of reading, see Steven Mailloux, "Learning to Read: Interpretation and Reader-Response Criticism," pp. 99–107, and Didier Coste, "Trois conceptions du lecteur."

can achieve is a strong misreading—a reading that will in turn produce others. Most readings are weak misreadings, which also attain neither understanding nor self-knowledge but blindly trope upon the text while claiming not to trope. Bloom's account of the reader's anxious and belated involvement with the text denies that one may achieve through reading a mastery of that experience or a grasp of the reading self, though strong readers struggle to master the text by misreading it. His hyperbolic account makes us aware of the tenuous grounds on which critics construct their optimistic conclusions.[14] Certainly when we stop describing what "the reader" does and consider what particular prior readers have achieved, we tend to conclude that they failed to understand what they were doing, were influenced by assumptions they did not control, were misled in ways which we can describe but they cannot. Our dealings with prior readers reflect not the triumphant conclusions of most stories of reading but patterns of blindness and insight such as Paul de Man describes.

Stories of reading that refuse the idealizing *dénouements* stress instead the impossibility of reading. In his discussion of Rousseau, de Man writes,

> A text such as the *Profession de foi* can literally be called "unreadable" in that it leads to a set of assertions that radically exclude each other. Nor are these assertions mere neutral constations [sic]; they are exhortative performatives that require the passage from sheer enunciation to action. They compel us to choose while destroying the foundations of any choice. They tell the allegory of a judicial decision that can be neither judicious nor just. As in the plays of Kleist, the verdict repeats the crime it condemns. If, after reading the *Profession de foi*, we are tempted to convert to "theism," we stand convicted of foolishness in the court of the intellect. But if we decide that belief, in the most extensive use of the term (which must include all possible forms of idolatry and ideology), can once and forever be overcome by the enlightened mind, then this twilight of the idols will be all the more foolish in not recognizing itself as the first victim of its occurrence. One sees from this that the impossibility of reading should not be taken too lightly. [*Allegories of Reading*, p. 245]

[14]From a different point of view, Bloom's account of reading might itself be regarded as incurably optimistic in its celebration of heroic struggles of the will between individual subjects. See Culler, *The Pursuit of Signs*, pp. 107–11.

Such unreadability does not result simply from a central ambiguity or choice but from the way in which the system of
values in the text both urges choice and prevents that choice
from being made. The simplest examples of such unreadability
are paradoxical injunctions such as "Don't obey me all the time"
or "Be spontaneous," which establish a double bind: one must
choose between obedience and disobedience, but one cannot
choose, because to obey would be to disobey and to disobey
would be to obey. In the *Profession de foi* the theism which the
text ostensibly promotes is defined as assent to an inner voice,
which is that of Nature, and the choice one is urged to make
lies between this voice and judgment; but the possibility of
such a choice is undermined by the system of concepts within
the text, for on the one hand assent to the inner voice is defined as an act of judgment and, on the other hand, Rousseau's
account of judgment defines it as a process of analogizing and
substitution that is a source of error as well as of knowledge.
In undoing the oppositions on which it relies and between
which it urges the reader to choose, the text places the reader
in an impossible situation that cannot end in triumph but only
in an outcome already deemed inappropriate: an unwarranted
choice or a failure to choose.

Reading is an attempt to understand writing by determining
the referential and rhetorical modes of a text, translating the
figurative into the literal, for example, and removing obstacles
in the quest for a coherent result, but the construction of texts—
especially of literary works, where pragmatic contexts do not so
readily justify a confident distinction between the literal and
the figurative or the referential and the nonreferential—may
block this process of understanding. "The possibility of reading," writes de Man, "can never be taken for granted" (*Blindness and Insight*, p. 107). Rhetoric "puts an insurmountable obstacle in the way of any reading or understanding" (*Allegories of
Reading*, p. 131). The reader may be placed in impossible situations where there is no happy issue but only the possibility of
playing out roles dramatized in the text.

This possibility, discussed in Chapter Three below, is one
aspect of texts that deconstruction investigates, but it arises
from theories of reading that initially wish to give no such
power to the text. One might say, in schematic summary, that

theories such as we have been discussing note that one cannot authoritatively determine, by reading a text, what is in it and what is not, and they hope, by turning to the experience of the reader, to secure another basis for poetics and for particular interpretations. But it proves no easier to say what is in *the* reader's or *a* reader's experience than what is in the text: "experience" is divided and deferred—already behind us as something to be recovered, yet still before us as something to be produced. The result is not a new foundation but stories of reading, and these stories reinstate the text as an agent with definite qualities or properties, since this yields more precise and dramatic narratives as well as creating a possibility of learning that lets one celebrate great works. The value of a work is related to the efficacy granted it in these stories—an ability to produce stimulating, unsettling, moving, and reflective experiences. But these stories of provocation and manipulation lead one to ask what justifies the happy endings. Is it true that in completing a work readers transcend it and come to grasp, from a position outside it, what it did to them? Does the reader get outside the text or is the position of the reader, in which the attempt at understanding occurs, adumbrated in and by the text, which might create an untenable and inescapable position?

Deconstruction also addresses other issues raised by stories of reading, such as the relation between the curious divided structure of "experience" and the value of presence involved in appeals to experience: what is at stake in the claim that meaning is whatever is present in the reader's experience or in the notion that the end of reading is to make the reading self present to itself? Or why, to take one further issue, should we find an oscillation between the monism of theory and the dualism of narrative, in which oppositions that break down under theoretical scrutiny reassert themselves in accounts of our experience? What sort of system prevents the working out of a noncontradictory synthesis?

Taken together, these stories of reading adumbrate the paradoxical situation in which deconstruction operates. While addressing meaning as a problem of reading, as a result of applying codes and conventions, these stories come to rely on the text as a source of insight, suggesting that one must grant some authority to the text so as to try to learn from it, even when what one learns about texts and readings puts in question the claim that anything in particular is definitively in the text. Deconstruction explores the problematic situation to which stories of reading have led us. If it can be seen as the culmination of recent work on reading, it is because projects which began with something quite different in mind are brought up against the questions that deconstruction addresses.

Chapter Two

DECONSTRUCTION

DECONSTRUCTION has been variously presented as a philosophical position, a political or intellectual strategy, and
a mode of reading. Students of literature and literary theory
are doubtless most interested in its power as a method of reading and interpretation, but if our goal is to describe and evaluate the practice of deconstruction in literary studies, this is a
good reason for beginning elsewhere, with deconstruction as a
philosophical strategy.[1] Perhaps we should say, more precisely,
with deconstruction as a strategy within philosophy and a strategy for dealing with philosophy, for the practice of deconstruction aspires to be both rigorous argument within philosophy
and displacement of philosophical categories or philosophical
attempts at mastery. Here is Derrida describing "une stratégie générale de la déconstruction": "In a traditional philosophical opposition we have not a peaceful coexistence of facing terms but a violent hierarchy. One of the terms dominates
the other (axiologically, logically, etc.), occupies the commanding
 position. To deconstruct the opposition is above all, at a
particular moment, to reverse the hierarchy" (*Positions*, pp.
56–57/41).

This is an essential step, but only a step. Deconstruction must,
Derrida continues, "through a double gesture, a double science, a double writing, put into practice a *reversal* of the clas-

[1] I will not attempt to discuss the relationship of Derridian deconstruction
to the work of Hegel, Nietzsche, Husserl, and Heidegger. Gayatri Spivak's
introduction to *Of Grammatology* provides much useful information. See also
Rodolphe Gasché, "Deconstruction as Criticism."

sical opposition *and* a general *displacement* of the system. It is on that condition alone that deconstruction will provide the means of *intervening* in the field of oppositions it criticizes and which is also a field of non-discursive forces" (*Marges*, p. 392/SEC, p. 195). The practitioner of deconstruction works within the terms of the system but in order to breach it.

Here is another formulation: "To 'deconstruct' philosophy is thus to work through the structured genealogy of its concepts in the most scrupulous and immanent fashion, but at the same time to determine, from a certain external perspective that it cannot name or describe, what this history may have concealed or excluded, constituting itself as history through this repression in which it has a stake" (*Positions*, p. 15/6).

To these formulations let us add one more: to deconstruct a discourse is to show how it undermines the philosophy it asserts, or the hierarchical oppositions on which it relies, by identifying in the text the rhetorical operations that produce the supposed ground of argument, the key concept or premise. These descriptions of deconstruction differ in their emphases. To see how the operations they invoke might converge in practice, consider a case that lends itself to brief exposition, the Nietzschean deconstruction of causality.

Causality is a basic principle of our universe. We could not live or think as we do without taking for granted that one event causes another, that causes produce effects. The principle of causality asserts the logical and temporal priority of cause to effect. But, Nietzsche argues in the fragments of *The Will to Power*, this concept of causal structure is not something given as such but rather the product of a precise tropological or rhetorical operation, a *chronologische Umdrehung* or chronological reversal. Suppose one feels a pain. This causes one to look for a cause and spying, perhaps, a pin, one posits a link and reverses the perceptual or phenomenal order, *pain . . . pin*, to produce a causal sequence, *pin . . . pain*. "The fragment of the outside world of which we become conscious comes after the effect that has been produced on us and is projected *a posteriori* as its 'cause.' In the phenomenalism of the 'inner world' we invert the chronology of cause and effect. The basic fact of 'inner experience' is that the cause gets imagined after the effect has occurred" (*Werke*, vol. 3, p. 804). The causal scheme is produced by a metonymy or metalepsis (substitution of cause for effect); it is not an indubitable foundation but the product of a tropological operation.

Let us be as explicit as possible about what this simple example implies. First, it does not lead to the conclusion that the principle of causality is illegitimate and should be scrapped. On the contrary, the deconstruction itself relies on the notion of cause: the experience of pain, it is claimed, *causes* us to discover the pin and thus causes the production of a cause. To deconstruct causality one must operate with the notion of cause and apply it to causation itself. The deconstruction appeals to no higher logical principle or superior reason but uses the very principle it deconstructs. The concept of causation is not an error that philosophy could or should have avoided but is indispensable—to the argument of deconstruction as to other arguments.

Second, the deconstruction of causality is not the same as Hume's skeptical argument, though they have something in common. When we investigate causal sequences, Hume claims in his *Treatise of Human Nature*, we can discover nothing other than relations of contiguity and temporal succession. Insofar as "causation" means more than contiguity and succession it is something that can never be demonstrated. When we say that one thing causes another, what we have in fact experienced is "that like objects have always been placed in like relations of contiguity and succession" (I, III, vi). Deconstruction too puts causality in question in this way, but simultaneously, in a different movement, it employs the notion of cause in argument. If "cause" is an interpretation of contiguity and succession, then pain can be the cause in that it may come first in the sequence of experience.[2] This double procedure of systematically employ-

[2] One might object that sometimes we observe the cause first and then the effect: we see a baseball fly toward the window and then witness the breaking of the window. Nietzsche might reply that only the experience or expectation of the effect enables one to identify the phenomenon in question as a (possible) cause; but in any event, the *possibility* of an inverted temporal relation suffices to scramble the causal scheme by putting in doubt the inferring of causal relations from temporal relations. For further discussion of this Nietzschean deconstruction, see Paul de Man, *Allegories of Reading*, pp. 107–10. For extended discussion of another example, Nietzsche's deconstruction of the principle of identity, see de Man, pp. 119–31 and Sarah Kofman, *Nietzsche et la scène philosophique*, pp. 137–63.

ing the concepts or premises one is undermining puts the critic in a position not of skeptical detachment but of unwarrantable involvement, asserting the indispensability of causation while denying it any rigorous justification. This is an aspect of deconstruction which many find difficult to understand and accept.

Third, the deconstruction reverses the hierarchical opposition of the causal scheme. The distinction between cause and effect makes the cause an origin, logically and temporally prior. The effect is derived, secondary, dependent upon the cause. Without exploring the reasons for or the implications of this hierarchization, let us note that, working within the opposition, the deconstruction upsets the hierarchy by producing an exchange of properties. If the effect is what causes the cause to become a cause, then the effect, not the cause, should be treated as the origin. By showing that the argument which elevates cause can be used to favor effect, one uncovers and undoes the rhetorical operation responsible for the hierarchization and one produces a significant displacement. If either cause or effect can occupy the position of origin, then origin is no longer originary; it loses its metaphysical privilege. A nonoriginary origin is a "concept" that cannot be comprehended by the former system and thus disrupts it.

This Nietzschean example poses numerous problems, but for the moment it can serve as a compact instance of the general procedures we encounter in the work of Jacques Derrida. Derrida's writings consist of engagements with a series of texts, mostly by the great philosophers but also by others: Plato (*La Dissémination*), Rousseau (*De la grammatologie*), Kant ("Economimésis," *La Vérité en peinture*), Hegel (*Marges, Glas*), Husserl (*L'Origine de la géométrie, La Voix et le phénomène, Marges*), Heidegger (*Marges*), Freud (*L'Ecriture et la différence, La Carte postale*), Mallarmé (*La Dissémination*), Saussure (*De la grammatologie*), Genet (*Glas*), Lévi-Strauss (*L'Ecriture et la différence, De la grammatologie*), Austin (*Marges*). Most of these encounters display a concern with a problem that he identifies succinctly in "La Pharmacie de Platon" ("Plato's Pharmacy"): in writing philosophy Plato condemns writing. Why?

Quelle loi commande cette "contradiction," cette opposition à soi du dit contre l'écriture, dit qui se dit contre soi-même dès lors qu'il s'écrit, qu'il écrit son identité à soi et enlève sa propriété *contre* ce fond d'écriture? Cette "contradiction," qui n'est autre que le rapport à soi de la diction s'opposant à la scription, . . . cette contradiction n'est pas contingente. [*La Dissémination*, p. 182]

What law governs this "contradiction," this opposition to itself of what is said against writing, of a dictum that pronounces itself against itself as soon as it finds its way into writing, as soon as it writes down its self-identity and carries away what is proper to it *against* this ground of writing? This "contradiction," which is nothing other than the relation-to-self of diction as it opposes itself to scription, . . . this contradiction is not contingent. [*Dissemination*, p. 158]

Philosophical discourse defines itself in opposition to writing and thus in opposition to itself, but this self-division or self-opposition is not, Derrida claims, a mistake or accident that sometimes occurs in philosophical texts. It is a structural property of the discourse itself.

Why should this be? As a point of departure for the discussion of Derrida, this claim poses several questions. Why should philosophy resist the idea that it is a kind of writing? Why should this question of the status of writing be important? To answer these questions we must cover considerable ground.

1. WRITING AND LOGOCENTRISM

In *De la grammatologie* and elsewhere, Derrida has documented the devaluation of writing in philosophical writings. The American philosopher Richard Rorty has suggested that we think of Derrida as answering the question, "'Given that philosophy *is* a kind of writing, why does this suggestion meet with such resistance?' This becomes, in his work, the slightly more particular question, 'What must philosophers who object to this characterization think *writing* is, that they should find the notion that this is what they are doing so offensive?'" ("Philosophy as a Kind of Writing," p. 144).

Philosophers write, but they do not think that philosophy ought to be writing. The philosophy they write treats writing as a means of expression which is at best irrelevant to the thought it expresses and at worst a barrier to that thought. For philosophy, Rorty continues, "Writing is an unfortunate necessity; what is really wanted is to show, to demonstrate, to point out, to exhibit, to make one's interlocutor stand at gaze before the world. . . . In a mature science, the words in which the investigator 'writes up' his results should be as few and as transparent as possible. . . . Philosophical writing, for Heidegger as for the Kantians, is really aimed at putting an end to writing. For Derrida, writing always leads to more writing, and more, and still more" (p. 145).

Philosophy characteristically hopes to solve problems, to show how things are, or to untangle a difficulty, and thus to put an end to writing on a topic by getting it right. Of course, philosophy is by no means alone in this hope. Any discipline must suppose the possibility of solving a problem, finding the truth, and thus writing the last words on a topic. The idea of a discipline is the idea of an investigation in which writing might be brought to an end. Literary critics, dismayed by the proliferation of interpretations and the prospect of a future in which writing will breed ever more writing so long as academic journals and university presses survive, frequently attempt to imagine ways of bringing writing to an end by reformulating the goals of literary criticism to make it a true discipline. Claims about the true purpose of criticism usually define tasks that could in principle be completed. They invoke the hope of saying the last word, arresting the process of commentary. In fact, this hope of getting it right is what inspires critics to write, even though they simultaneously know that writing never puts an end to writing. Paradoxically, the more powerful and authoritative an interpretation, the more writing it generates.

Whatever its discomforts for critics, this is a particularly awkward situation for philosophers. If they are seeking to solve problems about the conditions of truth, the possibility of knowledge, and the relationship between language and the world, then the relation of their own language to truth and to the world is part of the problem. To treat philosophy as a species of writing would create difficulties. If philosophy is to define the relation of writing to reason, it must not itself be writing, for it wants to define the relation not from the perspective of writing but from the perspective of reason. If it is to determine the truth about the relation of writing to truth, it must be on the side of truth, not of writing. To return to Derrida's remark quoted earlier concerning the dictum that pronounces against itself as soon as it writes itself or is written, it is precisely because it is written that philosophy must condemn writing, must define itself against writing. To claim that its statements are structured by logic, reason, truth, and not by the rhetoric of the language in which they are "expressed," philosophical discourse defines itself against writing.

Writing, from this perspective, is the external, the physical, the nontranscendental, and the threat posed by writing is that the operations of what should be merely a means of expression might affect or infect the meaning it is supposed to represent. We can glimpse here the outlines of a familiar model. There is thought—the realm of philosophy, for example—and then mediating systems through which thought is communicated. In speech there is already mediation but the signifiers disappear as soon as they are uttered; they do not obtrude, and the speaker can explain any ambiguities to insure that the thought has been conveyed. It is in writing that the unfortunate aspects of mediation become apparent. Writing presents language as a series of physical marks that operate in the absence of the speaker. They may be highly ambiguous or organized in artful rhetorical patterns.

The ideal would be to contemplate thought directly. Since this cannot be, language should be as transparent as possible. The threat of nontransparency is the danger that, instead of permitting direct contemplation of thought, linguistic signs might arrest the gaze and, by interposing their material form, affect or infect the thought. Worse still, philosophical thinking, which should lie beyond the contingencies of language and expression, might be affected by the forms of the signifiers of a language, which suggest, for example, a connection between the desire to write and to get it right. Can we be certain that our philosophical thinking about the relation between subject and object has not been influenced by the visual or morphological symmetry of these terms and the fact that they sound very similar? The extreme case, a sin against reason itself, is the pun, in which an "accidental" or external relationship between signifiers is treated as a conceptual relationship, identifying "history" as "his story" or connecting meaning (*sens*) and absence (*sans*). We treat the pun as a joke, lest signifiers infect thought.

The rejection of the signifier takes the form of the rejection of writing. This is the move by which philosophy constitutes itself as a discipline unaffected by the machinations of words and their contingent relationships—a discipline of thought and reason. Philosophy defines itself as what transcends writing, and by identifying certain aspects of the functioning of language with writing, tries to rid itself of these problems by setting writing aside as simply an artificial substitute for speech. This condemnation of writing, in Plato and elsewhere, is of considerable importance because the "phonocentrism" that treats writing as a representation of speech and puts speech in a direct and natural relationship with meaning is inextricably associated with the "logocentrism" of metaphysics, the orientation of philosophy toward an order of meaning—thought, truth, reason, logic, the Word—conceived as existing in itself, as foundation. The problem Derrida identifies involves not only the relation of speech and writing in philosophical discourse but also the claim that competing philosophies are versions of logocentrism. Indeed, Derrida might say, it is only because they are united in this search for a foundation, for something beyond which we need not go, that they can become competing philosophies.

Philosophy has been a "metaphysics of presence," the only metaphysics we know. "It could be shown," Derrida writes, "that all names related to fundamentals, to principles, or to the center have always designated the constant of a presence" (*L'Ecriture et la différence* p. 411/279). Phonocentrism, the privileging of voice,

> merges with the determination through history of the meaning of being in general as *presence*, with all the sub-determinations that depend on this general form and organize within it their system and their historical linkage (presence of the object to sight as *eidos*, presence as substance/essence/existence (*ousia*), temporal presence as the point (*stigmè*) of the now or the instant (*nun*), self-presence of the cogito, consciousness, subjectivity, co-presence of the self

and the other, intersubjectivity as an intentional phenomenon of the ego, etc.). Logocentrism would thus be bound up in the determination of the being of the existent as presence. [*De la grammatologie*, p. 23/12]

Each of these concepts, all of which involve a notion of presence, has figured in philosophical attempts to describe what is fundamental and has been treated as a centering, grounding force or principle. In oppositions such as meaning/form, soul/body, intuition/expression, literal/metaphorical, nature/culture, intelligible/sensible, positive/negative, transcendental/empirical, serious/nonserious, the superior term belongs to the logos and is a higher presence; the inferior term marks a fall. Logocentrism thus assumes the priority of the first term and conceives the second in relation to it, as a complication, a negation, a manifestation, or a disruption of the first. Description or analysis thus becomes

the enterprise of returning "strategically," in idealization, to an origin or to a "priority" seen as simple, intact, normal, pure, standard, self-identical, in order *then* to conceive of [pour pensor *ensuite*] derivation, complication, deterioration, accident, etc. All metaphysicians have proceeded thus, from Plato to Rousseau, from Descartes to Husserl: good before evil, the positive before the negative, the pure before the impure, the simple before the complex, the essential before the accidental, the imitated before the imitation, etc. This is not just *one* metaphysical gesture among others; it is the metaphysical exigency, the most constant, profound, and potent procedure. [*Limited Inc.*, p. 66/236]

Indeed, we generally assume that this is the procedure to follow in any "serious" analysis: to describe, for example, the simple, normal, standard case of deconstruction, illustrating its "essential" nature, and proceeding from there to discuss other cases that can then be defined as complications, derivations, and deteriorations. The difficulty of imaging and practicing different procedures is an indication of the ubiquity of logocentrism.

Among the familiar concepts that depend on the value of presence are: the immediacy of sensation, the presence of ultimate truths to a divine consciousness, the effective presence of

93

an origin in a historical development, a spontaneous or un-
mediated intuition, the transumption of thesis and antithesis in
a dialectical synthesis, the presence in speech of logical and
grammatical structures, truth as what subsists behind appearances, and the effective presence of a goal in the steps that lead
to it. The authority of presence, its power of valorization, structures all our thinking. The notions of "making clear," "grasping," "demonstrating," "revealing," and "showing what is the
case" all invoke presence. To claim, as in the Cartesian *cogito*,
that the "I" resists radical doubt because it is present to itself in
the act of thinking or doubting is one sort of appeal to presence. Another is the notion that the meaning of an utterance is
what is present to the consciousness of the speaker, what he or
she "has in mind" at the moment of utterance.

As these examples indicate, the metaphysics of presence is
pervasive, familiar, and powerful. There is, however, a problem that it characteristically encounters: when arguments cite
particular instances of presence as grounds for further development, these instances invariably prove to be already complex
constructions. What is proposed as a given, an elementary con-
stituent, proves to be a product, dependent or derived in ways
that deprive it of the authority of simple or pure presence.

Consider, for example, the flight of an arrow. If reality is
what is present at any given instant, the arrow produces a paradox. At any given moment it is in a particular spot; it is always
in a particular spot and never in motion. We want to insist,
quite justifiably, that the arrow *is* in motion at every instant
from the beginning to the end of its flight, yet its motion is
never present at any moment of presence. The presence of
motion is conceivable, it turns out, only insofar as every instant
is already marked with the traces of the past and future. Motion can be present, that is to say, only if the present instant is
not something given but a product of the relations between
past and future. Something can be happening at a given instant
only if the instant is already divided within itself, inhabited by
the nonpresent.

This is one of Zeno's paradoxes, purported to demonstrate
the impossibility of motion, but what it illustrates more convincingly are the difficulties of a system based on presence. We
think of the real as what is present at any given instant because

the present instant seems a simple, indecomposable absolute. The past is a former present, the future an anticipated present, but the present instant simply is: an autonomous given. But it turns out that the present instant can serve as ground only insofar as it is not a pure and autonomous given. If motion is to be present, presence must already be marked by difference and deferral. We must, Derrida says, "penser le présent à partir du temps comme différance" [think the present starting from/in relation to time as difference, differing, and deferral] (*De la grammatologie*, p. 237/166). The notion of presence and of the present is derived: an effect of differences. "We thus come," Derrida writes, "to posit presence . . . no longer as the absolute matrix form of being but rather as a 'particularization' and 'effect.' A determination and effect within a system that is no longer that of presence but of differance" (*Marges*, p. 17/"Differance," p. 147).

Here the issue has been the hierarchical opposition presence/absence. A deconstruction would involve the demonstration that for presence to function as it is said to, it must have the qualities that supposedly belong to its opposite, absence. Thus, instead of defining absence in terms of presence, as *its* negation, we can treat "presence" as the effect of a generalized absence or, as we shall see shortly, of *différance*. This operation may become clearer if we consider another example of the difficulties that arise within the metaphysics of presence. This one bears on signification and might be called the paradox of structure and event.

The meaning of a word, it is plausible to claim, is what speakers mean by it. A word's meaning within the system of a language, what we find when we look a word up in a dictionary, is a result of the meaning speakers have given it in past acts of communication. And what is true of a word is true of language in general: the structure of a language, its system of norms and regularities, is a product of events, the result of prior speech acts. However, when we take this argument seriously and begin to look at the events which are said to determine structures, we find that every event is itself already determined and made possible by prior structures. The possibility of meaning something by an utterance is already inscribed in the structure of the language. The structures themselves are always products, but however far back we try to push, even when we try to imagine the "birth" of language and describe an originary event that might have produced the first structure, we discover that we must assume prior organization, prior differentiation.

As in the case of causality, we find only nonoriginary origins. If a cave man is successfully to inaugurate language by making a special grunt signify "food," we must suppose that the grunt is already distinguished from other grunts and that the world has already been divided into the categories "food" and "nonfood." Acts of signification depend on differences, such as the contrast between "food" and "nonfood" that allows food to be signified, or the contrast between signifying elements that allows a sequence to function as a signifier. The sound sequence *bat* is a signifier because it contrasts with *pat, mat, bad, bet,* etc. The noise that is "present" when one says *bat* is inhabited by the traces of forms one is not uttering, and it can function as a signifier only insofar as it consists of such traces. As in the case of motion, what is supposedly present is already complex and differential, marked by difference, a product of differences.

An account of language, seeking solid foundation, will doubtless wish to treat meaning as something somewhere present—say, present to consciousness at the moment of a signifying event; but any presence it invokes turns out to be already inhabited by difference. However, if one tries instead to ground an account of meaning on difference, one fares no better, for differences are never given as such and are always products. A scrupulous theory must shift back and forth between these perspectives, of event and structure or *parole* and *langue,* which never lead to a synthesis. Each perspective shows the error of the other in an irresolvable alternation or aporia. As Derrida writes,

> We can extend to the system of signs in general what Saussure says about language: "The linguistic system (*langue*) is necessary for speech events (*parole*) to be intelligible and produce their effects, but the latter are necessary for the system to establish itself. . . . " There is a circle here, for if one distinguishes rigorously *langue* and *parole,* code and message, schema and usage, etc. and if one is to do justice to the two principles here enunciated, one does not know where to begin and how something can in general begin, be it *langue* or *parole.* One must therefore recognize, prior

to any dissociation of *langue* and *parole*, code and message, and what goes with it, a systematic production of differences, the *production* of a system of differences—a *différance* among whose effects one might later, by abstraction and for specific reasons, distinguish a lingusitics of *langue* from a linguistics of *parole*. [*Positions*, pp. 39–40/28]

The term *différance*, which Derrida introduces here, alludes to this undecidable, nonsynthetic alternation between the perspectives of structure and event. The verb *différer* means to differ and to defer. *Différance* sounds exactly the same as *différence*, but the ending *ance*, which is used to produce verbal nouns, makes it a new form meaning "difference-differing-deferring." *Différance* thus designates both a "passive" difference already in place as the condition of signification and an act of differing which produces differences. An analogous English term is *spacing*, which designates both an arrangement and an act of distribution or arranging. Derrida occasionally uses the corresponding French term *espacement*, but *différance* is more powerful and apposite because *difference* has been a crucial term in the writings of Nietzsche, Saussure, Freud, Husserl, and Heidegger. Investigating systems of signification, they have been led to emphasize difference and differentiation, and Derrida's silent deformation of the term, as well as showing that writing cannot be seen as simply the representation of speech, makes apparent the problem that both determines and subverts every theory of meaning.

Différance, he writes,

is a structure and a movement that cannot be conceived on the basis of the opposition presence/absence. *Différance* is the systematic play of differences, of traces of differences, of the spacing [*espacement*] by which elements relate to one another. This spacing is the production, simultaneously active and passive (the *a* of *différance* indicates this indecision as regards activity and passivity, that which cannot yet be governed and organized by that opposition), of intervals without which the "full" terms could not signify, could not function [*Positions*, pp. 38–39/27]

These problems are explored further in Derrida's reading of Saussure in *De la grammatologie*. Saussure's *Cours de linguistique générale,* which has inspired both structuralism and semiotics, can be shown to contain, on the one hand, a powerful critique of the metaphysics of presence and, on the other hand, an explicit affirmation of logocentrism and unavoidable involvement with it. Derrida thus shows how Saussure's discourse deconstructs itself, but he also argues, and this is a point that must not be missed, that, far from invalidating the *Cours,* this self-deconstructive movement is essential to its power and pertinence. The value and force of a text may depend to a considerable extent on the way it deconstructs the philosophy that subtends it.

Saussure begins by defining language as a system of signs. Noises count as language only when they serve to express or communicate ideas, and thus the central question for him becomes the nature of the sign: what gives it its identity and enables it to function as sign. He argues that signs are arbitrary and conventional and that each is defined not by essential properties but by the differences that distinguish it from other signs. A language is thus conceived as a system of differences, and this leads to the development of the distinctions on which structuralism and semiotics have relied: between a language as a system of differences (*langue*) and the speech events which the system makes possible (*parole*), between the study of the language as a system at any given time (synchronic) and study of the correlations between elements from different historical periods (diachronic), between two types of differences within the system, syntagmatic and paradigmatic relations, and between the two constituents of the sign, signifier and signified. These basic distinctions together constitute the linguistic and semiotic project of accounting for linguistic events by making explicit the system of relations that makes them possible.

Now the more rigorously Saussure pursues his investigations, the more he is led to insist on the purely relational nature of the linguistic system. Sound itself, he argues convincingly, cannot belong to the system; it permits the manifestation of units of the system in acts of speech. Indeed, he concludes that "in the linguistic system there are only differences, *without positive terms*" (*Cours,* p. 166/120). This is a radical formulation. The common view is doubtless that a language consists of words, positive entities, which are put together to form a system and thus acquire relations with one another, but Saussure's analysis of the nature of linguistic units leads to the conclusion that, on the contrary, signs are the product of a system of differences; indeed, they are not positive entities at all but effects of difference. This is a powerful critique of logocentrism; as Derrida explains, to conclude that the system consists only of differences undermines the attempt to found a theory of language on positive entities which might be present either in the speech event or in the system. If in the linguistic system there are only differences, Derrida notes,

> the play of differences involves syntheses and referrals that prevent there from being at any moment or in any way a simple element that is present in and of itself and refers only to itself. Whether in written or in spoken discourse, no element can function as a sign without relating to another element which itself is not simply present. This linkage means that each "element"—phoneme or grapheme—is constituted with reference to the trace in it of the other elements of the sequence or system. This linkage, this weaving, is the *text*, which is produced only through the transformation of another text. Nothing, either in the elements or in the system, is anywhere simply present or absent. There are only, everywhere, differences and traces of traces. [*Positions*, pp. 37–38/26]

The arbitrary nature of the sign and the system with no positive terms give us the paradoxical notion of an "instituted trace," a structure of infinite referral in which there are only traces— traces prior to any entity of which they might be the trace.

At the same time, however, there is in Saussure's argument an affirmation of logocentrism. The concept of the sign itself, from which Saussure starts, is based on a distinction between the sensible and the intelligible; the signifier exists to give access to the signified and thus seems to be subordinated to the concept or meaning that it communicates. Moreover, in order to distinguish one sign from another, in order to tell when material variations are significant, the linguist must assume the possibility of grasping signifieds, making them his point of departure. The concept of the sign is so involved with the basic concepts of logocentrism that it would be difficult for Saussure to shift it even if he wished to. Though much of his analysis does work to this end, he explicitly affirms a logocentric conception of the sign and thus inscribes his analysis within logocentrism. This emerges, most interestingly for Derrida, in Saussure's treatment of writing, which he relegates to a secondary and derivative status. Although he had specifically excluded sound as such from the linguistic system and insisted on the formal character of linguistic units, he maintains that "the object of linguistic analysis is not defined by the combination of the written word and the spoken word: the spoken word alone constitutes the object" (*Cours*, pp. 45/23–24). Writing is simply a means of representing speech, a technical device or external accessory that need not be taken into consideration when studying language.

This may seem a relatively innocuous move, but in fact, as Derrida shows, it is crucial to the Western tradition of thinking about language, in which speech is seen as natural, direct communication and writing as an artificial and oblique representation of a representation. In defense of this ranking, one may cite the fact that children learn to speak before they learn to write or that millions of people, even entire cultures, have speech without writing; but when such facts are adduced they are taken to demonstrate not just a factual or local priority of speech to writing but a more portentous general and comprehensive priority. Speech is seen as in direct contact with meaning: words issue from the speaker as the spontaneous and nearly transparent signs of his present thought, which the attendant listener hopes to grasp. Writing, on the other hand, consists of physical marks that are divorced from the thought that may have produced them. It characteristically functions in the absence of a speaker, gives uncertain access to a thought, and can even appear as wholly anonymous, cut off from any speaker or author. Writing thus seems to be not merely a technical device for representing speech but a distortion of speech. This judgment of writing is as old as philosophy itself. In the *Phaedrus* Plato condemns writing as a bastardized form of communication; separated from the father or moment of origin, writing can give rise to all sorts of misunderstandings since the speaker is not there to explain to the listener what he has in mind.

Privileging speech by treating writing as a parasitic and imperfect representation of it is a way of setting aside certain features of language or aspects of its functioning. If distance, absence, misunderstanding, insincerity, and ambiguity are features of writing, then by distinguishing writing from speech one can construct a model of communication that takes as its norm an ideal associated with speech—where the words bear a meaning and the listener can in principle grasp precisely what the speaker has in mind. The moral fervor that marks Saussure's discussion of writing indicates that something important is at stake. He speaks of the "dangers" of writing, which "disguises" language and even on occasion "usurps" the role of speech. The "tyranny of writing" is powerful and insidious, leading, for example, to errors of pronunciation that are "pathological," a corruption or infection of the natural spoken forms. Linguists who attend to written forms are "falling into the trap." Writing, supposedly a representation of speech, threatens the purity of the system it serves (*De la grammatologie*, pp. 51–63/34–43).

But if writing can affect speech, the relationship is more complicated than it at first appeared. The hierarchical scheme that gave speech priority and made writing dependent upon it is further skewed by Saussure's recourse to the example of writing to explain the nature of linguistic units. How can one illustrate the notion of a purely differential unit? "Since an identical state of affairs is observable in writing, another system of signs, we shall use writing to draw some comparisons that will clarify the whole issue" (*Cours*, p. 165/119). The letter *t*, for example, can be written in various ways so long as it remains distinct from *l*, *f*, *i*, *d*, etc. There are no essential features that must be preserved; its identity is purely relational.

Thus writing, which Saussure claimed ought not to be the object of linguistic enquiry, turns out to be the best illustration of the nature of linguistic units. Speech is to be understood as a form of writing, an instance of the basic linguistic mechanism manifested in writing. Saussure's argument brings about this reversal: the announced hierarchy that makes writing a derivative form of speech, a parasitic mode of representation added to speech, is inverted, and speech is presented, explained, as a form of writing. This gives us a new concept of writing: a generalized writing that would have as subspecies a vocal writing and a graphic writing.

Pursuing the interplay of speech and writing in the texts of Plato, Rousseau, Husserl, Lévi-Strauss, and Condillac, as well as Saussure, Derrida produces a general demonstration that if writing is defined by the qualities traditionally attributed to it, then speech is already a form of writing. For example, writing is often set aside as merely a technique for recording speech in inscriptions that can be repeated and circulated in the absence of the signifying intention that animates speech; but this iterability can be shown to be the condition of any sign. A sequence of sounds can function as a signifier only if it is repeatable, if it can be recognized as the "same" in different circumstances. It must be possible for me to repeat to a third party what someone said. A speech sequence is not a sign sequence unless it can be quoted and put into circulation among those who have no knowledge of the "original" speaker and his signifying intentions. The utterance "Ris-Orangis is a southern suburb of Paris" continues to signify as it is repeated, quoted, or, as here, cited as example; and it can continue to signify whether or not those who reproduce or quote it have anything "in mind." This possibility of being repeated and functioning without respect to a particular signifying intention is a condition of linguistic signs in general, not just of writing. Writing may be thought of as a material record, but as Derrida notes, "If 'writing' means inscription and especially the durable instituting of signs (and this is the only irreducible kernel of the concept of writing), then writing in general covers the entire domain of linguistic signs. . . . The very idea of institution, hence of the arbitrariness of the sign, is unthinkable prior to or outside the horizon of writing" (*De la grammatologie*, p. 65/44). Writing-in-general is an *archi-écriture*, an archi-writing or protowriting which is the condition of both speech and writing in the narrow sense.

The relationship between speech and writing gives us a structure which Derrida identifies in a number of texts and which he calls, using a term that Rousseau applies to writing, a logic of the "supplement." A supplement, Webster's tells us, is "something that completes or makes an addition." A supplement to a dictionary is an extra section that is added on, but the possibility of adding a supplement indicates that the dictionary itself is incomplete. "Languages are made to be spoken," writes Rousseau; "writing serves only as a supplement to speech." And this concept of the supplement, which appears everywhere in Rousseau, "harbors within it two significations whose cohabitation is as strange as it is necessary" (*De la grammatologie*, p. 208/144). The supplement is an inessential extra, added to something complete in itself, but the supplement is added in order to complete, to compensate for a lack in what was supposed to be complete in itself. These two different meanings of *supplement* are linked in a powerful logic, and in both meanings the supplement is presented as exterior, foreign to the "essential" nature of that to which it is added or in which it is substituted.

Rousseau describes writing as a technique added to speech, foreign to the nature of language, but the other sense of *supplement* also turns out to be at work here. Writing can be added to speech only if speech is not a self-sufficient, natural plenitude, only if there is already in speech a lack or absence that enables writing to supplement it. This emerges strikingly in Rousseau's discussion of writing, for while he condemns writing "as a destruction of presence and disease of speech," his own activity as a writer is presented, quite traditionally, as an attempt to restore through the absence of writing a presence that has been missing from speech. Here is a succinct formulation from the *Confessions*: "I would love society as others do if I were not sure of showing myself not just at a disadvantage but as completely different from what I am. The decision I have taken to write and to hide myself is precisely the one that suits me. If I were present people would never have known what I was worth" (*De la grammatologie*, p. 205/142).

Writing can be compensatory, a supplement to speech, only because speech is already marked by the qualities generally predicated of writing: absence and misunderstanding. As Derrida notes, though speaking of linguistic theory generally rather than of Rousseau's argument, writing can be secondary and derivative "only on one condition: that the 'original,' 'natural' etc. language never existed, was never intact or untouched by writing, that it has itself always been a writing," an archi-writing (*De la grammatologie*, p. 82/56). Derrida's discussion of "this dangerous supplement" in Rousseau describes this structure in a variety of domains: Rousseau's various external supplements are called in to supplement precisely because there is always a lack in what is supplemented, an originary lack.

For example, Rousseau discusses education as a supplement to nature. Nature is in principle complete, a natural plenitude to which education is an external addition. But the description of this supplementation reveals an inherent lack in nature; nature must be completed—supplemented—by education if it is to be truly itself: the right education is needed if human nature is to emerge as it truly is. The logic of supplementarity thus makes nature the prior term, a plenitude that is there at the start, but reveals an inherent lack or absence within it, so that education, the additional extra, also becomes an essential condition of that which it supplements.

Rousseau also speaks of masturbation as a "dangerous supplement." Like writing, it is a perverse addition, a practice or technique added to normal sexuality as writing is added to speech. But masturbation also replaces or substitutes for "normal" sexual activity. To function as substitute it must resemble in some essential way what it replaces, and indeed the fundamental structure of masturbation—desire as auto-affection focusing on an imagined object that one can never "possess"—is repeated in other sexual relationships, which can thus be seen as moments of a generalized masturbation.

However, it would be more exact to speak of a generalized substitution, for what Rousseau's supplements reveal is an endless chain of supplements. Writing is a supplement to speech, but speech is already a supplement: children, says *Emile*, quickly learn to use speech "to supplement their own weakness . . . for it does not need much experience to realize how pleasant it is to act through the hands of others and to move the world simply by moving the tongue" (*De la grammatologie*, p. 211/147). In the absence of Madame de Warens, his beloved "Maman," Rousseau has recourse to supplements, as the *Confessions* describes: "I would never finish if I were to describe in detail all the follies that the recollection of my dear Maman made me commit when I was no longer in her presence. How often I kissed my bed, recalling that she had slept in it, my curtains and all the furniture in the room, since they belonged to her and her beautiful hand had touched them, even the floor, on which I prostrated myself, thinking that she had walked upon it" (*De la grammatologie*, p. 217/152). These supplements function in her absence as substitutes for her presence, but, the text immediately continues, "Sometimes even in her presence I committed extravagances that only the most violent love seemed capable of inspiring. One day at table, just as she had put a piece of food in her mouth, I exclaimed that I saw a hair on it. She put the morsel back on her plate; I eagerly seized and swallowed it." Rousseau's passage astutely marks through the signifier the structure that is at work here. What he exclaims that he sees on the morsel of food is both something foreign and indifferent (*un cheveu*) and his own desire (*un je veux*), which functions through contingent supplements.

This chain of substitutions could be continued. Maman's "presence," as we have seen, does not arrest it. If he were to "possess her," as we say, this would still be marked by absence: "la possession physique," says Proust, "où d'ailleurs l'on ne possède rien." And Maman is herself a substitute for an unknown mother, who would herself be a supplement. "Through this sequence of supplements there emerges a law: that of an endless linked series, ineluctably multiplying the supplementary mediations that produce the sense of the very thing that they defer: the impression of the thing itself, of immediate presence, or originary perception. Immediacy is derived. Everything begins with the intermediary . . ." (*De la grammatologie*, p. 226/157).

Rousseau's texts, like many others, teach that presence is always deferred, that supplementation is possible only because of an originary lack, and they thus propose that we conceive what we call "life" on the model of the text, on the model of supplementation figured by signifying processes. What these writings maintain is not that there is nothing outside the empirical texts—the writings—of a culture, but that what lies outside are more supplements, chains of supplements, thus putting in question the distinction between inside and outside. The matrix of what we call Rousseau's real life, with its socioeconomic conditions and public events, its private sexual experiences and its acts of writing, would prove on examination to be constituted by the logic of supplementarity, as do the physical objects he invokes in the passage about Maman in the *Confessions*. Derrida writes,

> What we have tried to show in following the connecting thread of the "dangerous supplement," is that in what we call the real life

of these "flesh and blood" creatures, beyond and behind what we believe we can circumscribe as Rousseau's *oeuvre*, there has never been anything but writing, there have never been anything but supplements and substitutional significations which could only arise in a chain of differential references. The "real" supervenes or is added only in taking meaning from a trace or an invocation of supplements [*un appel de supplément*]. And so on indefinitely, for we have read *in the text* that the absolute present, Nature, what is named by words like "real mother" etc., have always already escaped, have never existed; that what inaugurates meaning and language is writing as the disappearance of natural presence. [*De la grammatologie*, pp. 228/158–59]

This ubiquity of the supplement does not mean that there is no difference between the "presence" of Maman or Thérèse and their "absence," or between a real event and a fictional one. These differences are crucial and play a powerful role in what we call our experience. But effects of presence and of historical reality arise within and are made possible by supplementation, by difference, as particular determinations of this structure. Maman's "presence" is a certain type of absence, and a real historical event, as numerous theorists have sought to show, is a particular type of fiction. Presence is not originary but reconstituted (*L'Ecriture et la différence*, p. 314/212).

The metaphysical strategy at work in Rousseau's texts, which at the same time prove its undoing, has consisted "of excluding non-presence by determining the supplement as simple exteriority, pure addition or pure absence. . . . What is added is nothing because it is added to a full presence to which it is exterior. Speech comes to be added to intuitive presence (of the entity, of essence, of the *eidos*, of *ousia*, and so forth); writing comes to be added to a living self-present speech; masturbation comes to be added to so-called normal sexual experience; culture to nature, evil to innocence, history to origin, and so forth" (*De la grammatologie*, pp. 237–38/167). The importance of these structures and valuations in our thinking indicates that the privileging of speech over writing is not a mistake. that authors might have avoided. The setting aside of writing as supplement is, Derrida insists, an operation underwritten by the entire history of metaphysics and is even the crucial operation in the "economy" of metaphysical concepts.

The privilege of the *phonè* does not depend upon a choice that might have been avoided. It corresponds to a moment of the system (let us say, of the "life" of "history" or of "being-as-self-relationship"). The system of "hearing/understanding-oneself-speak" [*s'entendre parler*] through the phonic substance—which *presents itself* as a non-exterior, non-worldly and therefore non-empirical or non-contingent signifier—has necessarily dominated the history of the world during an entire epoch, and has even produced the idea of the world, the idea of world-origin, arising from the difference between the worldly and the non-worldly, the outside and the inside, ideality and non-ideality, universal and non-universal, transcendental and empirical, etc. [*De la grammatologie*, pp. 17/7–8]

These are large claims. They become more comprehensible if one notes that the idea of the "world," as that which is outside consciousness, depends on distinctions such as inside/outside, and each of these oppositions depends upon a point of differentiation, a point where outside becomes differentiated from inside. The distinction is controlled by a point of differentiation. Derrida's claim is twofold. First, the moment of speech, or rather the moment of one's own speech, where signifier and signified seem simultaneously given, where inside and outside, material and spiritual seem fused, serves as a point of reference in relation to which all these essential distinctions can be posited. Second, this reference to the moment of one's own speech enables one to treat the resulting distinctions as hierarchical oppositions, in which one term belongs to presence and the logos and the other denotes a fall from presence. To tamper with the privilege of speech would be to threaten the entire edifice.

Speech can play this role because at the moment when one speaks material signifier and spiritual signified seem to present themselves as an undissociated unity, where the intelligible controls the sensible. Written words may appear as physical marks which the reader must interpret and animate; one can see them without understanding them, and this possibility of a gap is part of their structure. But when I speak, my voice does not seem to be something external that I first hear and then understand. Hearing and understanding my speech as I speak are the same thing. This is what Derrida calls the system of *s'enten-*

dre parler, the French verb efficiently fusing the acts of hearing oneself and understanding oneself. In speech I seem to have direct access to my thoughts. The signifiers do not separate me from my thought, but efface themselves before it. Nor do the signifiers seem to be external devices taken from the world and put to use. They arise spontaneously from within and are transparent to the thought. The moment of hearing/understanding oneself speak offers "the unique experience of the signified producing itself spontaneously, from within the self, and yet nevertheless, as signified concept, in the element of ideality or universality. The unworldly character of this substance of expression is constitutive of this ideality. This experience of the effacement of the signifier in voice is not one illusion among others—since it is the condition of the very idea of truth . . ." (*De la grammatologie*, p. 33/20).

The effacement of the signifier in speech is a condition of the idea of truth because it combines the possibility of objectivity—repeatable manifestation, a constant meaning present in numerous appearances—with dominance of meaning over appearance. Insofar as truth requires the possibility of a constant signification which can manifest itself and remains unchanged or unaffected by the vehicles that manifest it, voice provides us with the necessary model. By this model in which the distinction between meaning and form is a hierarchical opposition, truth dominates the opposition between truth and appearances.

But of course this model does involve an illusion. The evanescence of the signifier in speech creates the impression of the direct presence of a thought, but however swiftly it vanishes, the spoken word is still a material form which, like the written form, works through its differences from other forms. If the vocal signifier is preserved for examination, as in a tape recording, so that we can "hear ourselves speak," we find that speech is a sequence of signifiers just as writing is, similarly open to the process of interpretation. Though speech and writing may produce different sorts of effects of signification, there are no grounds for claiming that voice delivers thoughts directly, as may seem to be the case when one hears oneself speak at the moment of speaking. A recording of one's own speech makes clear that speech too works by the differential play of signifiers, though it is precisely this work of difference that the privileging of speech seeks to suppress. "Speech and the consciousness of speech—that is to say, simply consciousness as self-presence—are the phenomena of an auto-affection experienced as the suppression of differance. This *phenomenon*, this presumed suppression of differance, this lived reduction of the opacity of the signifier, are the origin of what we call presence" (*De la grammatologie*, p. 236/166).

In seeing how the system of *s'entendre parler* serves as a model of presence and reveals the solidarity of phonocentrism, logocentrism, and metaphysics of presence, we have explored the reasons why speech has been set above writing. This opposition, in all its strategic importance, is deconstructed in the texts that affirm it, as speech turns out to depend upon those very qualities that have been predicated of writing. Theories grounded on presence—whether of meaning as a signifying intention present to consciousness at the moment of utterance or of an ideal norm that subsists behind all appearances—undo themselves, as the supposed foundation or ground proves to be the product of a differential system, or rather, of difference, differentiation, and deferral. But the operation of deconstruction or the self-deconstruction of logocentric theories does not lead to a new theory that sets everything straight. Even theories like Saussure's, with its powerful critique of logocentrism in its concept of a purely differential system, do not escape the logocentric premises they undermine; and there is no reason to believe that a theoretical enterprise could ever free itself from those premises. Theory may well be condemned to a structural inconsistency.

The question that now arises, especially for literary critics who are more concerned with the implications of philosophical theories than with their consistency or affiliations, is what this has to do with the theory of meaning and the interpretation of texts. The examples we have examined so far permit at least a preliminary reply: deconstruction does not elucidate texts in the traditional sense of attempting to grasp a unifying content or theme; it investigates the work of metaphysical oppositions in their arguments and the ways in which textual figures and relations, such as the play of the supplement in Rousseau, produce a double, aporetic logic. The examples we have considered give no reason to believe, as is sometimes suggested, that deconstruction makes interpretation a process of free association in which anything goes, though it does concentrate on conceptual and figural implications rather than on authorial intentions. However, the deconstruction of the opposition between speech and writing, by making central to language predicates often associated with the written character alone, may have implications that we have not yet explored. If, for example, meaning is thought of as the product of language rather than its source, how might that affect interpretation? A good way to approach the implications of deconstruction for models of signification is through Derrida's reading of J. L. Austin in "Signature événement contexte" (*Marges*) and the subsequent dispute with the American theorist of speech acts, John Searle.

2. Meaning and Iterability

In the Saussurian perspective meaning is the product of a linguistic system, the effect of a system of differences. To account for meaning is to set forth the relations of contrast and the possibilities of combination that constitute a language. This procedure is essential to the analysis of signifying processes, but two observations must be made about the theory that proposes it. First, as we have seen in following Saussure's self-deconstruction, a theory based on difference does not escape logocentrism but finds itself appealing to presence, not only because concepts of analysis, demonstration, and objectivity involve such reference but also because in order to identify differences responsible for meanings one needs to treat some meanings as if they were given, as if they were somewhere "present" as a point of departure.

Second, a theory that derives meaning from linguistic structure, though it contributes much to the analysis of meaning, does not account for it completely. If one conceives of meaning as the effect of linguistic relations manifested in an utterance, then one must contend with the fact that, as we say, a speaker can mean different things by the same linguistic sequence on different occasions. "Could you move that box?" may be a request, or a question about one's interlocutor's strength, or even, as rhetorical question, the resigned indication of an impossibility.

Such examples seem to reinstate a model in which the subject—the consciousness of the speaker—is made the source of meaning: despite the contribution of linguistic structure, the meaning of the utterance varies from case to case; its meaning is what the speaker means by it. Confronted with such a model, the partisan of structural explanation will ask what makes it possible for the speaker to mean these several things by the one utterance. Just as we account for the meaning of sentences by analyzing the linguistic system, so we should account for the meaning of utterances (or as Austin calls it, their illocutionary force) by analyzing another system, the system of speech acts. As the founder of speech act theory, Austin is in fact repeating at another level (though less explicitly) the crucial move made by Saussure: to account for signifying events (*parole*) one attempts to describe the system that makes them possible.

Thus Austin argues, for example, that to mean something by an utterance is not to perform an inner act of meaning that accompanies the utterance. The notion that I may mean different things by "Could you move that box?" seems to urge that we explain meaning by inquiring what the speaker has in mind, as though this were the determining factor, but this is what Austin denies. What makes an utterance a command or a promise or a request is not the speaker's state of mind at the moment of utterance but conventional rules involving features of the context. If in appropriate circumstances I say "I promise to return this to you," I have made a promise, whatever was running through my mind at the time, and conversely, when earlier in this sentence I wrote the words "I promise to return this to you" I did not succeed in making a promise, even if the thoughts in my mind were similar to those that occurred on an occasion when I did make a promise. Promising is an act governed by certain conventions that the theorist of speech acts attempts to make explicit.

Austin's project is thus an attempt at structural explanation which offers a pertinent critique of logocentric premises, but in his discussion he reintroduces precisely those assumptions that his project puts in question. Derrida outlines this self-deconstructive movement in a section of "Signature événement contexte" (*Marges*), but John Searle's egregious misunderstanding in his "Reiterating the Differences: A Reply to Derrida" indicates that it may be important to proceed more slowly than Derrida does, with fuller discussion of Austin's project and Derrida's observations.

Austin begins *How to Do Things with Words* with the observation that "It was for too long the assumption of philosophers that the business of a 'statement' can only be to 'describe' some state of affairs, or to 'state some fact,' which it must do either truly or falsely" (p. 1). The normal sentence was conceived as a true or false representation of a state of affairs, and numerous sentences which failed to correspond to this model were treated either as unimportant exceptions or as deviant "pseudo-statements." "Yet we, that is, even philosophers, set some limits to the amount of nonsense that we are prepared to admit we talk; so that it was natural to go on to ask, as a second stage, whether many apparently pseudo-statements really set out to be 'statements' at all" (p. 2).

Austin thus proposes to attend to cases previously ignored as marginal and problematic and to treat them not as failed statements but as an independent type. He proposes a distinction between statements, or *constative* utterances, which describe a state of affairs and are true or false, and another class of utterances which are not true or false and which actually perform the action to which they refer (for example, "I promise to pay you tomorrow" accomplishes the act of promising). These he calls *performatives*.

This distinction between *performative* and *constative* has proved very fruitful in the analysis of language, but as Austin presses further in his description of the distinctive features of the performative and the various forms it can take, he reaches a surprising conclusion. An utterance such as "I hereby affirm that the cat is on the mat" seems also to possess the crucial feature of accomplishing the act (of affirming) to which it refers. *I affirm X*, like *I promise X*, is neither true or false but performs the act it denotes. It would thus seem to count as a performative. But another important feature of the performative, Austin has shown, is the possibility of deleting the explicit performative verb. Instead of saying "I promise to pay you tomorrow" one can in appropriate circumstances perform the act of promising by saying "I will pay you tomorrow"—a statement whose illocutionary force remains performative. Similarly, one can perform the act of affirming or stating while omitting "I hereby affirm that." "The cat is on the mat" may be seen as a shortened version of "I hereby state that the cat is on the mat" and thus a performative. But, of course, "The cat is on the mat" is the classic example of a constative utterance.

Austin's analysis provides a splendid instance of the logic of supplementarity at work. Starting from the philosophical hierarchy that makes true or false statements the norm of language and treats other utterances as flawed statements or as extra— supplementary—forms, Austin's investigation of the qualities of the marginal case leads to a deconstruction and inversion of the hierarchy: the performative is not a flawed constative: rather, the constative is a special case of the performative. The possibility that a constative is a performative from which one of various performative verbs has been deleted has since been entertained by numerous linguists. John Lyons notes, "It is natural to consider the possibility of deriving all sentences from underlying structures with an optionally deletable main clause containing a first person subject, a performative verb of saying, and optionally an indirect-object expression referring to the addressee" (*Semantics*, vol. 2, p. 778).

This would be a way of extending grammar to account for part òf the force of utterances. Instead of saying that speakers can mean different things by the sentence "This chair is broken," linguists can extend the linguistic system to account for certain variations in meaning. "This chair is broken" can have different meanings because it can be derived from any of several underlying strings—strings which could be expressed as "I warn you that this chair is broken," "I inform you that this chair is broken," "I concede to you that this chair is broken," "I proclaim to you that this chair is broken," "I complain to you that this chair is broken."

Austin does not cast his theory in this form and would be skeptical of such attempts to extend grammar. He cites relationships between such pairs as "I warn you that this chair is broken" and "This chair is broken" to show that illocutionary force does not necessarily follow from grammatical structure. Indeed, he proposes a distinction between locutionary and illocutionary acts. When I say "This chair is broken," I perform the *locutionary* act of uttering a particular English sentence and the *illocutionary* act of stating, warning, proclaiming, or complaining. (There is also what Austin calls a *perlocutionary* act, the act I may accomplish by my performance of the locutionary and illocutionary acts: by arguing I may *persuade* you, by proclaiming something I may *bring you to know* it.) The rules of the linguistic system account for the meaning of the locutionary act; the goal of speech act theory is to account for the meaning of the illocutionary act or, as Austin calls it, the illocutionary force of an utterance.

To explain illocutionary force is to set forth the conventions that make it possible to perform various illocutionary acts: what one has to do in order to promise, to warn, to complain, to command. "Besides the uttering of the words of the so-called performative," Austin writes, "a good many other things have as a general rule to be right and to go off right if we are to be said to have happily brought off our action. What these are we may hope to discover by looking at and classifying types of cases in which something *goes wrong* and the act—marrying, betting, bequeathing, christening, or what not—is therefore at least to some extent a failure" (p. 14). Austin thus does not treat failure as an external accident that befalls performatives and has no bearing on their nature. The possibility of failure is internal to the performative and a point of departure for investigating it. Something cannot be a performative unless it can go wrong.

This approach may seem unusual, but in fact it accords with basic axioms of semiotics. "A sign," writes Umberto Eco in *A Theory of Semiotics*, "is everything which can be taken as significantly substituting for something else. Semiotics is in principle the discipline studying everything which can be used in order to lie. If something cannot be used to tell a lie, conversely it cannot be used to tell the truth" (p. 7). *The bat is on my hat* would not be a signifying sequence if it were not possible to utter it falsely. Similarly, *I now pronounce you man and wife* is not a performative unless it is possible for it to misfire, to be used in inappropriate circumstances and without the effect of performing a marriage.

For the smooth functioning of a performative, Austin says,

"(A.1) There must exist an accepted conventional procedure having a certain conventional effect, that procedure to include the uttering of certain words by certain persons in certain circumstances, and further, (A.2) the particular persons and circumstances in a given case must be appropriate for the invocation of the particular procedure invoked. (B.1) The procedure must be executed by all participants both correctly and (B.2) completely" (*How to Do Things with Words*, pp. 14–15). As this analysis suggests, to promise is to utter one of the conventional formulas in appropriate circumstances. It would be wrong, Austin argues, to think of the utterance "as (merely) the outward and visible sign, for convenience or other record or for information, of an inward and spiritual act" (p. 9). For example, "the act of marrying, like, say, the act of betting, is at least *preferably* . . . to be described as *saying certain words* rather than as performing a different, inward and spiritual action, of which these words are merely the outward and audible sign. That this is so can perhaps hardly be *proved*, but it is, I should claim, a fact" (p. 13).

Austin refuses to explain meaning in terms of a state of mind and proposes, rather, an analysis of the conventions of discourse. Can such a program be carried out? Can his theory in fact avoid reinvoking the notion of presence? Saussure in his project reintroduces presence in his treatment of voice; can Austin proceed without also reinstating the notion of meaning as a signifying intention present to consciousness at the moment of utterance and thus treating the meaning of a speech act as ultimately determined by or grounded in a consciousness whose intention is fully present to itself? Derrida's reading focuses on the way in which this reintroduction occurs. An especially interesting moment in which the argument can be shown to involve such an appeal occurs in the opening pages of *How to Do Things with Words*, as Austin is staking out the ground for his enterprise. After chastising philosophers for treating as marginal any utterances that are not true or false statements and thus leading us to suppose that he himself will be concerned with such things as fictional utterances which are neither true or false, Austin proposes an objection to the notion of performative utterance: "Surely the words must be spoken 'seriously' and so as to be taken 'seriously'? This is, though vague, true enough in general—it is an important commonplace in discussing the purport of any utterance whatsoever. I must not be joking, for example, nor writing a poem" (p. 9).

The rhetorical structure of this passage is itself quite revealing. Although he proposes to exclude the nonserious, Austin offers no characterization of it, presumably because he is particularly anxious at this point to avoid the reference to an inner intention that such description would doubtless involve. Instead his text posits an anonymous objection which introduces "seriously" in quotation marks, as if it were itself not altogether serious. Doubling itself to produce this objection whose key term remains unanchored, the text can then grant the objection as something to be taken for granted.

Once, Austin has already told us, it was customary for philosophers to exclude—unjustifiably—utterances that were not true or false statements. Now his own text makes it appear customary to exclude utterances that are not serious. We have here, as the remark about the vagueness of the "serious" indicates, not a rigorous move within philosophy but a customary exclusion on which philosophy relies. Elsewhere Austin writes, in a comment that might pertain to the complexities of the nonserious and the perhaps-not-quite-serious, "it's not things, it's philosophers that are simple. You will have heard it said, I expect, that oversimplification is the occupational disease of philosophers, and in a way one might agree with that. But for a sneaking suspicion that it's their occupation" (*Philosophical Papers*, p. 252).[3]

The exclusion of the nonserious is repeated in a longer passage that helps to indicate what is at stake. After listing various failures that may prevent the accomplishment of a performative, Austin notes that performatives are subject

[3] Of course, this simplification is designed to permit complex investigations. Austin's shrewd diagnosis captures the structure of supplementarity that we have been discussing: the supposed occupational hazard—an external ailment that might afflict or infect the analyst—may prove to be essential, to be the occupation itself, without losing its quality of ailment. In fact, Austin's successors have attempted to improve his analysis by more radical exclusions and simplifications. Jerrold Katz, in *Propositional Structure and Illocutionary Force* (New York: Harper & Row, 1977), undertakes to show, in a chapter entitled "How to save Austin from Austin," that a more thorough idealization will protect the distinction between performative and constative from the insightful self-deconstruction accomplished by Austin (pp. 184–85). See Shoshana Felman's excellent discussion in *Le Scandale du corps parlant*, pp. 190–201.

to certain other kinds of ill which infect *all* utterances. And these likewise, though again they might be brought into a more general account, we are deliberately at present excluding. I mean, for example, the following: a performative utterance will, for example, be *in a peculiar way* hollow or void if said by an actor on the stage or introduced in a poem, or spoken in a soliloquy. This applies in a similar manner to any and every utterance—a sea-change in special circumstances. Language in such circumstances is in special ways—intelligibly—used not seriously, but in ways *parasitic* upon its normal use—ways which fall under the doctrine of the *etiolations* of language. All this we are *excluding* from consideration. Our performative utterances, felicitous or not, are to be understood as issued in ordinary circumstances. [*How to Do Things with Words*, pp. 21–22]

As the image of the parasite suggests, we have here a familiar relationship of supplementarity: the nonserious use of language is something extra, added to ordinary language and wholly dependent upon it. It need not be taken into consideration in discussing ordinary language use since it is only a parasite.

John Searle argues in his reply to Derrida that this exclusion is of no importance but purely provisional.

Austin's idea is simply this: if we want to know what it is to make a promise or to make a statement, we had better not *start* our investigation with promises made by actors on a stage in the course of a play or statements made in a novel by novelists about characters in the novel, because in a fairly obvious way such utterances are not standard cases of promises and statements. . . . Austin correctly saw that it was necessary to hold in abeyance one set of questions, about parasitic discourse, until one has answered a logically prior set of questions about "serious" discourse. ["Reiterating the Differences," pp. 204–5]

This may well have been "Austin's idea," but the appropriateness of such an idea is precisely what is in question. "What is at stake," writes Derrida, "is above all the structural impossibility and illegitimacy of such an 'idealization,' even one which is methodological and provisional" (*Limited Inc.*, p. 39/206). Indeed, Austin himself, who begins his investigation of performatives by looking at ways in which they can go wrong, contests Searle's notion of simple logical priority: "The project of clarifying all possible ways and varieties of *not exactly doing things* . . . has to be carried through if we are to understand properly what doing things is" (*Philosophical Papers*, p. 27, Austin's italics). To set aside as parasitic certain uses of language in order to base one's theory on other, "ordinary" uses of language is to beg precisely those questions about the essential nature of language that a theory of language ought to answer. Austin objected to such an exclusion by his predecessors: in assuming that the ordinary use of language was to make true or false statements, they excluded precisely those cases that enable him to conclude that statements are a particular class of performative. When Austin then performs a similar exclusion, his own example prompts us to ask whether it is not equally illicit, especially since both he and Searle, by putting "serious" in quotation marks, suggest the dubiousness of the hierarchical opposition, serious/nonserious. The fact that Austin's own writing is often highly playful and seductive, or that he does not hesitate to undermine distinctions that he proposes, only emphasizes the inappropriateness of excluding nonserious discourse from consideration.[4]

Searle uses his "Reply to Derrida" not to explore this problem but dogmatically to reaffirm the structure in question. "The existence of the pretended form of the speech act is logically dependent on the possibility of the nonpretended speech act in the same way that any pretended form of behavior is dependent on nonpretended forms of behavior, and in this sense the pretended forms are *parasitical* on the nonpretended forms" ("Reiterating the Differences," p. 205).

In what sense is the pretended dependent upon the nonpre-

[1]Shoshana Felman, in a fascinating discussion, casts Austin in the role of a Don Juan who seduces readers and disrupts all norms. She attempts to set aside Austin's exclusion of nonserious discourse by suggesting that when Austin writes, "I must not be joking, for example, or writing a poem," "cette phrase ne pourrait-elle pas être considérée elle-même comme une dénégation—comme une plaisanterie?" [Could not this sentence itself be considered as a denial—as a joke?] (*Le Scandale du corps parlant*, p. 188). This is a clever suggestion, part of Felman's sustained attempt to attribute to Austin everything she has learned from Derrida, in order then to accuse Derrida of misreading Austin. Still, to treat the exclusion of jokes as a joke prevents one from explaining the logical economy of Austin's project, which can admit infelicities and exploit them so profitably only by excluding the fictional and the nonserious. This logic is what is at stake, not Austin's attitude or his liking for what Felman calls "le fun."

tended? Searle gives an example: "there could not, for example, be promises made by actors in a play if there were not the possibility of promises made in real life." We are certainly accustomed to thinking in this way: a promise I make is real; a promise in a play is a fictional imitation of a real promise, an empty iteration of a formula used to make real promises. But in fact one can argue that the relation of dependency works the other way as well. If it were not possible for a character in a play to make a promise, there could be no promises in real life, for what makes it possible to promise, as Austin tells us, is the existence of a conventional procedure, of formulas one can repeat. For me to be able to make a promise in "real life," there must be iterable procedures or formulas, such as are used on stage. "Serious" behavior is a special case of role-playing.

"Could a performative utterance succeed," Derrida asks or pretends to ask, "if its formulation did not repeat a 'coded' or iterable utterance, or in other words, if the formula I pronounce in order to open a meeting, to launch a ship or a marriage were not identifiable as *conforming* with an iterable model, if it were not thus identifiable in some way as 'citation'?" (*Marges*, p. 389/SEC, pp. 191–92). For the "standard case" of promising to occur, it must be recognizable as the repetition of a conventional procedure, and the actor's performance on the stage is an excellent model of such repetition. The possibility of "serious" performatives depends upon the possibility of performances, because performatives depend upon the iterability that is most explicitly manifested in performances.[5] Just as Aus-

---

[5]Searle accuses Derrida of "confusing no less than three separate and distinct phenomena: iterability, citationality, and parasitism." "There is a basic difference in that in parasitic discourse the expressions are being *used*, not *mentioned*"— a difference Derrida is said not to understand ("Reiterating the Differences," p. 206). But the distinction between *use* and *mention* is precisely one of the hierarchizations that Derrida's argument contests. The distinction seems clear and important in the classic examples: *Boston is populous* uses the word or expression *Boston*, while "*Boston*" *is disyllabic* does not use the expression but mentions it—mentions the word "Boston" by using an expression which is a metaname. Here the distinction seems clear because it points to the difference between using a word to talk about a city and talking about a word. But when we turn to other examples of citation the problem becomes more complicated. If I write of a scholar, "Some of my colleagues think his work 'boring and incompetent' or 'pointless,'" what have I done? Have I used the expressions "boring and incompetent" and "pointless" as well as mentioned them? If we wish to preserve the distinction between use and mention here, we shall fall back on those

tin reversed his predecessors' hierarchical opposition by showing that constatives were a special case of performatives, so we
can reverse Austin's opposition between the serious and the
parasitic by showing that his so-called "serious" performatives
are only a special case of performances.

This is a principle of considerable breadth. Something can be
a signifying sequence only if it is iterable, only if it can be
repeated in various serious and nonserious contexts, cited, and
parodied. Imitation is not an accident that befalls an original
but its condition of possibility. There is such a thing as an
original Hemingway style only if it can be cited, imitated, and
parodied. For there to be such a style there must be recognizable features that characterize it and produce its distinctive
effects; for features to be recognizable one must be able to
isolate them as elements that could be repeated, and thus the
iterability manifested in the inauthentic, the derivative, the im-
itative, the parodic, is what makes possible the original and the
authentic. Or, to take a more pertinent example, deconstruction exists only by virtue of iteration. One is tempted to speak
of an original practice of deconstruction in Derrida's writings
and to set aside as derivative the imitations of his admirers, but
in fact these repetitions, parodies, "etiolations," or distortions
are what bring a method into being and articulate, within Derrida's work itself, a practice of deconstruction.

---

notions of seriousness and of intention which Derrida claims are involved. I *use*
the expressions insofar as I seriously intend the meanings of the sign sequences
I utter; I mention them when I reiterate some of these signs (within quotation
marks, for example), without committing myself to the meaning they convey.
Mentioning, for Searle, would thus be parasitic upon use, and the distinction
would separate the proper use of language, where I seriously intend the meaning of the signs I use, from a derivative reiteration that only mentions. We thus
have a distinction—am I "seriously" applying the expressions "boring," "pointless," and "incompetent," or only mentioning them?—between two sorts of
iteration, apparently based on intention; and Derrida is quite right to claim that
use/mention is ultimately a hierarchy of the same sort as serious/nonserious and
speech/writing. All attempt to control language by characterizing distinctive
aspects of its iterability as parasitic or derivative. A deconstructive reading
would demonstrate that the hierarchy should be reversed and that *use* is but a
special case of *mentioning*.

The distinction is still useful: among other things it helps us to describe how
language subverts it. However much I may wish only to mention to a friend
what others say about him, I effectively use those expressions, giving them
meaning and force in my discourse. And no matter how wholeheartedly I may
wish to "use" certain expressions, I find myself mentioning them: "I love you"
is always something of a quotation, as many lovers have attested.

A deconstructive reading of Austin focuses on the way he repeats the move he identifies and criticizes in others and on the way in which the distinction between the serious and the parasitic, which makes it possible for him to undertake an analysis of speech acts, is undone by the implications of that analysis. Since any serious performative can be reproduced in various ways and is itself a repetition of a conventional procedure, the possibility of repetition is not something external that may afflict serious performatives. On the contrary, Derrida insists, the performative is from the outset structured by this possibility. "This *possibility* is part of the so-called 'standard' case. It is an essential, internal, and permanent part, and to exclude what Austin himself admits is a *constant* possibility from one's description is to describe something other than the so-called standard case" (*Limited Inc.*, p. 61/231).

Nevertheless, like Saussure's exclusion of writing, Austin's exclusion of the parasitic is not simply an error, an error he might have avoided. It is a strategic part of his enterprise. As we saw above, for Austin an utterance can function as a performative and thus have a certain meaning or illocutionary force when there exists a conventional procedure involving "the utterance of certain words by certain persons in certain circumstances" and when these specified conditions are actually fulfilled. Illocutionary force is thus held to depend upon context, and the theorist must, in order to account for meaning, specify the necessary features of the context—the nature of the words, persons, and circumstances required. What happens when one attempts such specification? Marriage is an example Austin cites. When the minister says "I now pronounce you man and wife," his utterance successfully performs the act of uniting a couple in marriage if the context meets certain conditions. The speaker must be one authorized to perform weddings; the persons he addresses must be a man and a woman who are not married, who have obtained a license to marry, and who have uttered the required phrases in the preceding ceremony. But when one formulates such conditions regarding the words, persons, and circumstances that are necessary for an utterance to have a particular meaning or force, a listener or critic can usually without great difficulty imagine circumstances that fit these conditions but in which the utterance would not have the illocutionary force that is supposed to follow from them. Suppose that the requirements for a marriage ceremony were met but that one of the parties were under hypnosis, or again that the ceremony were impeccable in all respects but had been called a "rehearsal," or finally, that while the speaker was a minister licensed to perform weddings and the couple had obtained a license, the three of them were on this occasion acting in a play that, coincidentally, included a wedding ceremony.

When anyone proposes an example of a meaningless sentence, listeners can usually imagine a context in which it would in fact have meaning; by placing a frame around it, they can make it signify. This aspect of the functioning of language, the possibility of grafting a sequence onto a context that alters its functioning, is also at work in the case of performatives. For any specification of the circumstances under which an utterance counts as a promise we can either imagine further details that would make a difference or else place a further frame around the circumstances. (We imagine that the conditions are fulfilled on a stage or in an example).

In order to arrest or control this process, which threatens the possibility of a successful theory of speech acts, Austin is led to reintroduce the notion, previously rejected, that the meaning of an utterance depends on the presence of a signifying intention in the consciousness of the speaker. First, he sets aside the nonserious—a notion not explicitly defined but which clearly would involve reference to intention: a "serious" speech act is one in which the speaker consciously assents to the act he appears to be performing. Second, he introduces intention as one feature of the circumstances by setting aside speech acts performed unintentionally—"done under duress, or by accident, or owing to this or that variety of mistakes, say, or otherwise unintentionally" (p. 21).

However, this reintroduction does not solve the problem; intention cannot serve as the decisive determinant or the ultimate foundation of a theory of speech acts. To see this one need only consider what would happen if after apparently completing a marriage ceremony one of the parties said that he had been joking when he uttered his lines—only pretending, just rehearsing, or acting under duress. Assuming that the others believe his report of his intention, it will not in itself be decisive. What he had in mind at the moment of utterance does not determine what speech act his utterance performed. On the contrary, the question of whether a marriage did indeed take place will depend upon further discussion of the circumstances. If the minister had said that there would be a full dress rehearsal immediately before the real ceremony, or if the groom can sustain his claim that throughout the ceremony the bride's father was threatening him with a pistol, then one might reach a different conclusion about the illocutionary force of their utterances. What counts is the plausibility of the description of the circumstances: whether the features of the context adduced create a frame that alters the illocutionary force of the utterances.

Thus the possibility of grafting an utterance upon a new context, of repeating a formula in different circumstances, does not discredit the principle that illocutionary force is determined by context rather than by intention. On the contrary, it confirms this principle: in citation, iteration, or framing it is new contextual features that alter illocutionary force. We are here approaching a general principle of considerable importance. What the indissociability of performative and performance puts in question is not the determination of illocutionary force by context but the possibility of mastering the domain of speech acts by exhaustively specifying the contextual determinants of illocutionary force. A theory of speech acts must in principle be able to specify every feature of context that might affect the success or failure of a given speech act or that might affect what particular speech act an utterance effectively performed. This would require, as Austin recognizes, a mastery of the total context: "the total speech act in the total speech situation is the *only actual* phenomenon which, in the last resort, we are engaged in elucidating" (p. 148). But total context is unmasterable, both in principle and in practice. Meaning is context-bound, but context is boundless. Derrida declares, "This is my starting point: no meaning can be determined out of context, but no context permits saturation. What I am referring to here is not richness of substance, semantic fertility, but rather structure, the structure of the remnant or of iteration" ("Living On," p. 81).

Context is boundless in two senses. First, any given context is open to further description. There is no limit in principle to what might be included in a given context, to what might be shown to be relevant to the performance of a particular speech act. This structural openness of context is essential to all disciplines: the scientist discovers that factors previously disregarded are relevant to the behavior of certain objects; the historian brings new or reinterpreted data to bear on a particular event; the critic relates a passage or a text to a context that makes it appear in a new light. Striking instances of the possibilities of further specification of context, Derrida notes, are the displacements permitted by the notion of the unconscious. In his *Speech Acts* Searle proposes, as one of the conditions of promising, that "if the purported promise is to be non-defective, the thing promised must be something the hearer wants done, or considers to be in his interest" (p. 59). If unconscious desire becomes a contextual consideration, the status of some speech acts will thus change: an utterance that promises to do what the listener apparently wants but unconsciously dreads might thus cease to be a promise and become a threat; conversely, an utterance that Searle would deem a defective promise, because it "promises" something the listener claims not to want, might become a well-formed promise (*Limited Inc.*, p. 47/215). Meaning is determined by context and for that very reason is open to alteration when further possibilities are mobilized.

Context is also unmasterable in a second sense: any attempt to codify context can always be grafted onto the context it sought to describe, yielding a new context which escapes the previous formulation. Attempts to describe limits always make possible a displacement of those limits, so that Wittgenstein's suggestion that one cannot say "bububu" and mean "if it does not rain I shall go out for a walk," has, paradoxically, made it possible to do just that. Its denial establishes a connection that can be exploited. Adepts of speech act theory, interested in excluding nonserious utterances from the corpus they are attempting to master, might admire the principle at work in a sign displayed in certain American airports at the spot where passengers and hand luggage are searched: "All remarks concerning bombs and weapons will be taken seriously." Designed to master signification by specifying the illocutionary force of certain statements in this context, it attempts to preclude the possibility of saying in jest "I have a bomb in my shoe" by

identifying such utterances as serious statements. But this codification fails to arrest the play of meaning, nor is its failure an
accident. The structure of language grafts this codification onto
the context it attempts to master, and the new context creates
new opportunities for obnoxious behavior. "If I were to remark that I had a bomb in my shoe, you would have to take it
seriously, wouldn't you?" is only one of the numerous remarks
whose force is a function of context but which escape the prior
attempt to codify contextual force. A metasign, "All remarks
about bombs and weapons, including remarks about remarks
about bombs and weapons, will be taken seriously" would escal-
ate the struggle without arresting it, engendering the possibility
of obnoxious remarks about this sign about remarks.

But if this seems a nonserious example, let us consider a
more serious instance. What speech act is more serious than the
act of signing a document, a performance whose legal, finan-
cial, and political implications may be enormous? Austin cites
the act of signature as the equivalent in writing of explicit performative utterances with the form "I hereby . . . ," and indeed
it is in appending a signature that one can in our culture most
authoritatively take responsibility for an utterance. By signing a
document one intends its meaning and seriously performs the
signifying act it accomplishes.

Derrida concludes "Signature événement contexte" with what
he calls an "improbable signature," the "reproduction" of a "J.
Derrida" in script above a printed "J. Derrida," accompanied
by the following "Remark": "(Remark: the—written—text of
this—oral—communication should have been sent to the Association des sociétés de philosophie de langue francaise before the
meeting. That dispatch should thus have been signed. Which
I do, and counterfeit, here. Where? There. J.D.)" (*Marges*, p.
393/SEC, p. 196). Is the cursive "J. Derrida" a signature even
if it is a citation of the signature appended to the copy of
this text sent through the mails? Is it still a signature when
the supposed signatory calls it counterfeit? Can one counterfeit
one's own signature? What, in sum, is a signature?

Traditionally, as Austin's remarks suggest, a signature is supposed to attest to the presence to consciousness of a signifying
intention at a particular moment. Whatever my thoughts before or after, there was a moment when I fully intended a

particular meaning. The notion of signature thus seems to imply a moment of presence to consciousness which is the origin of subsequent obligations or other effects. But if we ask what enables a signature to function in this way, we find that effects of signature depend on iterability. As Derrida writes, "the condition of possibility of those effects is simultaneously, once again, the condition of their impossibility, of the impossibility of their rigorous purity. In order to function, that is, to be readable, a signature must have a repeatable, iterable, imitable form; it must be able to be detached from the present and singular intention of its production. It is its sameness which, by corrupting its identity and its singularity, divides its seal" (*Marges*, pp. 391–2/SEC, p. 194).

A proper signature, one that will validate a check or some other document, is one that conforms to a model and can be recognized as a repetition. This iterability, an essential feature of the structure of the signature, introduces as part of its structure an independence from any signifying intention. If the signature on a check corresponds to the model, the check can be cashed whatever my intentions at the moment of signature. So true is this that the empirical presence of the signatory is not even an essential feature of the signature. It is part of the structure of the signature that it can be produced by a stamp or by a machine. We can, fortunately, cash checks signed by a machine and receive a salary even though the signatory never saw the check nor entertained a specific intention to pay us the sum in question.

It is tempting to think of checks signed by a machine as perverse exceptions irrelevant to the fundamental nature of signatures. Logocentric idealization sets aside such cases as accidents, "supplements," or "parasites" in its attempt to preserve a model predicated upon the presence of a full intention to consciousness at the moment of signature. But such cases could not occur if they did not belong to the structure of the phenomenon in question, and far from being a perverse exception, the check signed by machine is a logical and explicit example of the fundamental iterability of signatures. The requirement that a signature be recognizable as a repetition introduces the possibility of a machine as part of the structure of the signature at the same time as it eliminates the need for any particular intention at the point of signature.

Signatures thus ought to be included in what Derrida calls "a typology of forms of iteration":

> In such a typology the category of intention will not disappear: it will have its place, but from that place it will no longer be able to govern the entire scene and system of utterance. Above all, we will then be dealing with different kinds of marks or chains of iterable marks and not with an opposition between citational utterances on the one hand and singular and original event-utterances on the other. The first consequence of this will be the following: given that structure of iteration, the intention animating the utterance will never be through and through present to itself and to its content. The iteration structuring it introduces into it *a priori* an essential dehiscence and cleft [*brisure*]. [*Marges*, p. 389/SEC, p. 192]

It is not a matter of denying that signatories have intentions, but of situating those intentions. One way of doing this would be to take the unconscious, as Vincent Descombes has argued, "not as a phenomenon of the will but as a phenomenon of enunciation" (*L'Inconscient malgré lui*, p. 85). The thesis of the unconscious "makes sense only in relation to the subject of enunciation: he does not know what he says" (p. 15). The unconscious is the excess of what one says over what one knows, or of what one says over what one wants to say. Either the speaker's intention is whatever content is present to his consciousness at the moment of utterance, in which case it is variable and incomplete, unable to account for the illocutionary force of utterances, or else it is comprehensive and divided— conscious and unconscious—a structural intentionality which is never anywhere present and which includes implications that never, as we say, entered my mind. This latter notion of intention, marked by what Derrida calls an essential cleft or division, is indeed quite common. When questioned about the implications of an utterance I may quite routinely include in my intention implications that had never previously occurred to me. My intention is the sum of further explanations I might give when questioned on any point and is thus less an origin that a product, less a delimited content than an open set of discursive possibilities linked to the consequences of iterable acts and to contexts that pose particular questions about those acts.

The example of the signature thus presents us with the same structure we encountered in the case of other speech acts: (1) the dependence of meaning on conventional and contextual factors, but (2) the impossibility of exhausting contextual possibilities so as to specify the limits of illocutionary force, and thus (3) the impossibility of controlling effects of signification or the force of discourse by a theory, whether it appeal to intentions of subjects or to codes and contexts. Austin, like other philosophers and literary theorists, attempts to make signification masterable by defining what escapes his theory as marginal—by excluding it, Derrida says, "in the name of a kind of ideal regulation" (*Marges*, p. 385/ SEC, p. 118). Like other attempts at mastery, taken individually or collectively, Austin's oscillate between attempts to define determining contexts—his inventory of the conditions for the performance of various speech acts—and recourse to versions of intention when the description of contexts fails to exhaust contextual possibilities. Our earlier formula, "meaning is context-bound but context is boundless," helps us recall why both projects fail: meaning is context-bound, so intentions do not in fact suffice to determine meaning; context must be mobilized. But context is boundless, so accounts of context never provide full determinations of meaning. Against any set of formulations, one can imagine further possibilities of context, including the expansion of context produced by the reinscription within a context of the description of it.

This account of meaning and context can clarify deconstruction's dealings with the notion of history, which remain for many an obscure point. Those who invoke history adduce it as a ground that determines meaning, and since Derrida does not use it in this way, they see him as a "textualist" who denies that historical contexts determine meaning. But in its critique of philosophy and of other essentializing theories, deconstruction emphasizes that discourse, meaning, and reading are historical through and through, produced in processes of contextualization, decontextualization, and recontextualization. When Derrida writes that we must attempt to think presence (including meaning as a presence to consciousness) "à partir du temps comme différance" [starting from/in relation to time as difference, differing, and deferral], he makes clear both the historicity of articulations and the impossibility of making this historicity a ground or a foundation (*De la grammatologie*, p. 237/166). Time as differing and deferral undermines presence by making it a construct rather than a given, but time is not a foundation. "We shall distinguish by the term *differance*," Derrida writes, "the movement by which language, or any code, any system of reference in general, becomes 'historically' constituted as a fabric of differences." "If the word *history* did not carry with it the theme of a final repression of difference, we could say that differences alone could be 'historical' through and through and from the start" (*Marges*, p. 12/"Differance," p. 141).

Those who champion a "historical approach" or chide deconstruction for refusing to appreciate the historical determination of meaning offer a dubious alternative. A "historical approach" appeals to historical narratives—stories of changes in thinking and of the thoughts or beliefs appropriate to distinguishable historical periods—in order to control the meaning of rich and complex works by ruling out possible meanings as historically inappropriate. These historical narratives are produced by interpreting the supposedly less complex and ambiguous texts of a period, and their authority to authorize or control meanings of the most complex texts is certainly questionable. The history invoked as ultimate reality and source of truth manifests itself in narrative constructs, stories designed to yield meaning through narrative ordering. In *Positions* Derrida emphasizes his distrust of the concept of history, with its entire logocentric system of implications, but notes that he frequently uses the term *history* in a critical way, in order to reinscribe its force (pp. 77–78/56–57). Derrida uses history against philosophy: when confronted with essentialist, idealizing theories and claims to ahistorical or transhistorical understanding, he asserts the historicity of these discourses and theoretical assumptions. But he also uses philosophy against history and the claims of historical narratives. Deconstruction couples a philosophical critique of history and historical understanding with the specification that discourse is historical and meaning historically determined, both in principle and in practice.

History is not a privileged authority but part of what Derrida calls "le texte général"—the general text, which has no boundaries ("Avoir l'oreille de la philosophie," p. 310). We are always engaged in interpreting this general text, making determinations of meaning and halting, for practical reasons, the investigation and redescription of context. The meanings we determine in interpreting one another's speech, writing, and action are generally sufficient for our purposes, and some critics of deconstruction have argued that we should accept this relative determinacy as the nature of meaning. Meaning is what we understand; and instead of exposing its lack of foundation or decisive authority we should simply say, with Wittgenstein, "this language game is played."

In one sense this is an appropriate objection: we may quite reasonably deem the discussions of the preceding pages irrelevant to our concerns and try to ignore them (whether we will actually be able to ignore them is a different matter: a question of the historical force of these theoretical discourses). But those who offer this objection are seldom content just to ignore deconstruction. They begin by noting that we make determinations of meaning all the time but are tempted to argue from this that therefore meaning *is* determinate. They begin by noting that, whatever philosophers say, we have experiences of determining and grasping meanings, but they then go on to treat this experience as if it were a ground for the philosophical refutation of skepticism.[6] Wittgenstein asserts that "the language game is so to say something unpredictable. I mean, it is not based on grounds. It is not reasonable (or unreasonable). It is there—like our life" (*On Certainty*, p. 73). His admirers speak as though the language game were itself a ground—a true presence which determined meaning. But when one attempts to flesh out such an argument by setting forth the rules and conventions of the language game, one encounters all the problems we have been discussing. A Derridean would agree that the language game is played but might go on to point out that one can never be quite certain who is playing, or playing "seri-

[6]See Charles Altieri, *Act and Quality*, pp. 23–52, and "Wittgenstein on Consciousness and Language: A Challenge to Derridean Literary Theory." A similar argument is suggested by M. H. Abrams, "How to Do Things with Texts," pp. 570–71.

ously," what the rules are, or which game is being played. Nor is this uncertainty accidental or external. Those who cite Wittgenstein are inclined to adduce the language game and its rules as a simple given. "But—it is just a fact," Wittgenstein is reported as saying, "that people have laid down such and such rules" (*Lectures and Conversations*, p. 6n). It is always possible, though, that redescription will alter rules or place an utterance in a different language game. Discussing a sentence that appears in quotation marks in Nietzsche's *Nachlass*, "I have forgotten my umbrella," Derrida writes, "a thousand possibilities will always remain open" (*Limited Inc.*, p. 35/201). They remain open not because the reader can make the sentence mean anything whatever but because other specifications of context or interpretations of the "general text" are always possible.

As should now be clear, deconstruction is not a theory that defines meaning in order to tell you how to find it. As a critical undoing of the hierarchical oppositions on which theories depend, it demonstrates the difficulties of any theory that would define meaning in a univocal way: as what an author intends, what conventions determine, what a reader experiences. "There are two interpretations of interpretation," writes Derrida in a much-quoted passage of "La Structure, le signe, et le jeu dans le discours des sciences humaines."

> The one seeks to decipher, dreams of deciphering a truth or an origin which escapes play and the order of the sign and which lives the necessity of interpretation as an exile. The other, which is no longer turned toward the origin, affirms play and tries to pass beyond man and humanism, the name of man being the name of that being who, throughout the history of metaphysics and of onto-theology—in other words, throughout his entire history—has dreamed of full presence, of reassuring foundation, of the origin and the end of play. . . . We can see from various signs today that these two interpretations of interpretation—which are absolutely irreconcilable even if we live them simultaneously and reconcile them in an obscure economy—divide the field which we call, so problematically, the human sciences.
>
> I do not for my part believe, although these two interpretations must accentuate their difference and sharpen their irreducibility, that there can today be any question of *choosing*—in the first place because here we are in a region (let us say, provisionally, of histor-

icity) where the notion of choice is particularly trivial; and in the second place because we must first try to conceive of the common ground and the *differance* of this irreducible difference. [*L'Ecriture et la différence*, pp. 427–28/292–93]

Derrida has often been read as urging us to choose the second interpretation of interpretation, to affirm a free play of meaning;[7] but as he notes here, one cannot simply or effectively choose to make meaning either the original meaning of an author or the creative experience of the reader. As we saw in Chapter One, the attempt to make meaning the experience of the reader does not solve the problem of meaning but displaces it, producing a divided and deferred concept of experience, and the notion of the reader's creative freedom breaks down rather swiftly. One can, of course, choose or claim to have chosen this second interpretation of interpretation, but there is no guarantee that such a choice can be effectively realized in the economy of one's discourse. The notion of choice here is "bien légère," as Derrida says, because whatever the theorist's choice, the theory seems to present a divided meaning or interpretation— divided, for example, between meaning as a property of a text and meaning as the experience of the reader. What we call our experience is scarcely a reliable guide in these matters, but it would seem that in one's experience of interpretation meaning is both the semantic effects one experiences and a property of the text against which one seeks to check one's experience. It may be that what makes the notion of meaning indispensable is this divided character and divided reference: to what one understands and to what one's understanding captures or fails to capture.

This double character of meaning is effectively presupposed in most of our dealings with it. If we say that the meaning of a work is the reader's response, we nevertheless show, in our descriptions of response, that interpretation is an attempt to discover meaning in the text. If we propose some other decisive determinant of meaning, we discover that the factors deemed

[7]Wayne Booth, for example, reports: "Jacques Derrida seeks a 'free play' amounting to a 'methodical craziness,' to produce a 'dissemination' of texts that, endless and treacherous and terrifying, liberates us to an *errance joyeuse*" (*Critical Understanding*, p. 216). Booth may have been helped to his understanding of Derrida by Geoffrey Hartman's articles, where similar formulations appear.

crucial are subject to interpretation in the same way as the text itself and thus defer the meaning they determine. What if, Derrida suggests, "the meaning of meaning (in the most general sense of meaning and not of indication) is infinite implication? the unchecked referral from signifier to signifier? If its force is a certain pure and infinite equivocalness, which gives signified meaning no respite, no rest, but engages it within its own economy to go on signifying and to differ/defer?" (*L'Ecriture et la différence*, p. 42/25).

The combination of context-bound meaning and boundless context on the one hand makes possible proclamations of the indeterminacy of meaning—though the smug iconoclasm of such proclamations may be irritating—but on the other hand urges that we continue to interpret texts, classify speech acts, and attempt to elucidate the conditions of signification. Even though one may have reasons to believe, as Derrida writes, that "the language of theory always leaves a residue that is neither formalizable nor idealizable in terms of that theory of language," this is no reason to stop work on theory (*Limited Inc.*, p. 41/209).[8] In mathematics, for example, Gödel's demonstration of the incompleteness of metamathematics (the impossibility of constructing a theoretical system within which all true statements of number theory are theorems) does not lead mathematicians to abandon their work. The humanities, however, often seem touched with the belief that a theory which asserts the ultimate indeterminacy of meaning makes all effort pointless. The fact that such assertions emerge from discussions that propose numerous particular determinations of meaning, specific interpretations of passages and texts, should cast doubts upon an impetuous nihilism. An opposition that is deconstructed is not destroyed or abandoned but reinscribed. Austin's discussion of the performative and the constative demonstrates the difficulty of making a principled distinction between two classes of utterance, but what this breakdown reveals is a difference *within* each speech act that had been treated as a difference *between* types of speech acts. The unstable difference between performative and constative becomes not the basis of a reliable typology but a characterization of language's unmasterable

[8] The first six words of this sentence are missing from the French text. A line of typescript has been omitted at line 35 of page 41 following "toujours."

oscillation between positing and corresponding. "The aporia between performative and constative language," writes Paul de Man in an extended reinscription of this opposition, "is merely a version of the aporia between trope and persuasion that both generates and paralyzes rhetoric and thus gives it the appearance of a history" (*Allegories of Reading*, p. 131).

What deconstruction proposes is not an end to distinctions, not an indeterminacy that makes meaning the invention of the reader. The play of meaning is the result of what Derrida calls "the play of the world," in which the general text always provides further connections, correlations, and contexts (*L'Ecriture et la différence*, p. 427/292). The notion of the "free play of meaning" has had a fine career, particularly in America, but a more useful concept, which elucidates the processes of signification we have been discussing as well as providing an approach to the structure of Derrida's own writing, is that of the graft. Meaning is produced by a process of grafting, and speech acts, both serious and nonserious, are grafts.

3. GRAFTS AND GRAFT

In "La Double Séance" Derrida offers grafting as a model for thinking about the logic of texts—a logic that combines graphic operations with processes of insertion and strategies for proliferation.

> One ought to explore systematically not only what appears to be a simple etymological coincidence uniting the graft and the graph (both from the Greek *graphion*: writing instrument, stylus), but also the analogy between the forms of textual grafting and so-called vegetal grafting, or even, more and more commonly today, animal grafting. It would not be enough to compose an encyclopedic catalogue of grafts (approach grafting, detached scion grafting; whip grafts, splice grafts, saddle grafts, cleft grafts, bark grafts; bridge grafting, inarching, repair grafting, bracing; T-budding, shield budding, etc.); one must elaborate a systematic treatise on the textual graft. [*La Dissémination*, p. 230/202]

Such a treatise would resemble a systematic typology of speech acts in its interest in what sorts of grafts will take—which will succeed, bear fruit, disseminate. But a theory of speech acts aims to be normative. It aims to describe, for example, the conditions that must be fulfilled in order for an utterance to count as a promise and is thus committed to a certain decidability: it seeks to draw a line between what is truly a promise and what is not. A treatise on textual grafting, on the other hand, would be probabilistic, an attempt to calculate probable forces.

What would such a treatise describe? It would treat discourse as the product of various sorts of combinations or insertions. Exploring the iterability of language, its ability to function in new contexts with new force, a treatise on textual grafting would attempt to classify various ways of inserting one discourse in another or intervening in the discourse one is interpreting. The fact that one has only the vaguest ideas of how to organize a typology of grafts indicates the novelty of this perspective, and perhaps the difficulty of making it productive.

It is clear, however, that deconstruction is, among other things, an attempt to identify grafts in the texts it analyzes: what are the points of juncture and stress where one scion or line of argument has been spliced with another? *Supplement* in Rousseau is one such point, at which a graft of logocentric and anti-logocentric arguments can be detected; the double treatment of writing in Saussure is another. Focusing on these moments, deconstruction elucidates the heterogeneity of the text. ("The motif of homogeneity," writes Derrida, "the theological motif par excellence, is what must be destroyed" [*Positions*, p. 86/64].) Writing on *The Critique of Judgment*, Derrida speaks of Kant's theory as the product of grafts. "Certain of its motifs belong to a long sequence, a powerful traditional chain stretching back to Plato or Aristotle. Woven in with them in a very strict and at first inextricable way are other, narrower sequences that would be inadmissible within a Platonic or Aristotelian politics of art. But it is not enough to sort or to measure lengths. Folded into a new system, the long sequences are displaced; their sense and function change" ("Economimesis," p. 57/3). If, in Derrida's aphorism, "toute thèse est une prothèse"—every thesis is an attached prothesis—one must identify grafts and analyze what they produce (*Glas*, p. 189).

One could also describe Derrida's writings themselves in terms of the techniques they employ for grafting discourses onto one another. A simple graft, though complex in its potential ramifications, binds two discourses side by side on the same page. "Tympan" (*Marges*, pp. i–xxv) grafts Michel Leiris's reflections on the associations of the name "Persephone" alongside Derrida's discussion of the limits of philosophy. This structure sets up reverberations, as does a tympanum: a membrane which at once divides and acts as a sounding board to transmit sound vibrations—connecting, by its transmission, the inside and the outside it separates.

Glas employs similar techniques on a larger scale. In the left-hand column of each page Derrida pursues an analysis of the concept of the family in Hegel (including the related questions of paternal authority, Absolute Knowledge, the Holy Family, Hegel's own family relations, and the Immaculate Conception). In the right-hand column, facing the author of *The Philosophy of Right*, is the thief and homosexual Jean Genet. Citations and discussions of his writings are woven together with remarks on the literary significance of proper names and signatures, the structure of double binds, the deconstruction of classical sign theory, and explorations of signifying links between words associated by phonological resemblance or etymological chains. Constantly at work in this book is the problematical relation between the two columns or texts. "Why pass a knife between two texts?" asks Derrida. "Or at least, why write two texts at once?" "On veut rendre l'écriture imprenable, bien sûr" (*Glas*, p. 76). Commentators are indeed tempted to suspect that *Glas*'s doubling is a strategy of evasion, designed to make the writing unmasterably elusive. While reading one column you are reminded that the gist lies elsewhere, in the relation between columns if not in the other column itself. One effect of this graft, though, is to produce chiasmus. The division between columns accentuates the most radical oppositions: between philosophy and literature (in the figures of the sublime philosopher and the obscene *littérateur*), spirit and body, orthodoxy and heterodoxy, paternal authority and maternal authority, the eagle (*Hegel-aigle*) and the flower (*Genet-genêt*), right and its subversion, property and theft. But the exploration of relations and connections between columns brings about reversals, an exchange of properties, not a deconstruction of oppositions but nevertheless a deconstructive effect.[9]

A perspicuous typology would doubtless distinguish *Glas*'s grafts from those of "Living On: Border Lines," which places one discourse above another and gives the lower something of the framing or parergonal character of commentary. The upper text, "Living On," is already a rather straggling graft of Blanchot's *L'Arrêt de mort* and "La Folie du jour" with Shelley's *The Triumph of Life*. The lower text, "Border Lines," in some ways a note on translation, effects in "telegraphic style" what it calls "a procession underneath the other one, going past it *in silence*, as if it did not see it, as if it had nothing to do with it" (p. 78). But before one accepts this text's description of its own graft one ought to take note of the concluding remark: "Never tell what you are doing, and, pretending to tell, do something else that immediately crypts, adds, entrenches itself. To speak of writing, of triumph, as *living on*, is to enunciate or denounce the manic fantasy. Not without repeating it, and that goes without saying" (p. 176). The complexity of grafts is indicated by this example: a graft that comments on another text and on itself, feigning or offering an explanation, is also an addition that exceeds that explanation. What goes without saying is said in the act of identifying it as what goes without saying, and a denunciation repeats what it denounces.

If a text's description of its own procedures is always a graft that adds something to those procedures, there is a related graft whereby the analyst applies the text's statements to its own processes of enunciation. Asking how what the text does relates to what it says, he often discovers an uncanny repetition. A striking example is Derrida's reading of *Beyond the Pleasure Principle* in "Spéculer—Sur 'Freud'" (*La Carte postale*, pp. 275–

[9]For a different account of *Glas*, see Geoffrey Hartman's *Saving the Text*. "I have looked at *Glas* as a work of art and bracketed specific philosophical concepts developed by Derrida," Hartman writes. "The place of the book in the history of art . . . is the focus I have found most fruitful" (p. 90). The result is "Derridadaism" (p. 33), which Hartman, engaged in *Saving the Text*, can ultimately reject as "somewhat self-involved" (p. 121). Since many may be willing to take Hartman's word about *Glas*, it is worth stressing that it contains considerable straightforward exposition of Hegel, Genet, and Saussure. For a specimen reading of the relations between columns, see Michael Riffaterre's "Syllepsis."

437). Since the matter Freud is discussing is the dominance of the pleasure principle—by what detours it dominates and whether anything escapes it—the question arises whether Freud's own writing is dominated by, or an instance of, the processes he describes. This issue takes on special pertinence in the chapter concerning his grandson Ernst's now famous "game" of *fort/da*. "Repliez," writes Derrida,

> Superimpose what he says his grandson does earnestly on what he is doing himself in saying so, in writing *Beyond the Pleasure Principle*, in playing so earnestly (in speculating) at writing it. For the speculative hetero-tautology here is that this "beyond" is *lodged* . . . in the repetition of repetition of the PP [Pleasure Principle and *Pépé* ("grandpa")].
>
> Superimpose: *he* (the grandson of his grandfather, the grandfather *of* his grandson) repeats repetition compulsively, but it all never goes anywhere, never advances by a single step. He repeats an operation that consists of dispatching, of pretending . . . to dispatch pleasure, the object of pleasure or the pleasure principle, represented here by the wooden reel that is supposed to represent the mother (and/or, we shall see, the father, in place of the son-in-law, the father as son-in-law, the other family name), to bring it back again and again. He pretends to dispatch the PP in order to make it return endlessly, . . . and to conclude: it is always there—I am always there. *Da.* The PP retains total authority, has never been away. [*La Carte postale*, p. 323/ "Coming into One's Own," pp. 118–19]

Freud's speculative dealings with the pleasure principle, as he casts it away in order to make it come back, are described by a graft that applies to them his remarks about his grandson. This relationship, Derrida continues, "is not strictly speaking a matter of superposition, nor of parallelism, nor of analogy, nor of coincidence. The necessity that links the two descriptions is of a different sort: we shall not find it easy to give a name to it, but clearly it is the main thing at stake for me in the sifting, interested reading I am repeating here."

Whatever we call it, we should beware of assuming that in exploiting the potential self-referentiality of the text Derrida is repeating the now familiar critical move in which the text is shown to describe its own signifying processes and thus said to stand free as a self-contained, self-explanatory aesthetic object that enacts what it asserts. The possibility of including the text's own procedures among the objects it describes does not, Derrida shows, lead to a presentational coherence and transparency. On the contrary, such self-inclusion blurs the boundaries of the text and renders its procedures highly problematical, since it is no longer possible to determine whether Freud's own procedure is an uncanny, transferential repetition of the structure he is investigating or whether the structure appears as it does as the result of a particular practice of composition. "Alors," writes Derrida, "ça boite et ça ferme mal" (*La Carte postale*, p. 418). "It limps and closes badly."

This sort of analysis, in which a discourse is shown to repeat the structures it is analyzing and in which the disruptive insights of this transference are explored, has become one of the major activities of deconstruction (see pp. 202–205 and 270–72 below). It is related to another graft involving the relation of a text's statements to its own procedures: the inversion of a previous interpretive graft. Where one text claims to analyze and elucidate another, it may be possible to show that in fact the relationship should be inverted: that the analyzing text is elucidated by the analyzed text, which already contains an implicit account of and reflection upon the analyst's moves. Derrida's most graphic instance, "Le Facteur de la vérité," inverts Lacan's reading of "The Purloined Letter" to show how Poe's story already analyzes and situates the psychoanalyst's attempt at mastery (*La Carte postale*, pp. 439–524/"The Purveyor of Truth"). But like most grafts, this is subject to further grafts. So Barbara Johnson goes on to argue, repeating Derrida's graft, that Derrida's moves in his discussion of Lacan are already repetitions of moves anticipated in the texts Derrida is reading and thus illustrate "the transfer of the repetition compulsion from the original text to the scene of its reading" ("The Frame of Reference," p. 154). "Each text," writes Derrida, "is a machine with multiple reading heads for other texts" ("Living On," p. 107).

Another common operation is that which takes a minor, unknown text and grafts it onto the main body of the tradition, or else takes an apparently marginal element of a text, such as a footnote, and transplants it to a vital spot. "*Ousia* et *Grammè*," an essay on Heidegger in *Marges,* is subtitled "Note sur une note de *Sein und Zeit*." The discussion of Kant's *Critique of Judg-*

ment focuses on a passage where Kant discusses ornaments such as picture frames ("Le Parergon," in *La Vérité en peinture*). The reading of Foucault's *L'Histoire de la folie* works exclusively from a brief discussion of Descartes's treatment of madness ("Cogito et histoire de la folie," in *L'Ecriture et la différence*). "Freud et la scène de l'écriture," an important and influential statement, deals with a previously ignored essay, Freud's "Note on the Mystic Writing Pad" (*L'Ecriture et la différence*). The discussion of Rousseau concentrates on an obscure essay of uncertain date, the "Essai sur l'origine des langues," and there focuses on an "extra" chapter on writing.

This concentration on the apparently marginal puts the logic of supplementarity to work as an interpretive strategy: what has been relegated to the margins or set aside by previous interpreters may be important precisely for those reasons that led it to be set aside. Indeed, the strategy of this graft is double. Interpretation generally relies on distinctions between the central and the marginal, the essential and the inessential: to interpret is to discover what is central to a text or group of texts. On the one hand, the marginal graft works within these terms to reverse a hierarchy, to show that what had previously been thought marginal is in fact central. But on the other hand, that reversal, attributing importance to the marginal, is usually conducted in such a way that it does not lead simply to the identification of a new center (as would, for example, the claim that the truly important thing about *The Critique of Judgment* is the attempt to relate different kinds of pleasure to the inside and the outside of the work of art), but to a subversion of the distinctions between essential and inessential, inside and outside. What is a center if the marginal can become central? "Disproportionate" interpretation is unsettling.

This double practice of relying on the terms of an opposition in one's argument but also seeking to displace that opposition yields a specific graft that Derrida identifies in discussions of the logic of "paleonymics": the retention of old names while grafting new meaning upon them. Arguing that, given the way writing has been characterized, speech is also a form of writing, Derrida in effect produces a new concept of writing, a generalized writing that includes speech as well, but he retains the old name as a "levier d'intervention"—to maintain leverage for intervention, to keep a handle on the hierarchical opposition (speech/writing) that he wishes to transform (*Positions*, p. 96/71). Here is a broad conclusion about the importance of the paleonymic graft for deconstruction.

> Deconstruction does not consist of moving from one concept to another but of reversing and displacing a conceptual order as well as the nonconceptual order with which it is articulated. For example, writing, as a classical concept, entails predicates that have been subordinated, excluded, or held in abeyance by forces and according to necessities to be analyzed. It is those predicates (I have recalled several of them) whose force of generality, generalization, and generativity is liberated, grafted onto a "new" concept of writing that corresponds as well to what has always *resisted* the prior organization of forces, always constituted the *residue* irreducible to the dominant force organizing the hierarchy that we may refer to, in brief, as logocentric. To leave this new concept the old name of writing is to maintain the structure of the *graft*, the transition and indispensable adherence to an effective *intervention* in the constituted historical field. It is to give everything at stake in the operations of deconstruction the chance, the force, the power of *communication*. [*Marges*, p. 393/SEC, p. 195]

The graft is the very figure of intervention.

Finally, Derrida's writings employ grafts related to poetic techniques for disrupting traditional habits of thought and forging new connections: the exploitation of phonetic, graphic, morphological, and etymological relations or of the semantic connections established by a single term. *Glas* explores the relations among various terms in *gl* and *cl*. *La Vérité en peinture*, which proposes to "abandon *gl*, deal with [*traiter avec*] *tr*" (p. 195), explains what might develop from this interest in the *trait* ("line," "feature," "connection," "stroke," "outline," "shaft," "projection," "stretch," "leash," "trace"):

> Plus tard, ailleurs, attirer tout ce discours sur les traits tirés, l'attirer du côté où se croisent les deux "familles," celle de *Riss* (*Aufriss*, l'entame, *Umriss*, le contour, le cadre, l'esquisse, *Grundriss*, le plan, le précis, etc.) et celle de *Zug*, de *Ziehen*, *Entziehen*, *Gezüge* (trait, tirer, attirer, retirer, le contrat qui rassemble tous les traits: "*Der Riss ist das einheitliche Gezüge von Aufriss und Grundriss, Durch-*

und Umriss," Heidegger, "L'Origine de l'oeuvre d'art"). [*La Vérité en peinture,* p. 222]

> Later, elsewhere, draw this whole discussion of drawn features [lines drawn through, run off], draw it toward the intersection of the two "families," that of *Riss* [rift] (*Aufriss*, draft, *Umriss*, outline, frame, sketch, *Grundriss*, plan, summary) and that of *Zug, Ziehen, Entziehen, Gezüge* (feature, draw, pull, withdraw, the contract that collects all features: "The rift is the unified drawing together of the draft and the plan, the breach and the outline," Heidegger, "The Origin of the Work of Art").

Linkings that stress the etymology or morphology of a word, bringing out the rift or gap at the heart of draft, outline, plan, are ways of applying torque to a concept and affecting its force. This is of particular interest when, as in the families cited here, the root element is a version of *différance*: the mark or feature as gap. Among the terms set in new perspective by their relation with other terms are *marge, marque, marche* (margin, mark, step), and perhaps most powerfully and appositely, the "family" *pharmakon, pharmakeus,* and *pharmakos* in "La Pharmacie de Platon." This case merits description as an example of the logic of signification revealed by deconstructive reading.

In the *Phaedrus* writing is described as a *pharmakon*, which means both "remedy" (a remedy for weakness of memory, for example) and "poison." Offered to mankind by its inventor as a remedy, writing is treated by Socrates as a dangerous drug. This double meaning of *pharmakon* proves essential to the logical placement of writing as a supplement: it is an artificial addition which cures and infects. *Pharmakon* is closely related to *pharmakeus* (magician, sorcerer, prisoner), a term that is applied in the dialogues to Socrates as well as to others. To his interlocutors Socrates is a magician who works by indirection and enchantment; in a strange town, it is suggested, he would swiftly be arrested as a sorcerer, and indeed, in Athens when he is arrested and led to drink poison (*pharmakon*) it is for seduction of youth.

But Socrates' sorcery is not a technique external to philosophy; it is the philosophical method itself, and a prayer at the beginning of the *Critias* asks the gods to "grant us that most effective medicine (*pharmakon teleôtaton*), that most effective of all medicines (*ariston pharmakôn*), knowledge (*epistēmēn*)." The text thus presents "the philosophical, epistemic order of the logos as an antidote, as a force inscribed within the general, alogical economy of the *pharmakon*" (*La Dissémination*, p. 142/ 124). Though writing and the *pharmakon* were presented as artifice marginal to the order of reason and nature, the signifying relations imply a reversal of this order and the identification of philosophy as a particular determination of the *pharmakon*. The *pharmakon* has no proper or determinate character but is rather the possibility of both poison and remedy (the poison Socrates takes is also for him a remedy). It thus becomes, Derrida argues, "the common element, the medium of any possible dissociation. . . . The *pharmakon* is 'ambivalent' because it constitutes the element in which opposites are opposed, the movement and play by which each relates back to the other, reverses itself and passes into the other: (soul/body, good/evil, inside/outside, memory/forgetfulness, speech/writing, etc.). It is on the basis of this play or this movement that Plato establishes the opposititions or distinctions. The *pharmakon* is the movement, the locus, and the play (the production) of difference" (pp. 145–46/127).

This role of *pharmakon* as a condition of difference is further confirmed by the link with *pharmakos*, "scapegoat." The exclusion of the *pharmakos* purifies the city, as the exclusion of the *pharmakon* of writing is meant to purify the order of speech and thought. The *pharmakos* is cast out as the representative of the evil that afflicts the city: cast out so as to make evil return to the outside from which it comes and to assert the importance of the distinction between inside and outside. But to play his role as representative of the evil to be cast out, the *pharmakos* must be chosen from *within* the city. The possibility of using the *pharmakos* to establish the distinction between a pure inside and a corrupt outside depends on its already being inside, just as the expulsion of writing can have a purificatory function only if writing is already within speech. "The ceremony of the *pharmakos*," Derrida writes, "is thus played out on the boundary line between the inside and outside, which it has as its function to trace and retrace repeatedly. *Intra muros/ extra muros*. Origin of difference and division, the *pharmakos* represents evil both introjected and projected" (p. 153/ 133). And representation here, as elsewhere, depends upon repetition. The significance of an expulsion depends upon the conventions of the ritual it repeats, and in Athens, Derrida notes, the ritual of expulsion was repeated every year, on the day that was also the birthday of that *pharmakeus* whose death by *pharmakon* made him a *pharmakos*—Socrates.

What is the status of such relations: the grafting onto one another of *pharmakon, pharmakeus,* and *pharmakos,* or the pun of *différance,* the play of *supplément?* Many might say that they are examples of graft in philosophy and that Derrida enjoys illgotten gains. "The most shocking thing about Derrida's work," writes Rorty, "is his use of multilingual puns, joke etymologies, allusions from anywhere, and phonic and typographical gimmicks" ("Philosophy as a Kind of Writing," pp. 146–47). They are shocking from a perspective that takes for granted the possibility of distinguishing on firm grounds between authentic philosophical operations and gimmicks, between show and substance, between contingent linguistic or textual configurations and logic or thought itself. The scandal of Derrida's writing would be the attempt to give "philosophical" status to "fortuitous" resemblances or connections. The fact that *pharmakon* is both poison and remedy, *hymen* a membrane and the penetration of that membrane, *dissemination* a scattering of semen, seeds, and *sèmes* (semantic features), and *s'entendre parler* both hearing and understanding oneself speak—these are contingent facts about languages, relevant to poetry but of no consequence for the universal discourse of philosophy.

It would be easy to answer that deconstruction denies the distinction between poetry and philosophy or between contingent linguistic features and thought itself, but that would be wrong, a simplifying response to a simplifying charge and a response that would carry with it a certain impotence. One writes with both hands, says Derrida. The answer, as one may by now expect, is double. Let us consider the example of *hymen,* which appears in a rich discussion of mime by Mallarmé:

> La scène n'illustre que l'idée, pas une action effective, dans un hymen (d'où procède le Rêve), vicieux mais sacré, entre le désir et l'accomplissement, la perpétration et son souvenir: ici devançant, la remémorant, au futur, au passé, *sous une apparence fausse de présent.* ["Mimique," quoted in *La Dissémination,* p. 201]

The scene illustrates only the idea, not any actual action, in a hymen (out of which flows Dream) tainted with vice yet sacred, between desire and fulfillment, perpetration and remembrance: here anticipating, there recalling, in the future, in the past, under the false appearance of a present. [P. 175]

"Hymen" is here a marriage between desire and its accomplishment, a fusion that abolishes contraries and also the difference between them. But, Derrida emphasizes, a hymen is also a membrane, and a hymen between desire and its accomplishment is precisely what keeps them separate. We have "an operation which 'at once' brings about a fusion or confusion *between* opposites and stands *between* opposites," a double and impossible operation which doubtless for that reason is "un hymen vicieux et sacré" (p. 240/212).

After developing the implications of this undecidable hymen, Derrida comments on his procedure and its implications, developing what we might call the right-handed reply to the charge of graft and frivolity:

It is not a question of repeating here with *hymen* what Hegel does with German words such as *Aufhebung, Urteil, Meinen, Beispiel*, etc., marveling at the happy accident that steeps a natural language in the element of speculative dialectic. What counts here is not the lexical richness, semantic openness of a word or concept, its depth or breadth, or the sedimentation in it of two contradictory significations (continuity and discontinuity, inside and outside, identity and difference, etc.). What counts here is the formal and syntactic activity [*pratique*] that composes and decomposes it. We have certainly seemed to bring everything back to the word *hymen*. Though everything seemed to make it an irreplaceable signifier, this is in fact something of a trap. This word, this syllepsis, is not indispensable; philology and etymology interest us only secondarily, and "Mimique" would not be irreparably harmed by the loss of "hymen." The effect is primarily produced by the syntax that disposes the *entre* ("between") in such a way that the suspense is due only to the place and not to the content of the words. "Hymen" only marks again what the place of *entre* already indicates and would still indicate even if the word "hymen" were not there. If one replaced "hymen" by "marriage" or "crime," "identity," or "difference," etc. the effect would be the same, except for the loss of an economic condensation or accumulation that we have not neglected. [Pp. 249–50/220]

Thus on the one hand, in keeping with the premises of philosophical argument, Derrida answers, yes, the fact that *hymen* has these two opposed meanings is a contingent fact about French (and also, as it happens, about Latin and English), a fact which I exploit because it presents forcefully and economically an underlying structure of some importance. *Différance* happily combines a structure of difference and an art of differing, but the argument does not depend on this feature of French morphology and lexis. The fact that Plato applies the term *pharmakon* to writing and *pharmakeus* to Socrates or that Austin speaks of fictional discourse as "parasitic" is important as a symptom of a deeper logic at work in their arguments, a logic which would doubtless have manifested itself in other ways if these particular terms had been omitted, since it involves the most fundamental articulations of the sphere of discourse.

On the one hand, deconstruction accepts the distinction between surface features of a discourse and its underlying logic or between empirical features of languages and thought itself. When it concentrates on the metaphors in a text or other apparently marginal features, they are clues to what is truly important. When it cites the range of meanings listed for a word in dictionaries or assembled around it by morphological and etymological links, it is in order to dramatize, through these contingent associations, connections that repeat themselves in various guises and contribute to a paradoxical logic. Of *dissémination* Derrida remarks, "ce mot a de la chance": "This word has good luck. . . . It has the power economically to condense, while unwinding their web, the question of semantic differance (the new concept of writing) and seminal drift, the impossible (monocentric, paternal, familial) reappropriation of the concept and of the sperm" ("Avoir l'oreille de la philosophie," p. 309). Derrida is not playing with words, he is betting with words, employing them strategically with an eye on larger stakes. It is only by doing this that he engages with philosophical discourse.

But on the other hand—the left hand—in relying on textual and linguistic configurations, as in "Plato's Pharmacy," one puts in question the possibility of distinguishing with surety between structures of language or texts and structures of thought, between the contingent and the essential. Might it not be that the relations identified and set aside as contingent also inhabit what is deemed essential? In arguing for the revelatory importance of poetic or contingent elements in philosophical texts, one is adumbrating the possibility of treating philosophy as a specific form of a generalized poetic discourse, and indeed, deconstructive readings have done just that. Treating philosophical writings not as statements of positions but as texts—heterogeneous discourses structured by a variety of canny and uncanny exigencies—they have taken seriously apparently trivial or gratuitous elements that philosophers might have dismissed as accidents of expression and presentation, and have revealed surprising performative dimensions of these supposedly constative writings. In analyzing the rhetorical strategies focused on *supplement* in Rousseau, *pharmakon* in Plato, and *parergon* in Kant, Derrida in effect makes philosophy a species of an architliterature, disrupting the hierarchy that treats literature as a nonserious margin of serious conceptual discourse.

Some of the best evidence for this deconstructive inversion comes from the consideration of metaphor in philosophy. In theory, metaphors are contingent features of philosophical discourse; though they may play an important role in expressing and elucidating concepts, they ought in principle to be separable from the concepts and their adequacy or inadequacy, and indeed separating essential concepts from the rhetoric in which they are expressed is a fundamental philosophical task. But when one attempts to perform this task, not only is it difficult to find concepts that are not metaphorical, but the very terms in which one defines this philosophical task are themselves metaphorical. In his *Topics* Aristotle provides various techniques for clarifying a discourse by identifying and interpreting metaphors, but as Derrida observes, "the appeal to criteria of clarity and obscurity would be enough to establish the point made above: that this whole philosophical delimitation of metaphor is already constructed and worked upon by 'metaphors.' How could a piece of knowledge or language be clear or obscure *properly* speaking? All the concepts which have played a part in the delimitation of metaphor always have an origin and a force which are themselves 'metaphorical'" (*Marges*, p. 301/"White Mythology," p. 54). The very notions of what in a discourse might be nonmetaphorical are concepts whose force owes much to their figural attractions.

The values of *concept, foundation,* and *theory* are metaphorical and resist a meta-metaphorical analysis. We need not insist on the optical metaphor that opens under the sun every theoretical point of view. The "fundamental" involves the desire for firm and final ground, for building land, the ground as support for an artificial structure. The force of this metaphor has its own history, of which Heidegger has suggested an interpretation. Finally, the concept of concept cannot fail to retain, though it would not be reducible to, the pattern of that gesture of power, the taking-now, the grasping and taking hold of the thing as an object. [P. 267/23–24]

Investigating Locke, Condillac, and Kant's attempts to identify and control figures (Kant notes that *Grund,* "ground," *abhängen,* "to depend," and *fliessen,* "to follow from," are metaphors), Paul de Man shows that attempts to control metaphor cannot extract themselves from metaphor and that in each case a crucial distinction between the literal and metaphorical breaks down. "The resulting undecidability is due to the asymmetry of the binary model" that opposes the figural to the literal or the literary to the philosophical ("The Epistemology of Metaphor," p. 28). The literal is the opposite of the figurative, but a literal expression is also a metaphor whose figurality has been forgotten. The philosophical is condemned to be literary in its dependence on figure even when it defines itself by its opposition to figure.

Thus the second half of the answer to the charge of exploiting contingencies would displace the opposition between the contingent and essential by arguing that the kind of relations identified as contingent and poetic already operate at the heart of the conceptual order. There may be no way for philosophy to free itself from rhetoric, since there seems no way to judge whether or not it has freed itself, the categories for such a judgment being inextricably entwined with the matter to be judged. Philosophical discourse has various particularities, which we invoke in labeling a text philosophical, but it occurs within a general textuality where the iterability of forms, their connections with other forms and contexts, and the extendibility of context itself preclude the rigorous circumscription of meaning. The *pharmakos* may be repeatedly cast out of the city to keep it pure, but casting out metaphor, poetry, the parasitic, the nonserious, is possible only because they already dwell in the heart of the city: and they are repeatedly discovered to dwell there, which is why they can be repeatedly cast out.

The left- and right-hand sides of the answer to the philosopher's charge are in some measure incompatible and cannot be brought together in a coherent synthesis. For this reason, it may not seem an answer at all to many, who would argue that logic forbids one to accept and employ a distinction on the one hand and to contest it on the other. The question then would be whether logic can enforce its interdiction and impose effective sanctions on deconstruction. Often, though, the objection to this double procedure is stated in a figure that invokes not the authority of a law or morality but a physical and empirical inappropriateness: deconstruction's procedure is called "sawing off the branch on which one is sitting." This may be, in fact, an apt description of the activity, for though it is unusual and somewhat risky, it is manifestly something one can attempt. One can and may continue to sit on a branch while sawing it. There is no physical or moral obstacle if one is willing to risk the consequences. The question then becomes whether one will succeed in sawing it clear through, and where and how one might land. A difficult question: to answer one would need a comprehensive understanding of the entire situation—the resilience of the support, the efficacy of one's tools, the shape of the terrain—and an ability to predict accurately the consequences of one's work. If "sawing off the branch on which one is sitting" seems foolhardy to men of common sense, it is not so for Nietzsche, Freud, Heidegger, and Derrida; for they suspect that if they fall there is no "ground" to hit and that the most clear-sighted act may be a certain reckless sawing, a calculated dismemberment or deconstruction of the great cathedral-like trees in which Man has taken shelter for millennia.[10]

I emphasize the double procedure of deconstruction since rumor is inclined to make every movement simple and treat deconstruction as an attempt to abolish all distinctions, leaving neither literature nor philosophy but only a general, undifferentiated textuality. On the contrary, a distinction between liter-

[10]I am grateful to William Warner for providing the formulations of this sentence in response to my remarks on "sawing off the branch on which one is sitting"—an activity he relates to Nietzsche's injunction in *The Gay Science* to "live dangerously!"

ature and philosophy is essential to deconstruction's power of intervention: to the demonstration, for example, that the most truly philosophical reading of a philosophical work—a reading that puts in question its concepts and the foundations of its discourse—is one that treats the work as literature, as a fictive, rhetorical construct whose elements and order are determined by various textual exigencies. Conversely, the most powerful and apposite readings of literary works may be those that treat them as philosophical gestures by teasing out the implications of their dealings with the philosophical oppositions that support them.

To sum up, one might say that to deconstruct an opposition, such as presence/absence, speech/writing, philosophy/literature, literal/metaphorical, central/marginal, is no' to destroy it, leaving a monism according to which there would be *only* absence or writing or literature, or metaphor, or marginality. To deconstruct an opposition is to undo and displace it, to situate it differently. Schematically, this involves several distinguishable moves: (A) one demonstrates that the opposition is a metaphysical and ideological imposition by (1) bringing out its presuppositions and its role in the system of metaphysical values—a task which may require extensive analysis of a number of texts—and (2) showing how it is undone in the texts that enunciate and rely on it. But (B) one simultaneously maintains the opposition by (1) employing it in one's argument (the characterizations of speech and writing or of literature and philosophy are not errors to be repudiated but essential resources for argument) and (2) reinstating it with a reversal that gives it a different status and impact. When speech and writing are distinguished as two versions of a generalized protowriting, the opposition does not have the same implications as when writing is seen as a technical and imperfect representation of speech. The distinction between the literal and the figurative, essential to discussions of the functioning of language, works differently when the deconstructive reversal identifies literal language as figures whose figurality has been forgotten instead of treating figures as deviations from proper, normal literality.

Working in this way, with a double movement, both inside and outside previous categories and distinctions, deconstruction is ambiguously or uncomfortably positioned and particularly open to attack and misunderstanding. Relying on distinctions that it puts in question, exploiting oppositions whose philosophical implications it seeks to evade, it can always be attacked both as an anarchism determined to disrupt any order whatever and, from the opposite perspective, as an accessory to the hierarchies it denounces. Instead of claiming to offer firm ground for the construction of a new order or synthesis, it remains implicated in or attached to the system it criticizes and attempts to displace. As we have seen in considering some Derridean graftings, the writings of deconstruction have a particularly problematical relation to the distinction between the serious and the nonserious. Unwilling to renounce the possibilities of serious argument or the claim to deal with "essential" matters, deconstruction nevertheless attempts to escape the confines of the serious since it also disputes the priority accorded to "serious" philosophical considerations over matters of, shall we say, linguistic "surface."

The implications of this ambidextrous relation to philosophy and philosophical projects are difficult to explicate, but they are essential to an understanding of deconstruction. In characterizing philosophy as logocentric, Derrida identifies its basic project as that of determining the nature of truth, reason, being, and of distinguishing the essential from the contingent, the well-grounded from the factitious. Since Descartes, the logocentrism of philosophy has emerged particularly in its concentration on epistemology. As Richard Rorty puts it in a powerful study of this tradition,

Philosophy as a discipline thus sees itself as the attempt to underwrite or debunk claims to knowledge made by science, morality, art or religion. It purports to do this on the basis of its special understanding of the nature of knowledge and of mind. Philosophy can be foundational in respect to the rest of culture because culture is the assemblage of claims to knowledge, and philosophy adjudicates such claims. It can do so because it understands the foundations of knowledge and it finds these foundations in a study of man-as-knower, of the "mental processes" or the "activity of representation" which make knowledge possible. To know is to represent accurately what is outside the mind; so to understand the possibility and nature of knowledge is to understand the way in which the mind is able to construct such representations. [*Philosophy and the Mirror of Nature*, p. 3]

Reality is the presence behind representations, what accurate representations are representations of, and philosophy is above all a theory of representation.

A theory of representation that seeks to establish foundations must take as given, must assume the presence of, that which accurate representations represent. There is thus always a question whether any supposed given may not in fact be a construct or product, dependent, for example, on the theory which it purports to support. Moreover, the characteristic problem of theories of truth or knowledge is why we should believe that we have more certain knowledge of the conditions of truth or of knowledge than we do of a particular truth. A pragmatic tradition has frequently argued that if we define truth as what simply *is* the case, then not only do we have no assurance that our present beliefs are true, since we must allow for the possibility that they will be invalidated by future discoveries, but we have no guarantee that our criteria for successful enquiry are the correct ones. Truth is better thought of, such thinkers have argued, as relative to a framework of argument and justification: truth, as John Dewey puts it, is "warrantable assertion."[11] Truth consists of propositions that can be justified according to currently accepted modes of justification. Instead of correspondence between propositions and some absolute state of affairs, we have a continuing conversation in which propositions are brought forth in defense of other propositions, in a potentially infinite process that is arrested only when those concerned are satisfied or become bored (Rorty, p. 159). For theorists who

[11]Cited by Rorty in *Philosophy and the Mirror of Nature*, p. 176. This book, especially chapters 3, 4, 6, 7, and 8, proves very useful for understanding Derrida, for it is an analytical philosopher's critique of what Derrida calls the logocentrism of Western philosophy. Using analytical arguments against the analytical enterprise, Rorty goes on to distinguish systematic philosophers from Gadamer, and Derrida. "Great systematic philosophers are constructive and offer arguments. Great edifying philosophers are reactive and offer satires, parodies, aphorisms" (p. 369). He recognizes that edifying philosophers do in fact propose arguments but maintains that they should not do so. However, as Derrida argues, if one is to engage with philosophy one must offer argument, and Rorty himself finds analytical argument indispensable to his edifying project of promoting the edifying tradition. The edifying philosopher necessarily writes hybrid texts.

treat truth as correspondence, there is a truth but we can never know whether we know it. Pragmatists hold that we can know truth, since truth is whatever is validated by our methods of validation, and while truth is relative to a set of institutional procedures and assumptions that may change, there can be no more secure foundation, they argue, than the sort of truth we possess.

One might be tempted to identify deconstruction with pragmatism since it offers a similar critique of the philosophical tradition and emphasizes the institutional and conventional constraints on discursive enquiry. Like pragmatism in Rorty's account, deconstruction sees representations as signs that refer to other signs, which refer to still other signs, and depicts enquiry as a process in which propositions are adduced to support other propositions and what is said to "ground" a proposition proves to be itself part of a general text. But there are two major obstacles to identifying deconstruction with pragmatism. First, deconstruction cannot be content with the pragmatist conception of truth. The appeal to consensus and convention—truth as what is validated by our accepted methods of validation—works to treat the norm as a foundation, and as Derrida's discussions of Austin and Searle suggest, norms are produced by acts of exclusion. Speech act theorists exclude nonserious examples so as to ground their rules on consensus and conventions. Moralists exclude the deviant so as to ground their precepts on a social consensus. If, as Rorty observes, to analyze propositions to determine their objectivity means "finding out whether there is general agreement among sane and rational men on what would count as confirming their truth" (p. 337), objectivity is constituted by excluding the views of those who do not count as sane and rational men: women, children, poets, prophets, madmen. One frequently finds general agreement, but consensuses adduced to serve as foundations are not given but produced—produced by exclusions of this sort.

Since deconstruction is interested in what has been excluded and in the perspective it affords on the consensus, there can be no question of accepting consensus as truth or restricting truth to what is demonstrable within a system. Indeed, the notion of truth as what is validated by accepted methods of validation is used to criticize what passes for truth. Since deconstruction attempts to view systems from the outside as well as the inside, it tries to keep alive the possibility that the eccentricity of women, poets, prophets, and madmen might yield truths about the system to which they are marginal—truths contradicting the consensus and not demonstrable within a framework yet developed.

Second, deconstruction differs from pragmatism in its attitude toward reflexive enquiry. At its most rigorous, pragmatism argues that we cannot by an effort of self-scrutiny or theoretical enquiry get outside the framework of beliefs and assumptions within which we operate—we cannot get outside our institutions and beliefs to evaluate them—and so we should not worry about these matters but should go pragmatically about our business. Deconstruction is, of course, skeptical about the possibility of solving epistemological problems or of actually breaking out of the logocentrism of Western thought, but it repudiates the complacency to which pragmatism may lead and makes reflection upon one's own procedures and institutional frameworks a necessary task. The questioning of one's categories and procedures may, of course, be carried out with considerable complacency, but the principle, the strategy, may be stated quite unequivocally: even if in principle we cannot get outside conceptual frameworks to criticize and evaluate, the practice of self-reflexivity, the attempt to theorize one's practice, works to produce change, as the recent history of literary criticism amply shows. Theoretical enquiry does not lead to new foundations—in this sense the pragmatists are right. But they are wrong to reject it on these grounds, for it does lead to changes in assumptions, institutions, and practices.

The preservation of the notion that truth might emerge from positions of marginality and eccentricity is part of this theoretical strategy, for while particular claims to have discovered a foundation or epistemologically authoritative position will be put in question, the critical project depends on resisting the notion that truth is only what can be demonstrated within an accepted framework. It may well be that "truth" plays such an indispensable role in argument and analysis precisely because it has this persistent duplicity, a double reference that is difficult to erase. Truth is both what can be demonstrated within an accepted framework and what simply is the case, whether or not anyone could believe it or validate it.

The resilience of this double function or play of "truth" can be seen in the fact that those who defend a pragmatist conception of truth do not generally maintain that their view is true because it is a warrantable assertion, demonstrable within the assumptions of our culture. They argue, on the contrary, that this is what truth *is*, that this is the truth about truth, even though people generally think truth is something else.

There is a paradox here which we encounter frequently in the domains of philosophy, literary criticism, and history, and which can doubtless be found elsewhere. The champions of an absolutist, correspondence theory of truth defend their position on pragmatic grounds: it has desirable consequences, is necessary to the preservation of essential values. We need not believe in the possibility of actually attaining truth, the argument runs, but we must believe that there is a truth—a way things are, a true meaning of a text or utterance—or else research and analysis lose all point; human enquiry has no goal. The proponents of a pragmatist view reply that, whatever the consequences of their relativism, we must live with them because this is the truth, the way things are: truth *is* relative, dependent on a conceptual framework. Both attempts to maintain a position give rise to a deconstructive movement in which the logic of the argument used to defend a position contradicts the position affirmed.

Deconstructive readings identify this paradoxical situation in which, on the one hand, logocentric positions contain their own undoing and, on the other hand, the denial of logocentrism is carried out in logocentric terms. Insofar as deconstruction maintains these positions, it might seem to be a dialetical synthesis, a superior and complete theory; but these two movements do not, when combined, yield a coherent position or a higher theory. Deconstruction has no better theory of truth. It is a practice of reading and writing attuned to the aporias that arise in attempts to tell us the truth. It does not develop a new philosophical framework or solution but moves back and forth, with a nimbleness it hopes will prove strategic, between nonsynthesizable moments of a general economy. It moves in and out of philosophic seriousness, in and out of philosophical demonstration. Working in and around a discursive framework rather than constructing on new ground, it nevertheless seeks to produce reversals and displacements. We have encountered a number of these reversals of hierarchies already but since there are several others of considerable practical and theoretical importance we might turn to them for an illustration of the implications of deconstruction before questioning the possible consequences for literary criticism.

4. INSTITUTIONS AND INVERSIONS

In "The Conflict of Faculties" Derrida writes:

> What is somewhat hastily called deconstruction is not, if it is of any consequence, a specialized set of discursive procedures, still less the rules of a new hermeneutic method that works on texts or utterances in the shelter of a given and stable institution. It is also, at the very least, a way of taking a position, in its work of analysis, concerning the political and institutional structures that make possible and govern our practices, our competencies, our performances. Precisely because it is never concerned only with signified content, deconstruction should not be separable from this politico-institutional problematic and should seek a new investigation of responsibility, an investigation which questions the codes inherited from ethics and politics. This means that, too political for some, it will seem paralyzing to those who only recognize politics by the most familiar road signs. Deconstruction is neither a methodological reform that should reassure the organization in place nor a flourish of irresponsible and irresponsible-making destruction, whose most certain effect would be to leave everything as it is and to consolidate the most immobile forces within the university.

The claim is that because deconstruction is never concerned only with signified content but especially with the conditions and assumptions of discourse, with frameworks of enquiry, it engages the institutional structures governing our practices, competencies, performances. The questioning of these structures, whatever its consequences—and they have not proved easy to calculate—can be seen as a politicizing of what might otherwise be thought a neutral framework. Questions of institutional force and structure prove to be involved in the problems deconstruction addresses. Kant's "The Conflict of Faculties," which Derrida analyzes in the essay of this name, discusses the relation of the Faculty of Philosophy to the other university faculties (Law, Medicine, and Theology) and to state power. Kant's attempt to define the Philosophy Faculty's sphere of operations and the limitations others' rights and powers might impose, proves to turn on a distinction between constative and performative language: the former a realm with which philosophy may make free, the latter reserved for the state and its university agents. And the problems that arise when a theory of speech acts attempts to define and sustain this opposition are precisely the issues that animate the institutional struggles of Kant's university and, in different forms, our own. "Il n'y a pas de hors texte" in that the realities with which politics is concerned, and the forms in which they are manipulated, are inseparable from discursive structures and systems of signification, or what Derrida calls "the general text." Dependent upon the hierarchical oppositions of our tradition, they are liable to be affected by inversions and displacements of those hierarchies, though such effects may be slow to work themselves out.

Derrida's most public involvement with institutions and politics has been his work with the Groupe de recherches sur l'enseignement philosophique (GREPH), which has undertaken a broad struggle against educational reforms that would reduce the role of philosophy in French schools and orient education toward the supposed technological requirements of the future job market. GREPH's defense of philosophy includes a critique of the conception of philosophy promoted by various institutions; a philosophical analysis of philosophy's involvement with interests and forces regarded as marginal to a purely philosophical enquiry expands the notion of philosophy as a critical discourse explicitly concerned with the politics of knowledge, representation, learning, and communication. By contesting the hierarchical oppositions within which philosophy and its role have been conceived, GREPH attempts to alter the ground and the stakes of its struggle. As Christopher Fynsk writes in a review of GREPH's *Qui a peur de la philosophie?*, the issue is not just the status of a discipline called "philosophy" but "a struggle between more or less determinate forces working *as philosophies* both inside and outside the institution" ("A Deceleration of Philosophy," p. 81).

The combination of sophisticated reflection on the nature of philosophy and the struggle for specific political goals is by no means easy to maintain, as the heterogeneity of contributions to *Qui a peur de la philosophie?* suggests. In an interview, "Entre crochets," Derrida emphasizes the paramount interest of this project "first because it is always difficult, because I don't know how to go about it: there is no program already constructed; it must be established or identified for each act; it can always fail; in each case, it does to some extent fail." But what interests me most, he continues, is to try to reduce a certain gap or delay:

> for example, between this work on or against the institution (to put it simply) and on the other hand what I perceive (to simplify again) as the most advanced version of philosophical or theoretical deconstruction. . . . We must take account of certain gaps and try to reduce them even if, for essential reasons, it is impossible to efface them: gaps, for example, between the discourses or practices of this immediately political deconstruction and a deconstruction of theoretical or philosophical aspect. These gaps are often so large as to conceal the connections [les relais] or make them unrecognizable to many. [P. 113]

Many theorists have a strong desire to eliminate these gaps. In *Marxism and Deconstruction*, for example, Michael Ryan outlines, with considerable polemical verve, ways in which deconstruction might be harnessed directly to political ends. Such projects risk bathos—does one need Derrida to unravel the contradictions of right-wing political rhetoric?—and, more important, beg numerous questions about what is truly progressive and what is not. There is no program already established, Derrida says, because attempts to reverse and thus displace major hierarchical oppositions of Western thought open possibilities of change that are incalculable. What seem at one stage the most abstract or recondite problems may have more disturbing consequences than immediate and intense political debates, and this radical potential may depend on a willingness to pursue theoretical investigations unchecked by the need to predict political benefits. If, as Derrida argues in *De la grammatologie*, the future deconstruction glimpses—a future that breaks with constituted normality—"can only be proclaimed or presented as a sort of monstrosity" (p. 14/5), then theoretical pursuits should perhaps be allowed to wax monstrous or grotesque and not be subjected to a teleology of political gain in the hope of eliminating the "gap" Derrida describes. Lest the necessary persistence of that gap excuse a conservative institutional complacency, one must, Derrida writes, continue "struggling as always upon two fronts, on two stages, and in two registers"—the critique of current institutions and the deconstruction of philosophical oppositions—while nevertheless contesting the distinction between the two ("Où commence et comment finit un corps enseignant," p. 67).

Deconstructive analyses, the claim is, have potentially radical institutional implications, but these implications, often distant and incalculable, are no substitute for immediate critical and political action, to which they may seem only indirectly related. Their radical potential may depend on the surprising resources they reveal in an excessive, uncalculating theoretical pursuit. If the force of theory depends upon possibilities of institutionalization—it becomes politically effective insofar as it can inform the practices by which we constitute, administer, and transmit a world—its most radical aspects are threatened by institutionalization and emerge precisely in a theoretical reflection that contests particular institutionalizations of a theoretical discourse. This is what one finds, for example, in the case of Freudian theory: its power is linked to the ability of its hierarchical reversals to transform thought and behavior, but the institutions of psychoanalysis have arguably been quite conservative, and the radical force of Freudian theory is linked not to those institutions but to the resources it provides for a continuing theoretical critique—a critique of institutions and assumptions, including those of psychoanalytic practice.

Indeed, Freudian theory is an excellent example of the way in which an apparently specialized or perverse investigation may transform a whole domain by inverting and displacing the oppositions that made its concerns marginal. One of the most productive intellectual enterprises of the 1970s has been the study of Freud's writings—from a deconstructive perspective—as theories and examples of textuality.[12] Detailing the consider-

---

[12]In addition to Derrida's "Spéculer—sur 'Freud'" in *La Carte postale* and "Freud et la scène de l'écriture" in *L'Ecriture et la différence*, see Sarah Kofman, *L'Enfance de l'art*, *Quatre Romans analytiques*, and *L'Enigme de la femme*;

able deconstructive and self-deconstructive force of his texts, these readings have given us a different view of Freudian theory.

One way to understand Freud's achievement is in the terms we have been exploring in this chapter. Freud begins with a series of hierarchical oppositions: normal/pathological, sanity/insanity, real/imaginary, experience/dream, conscious/unconscious, life/death. In each case the first term has been conceived as prior, a plenitude of which the second is a negation or complication. Situated on the margin of the first term, the second term designates an undesirable, dispensable deviation. Freud's investigations deconstruct these oppositions by identifying what is at stake in our desire to repress the second term and showing that in fact each first term can be seen as a special case of the fundamentals designated by the second term, which in this process is transformed. Understanding of the marginal or deviant term becomes a condition of understanding the supposedly prior term. The most general operations of the psyche are discovered, for example, through investigations of pathological cases. The logic of dreams and fantasies proves central to an account of the forces at work in all our experience. Investigation of neuroses is the key to the description of sane adaptation; it has even become something of a commonplace that "sanity" is only a particular determination of neurosis, a neurosis that accords with certain social demands. Or again, instead of treating sexuality as a highly specialized aspect of human experience, a force at work at certain moments in people's lives, Freud shows its pervasiveness, making a theory of sexual-

Jean-Michel Rey, *Parcours de Freud*; Philippe Lacoue-Labarthe, "Note sur Freud et la représentation"; Hélène Cixous, "La Fiction et ses fantômes"; Peter Brooks, "Fictions of the Wolfman"; Cynthia Chase, "Oedipal Textuality: Reading Freud's Reading of Oedipus"; Neil Hertz, "Freud and the Sandman"; Jeffrey Mehlman, "How to Read Freud on Jokes: The Critic as Schadchen" and "Trimethylamin: Notes on Freud's Specimen Dream"; Rodolphe Gasché, "La Sorcière métapsychologique"; David Carroll, "Freud and the Myth of Origins"; and Samuel Weber, *Freud-Legende*, "The Divaricator: Remarks on Freud's *Witz*," "The Sideshow, or: Remarks on a Canny Moment," and "It." Although Lacan's "return to Freud" has been a decisive stimulus to research and discussion, faithful Lacanians, taxed by the demands of discipleship, have not been the most astute and persuasive readers of Freud. The exception is, of course, Jean Laplanche, author of the classic *Vie et mort en psychanalyse*.

ity a precondition for understanding what might seem eminently nonsexual, such as the behavior of children. The "nonsexual" becomes a particular version of what Freud calls an
"enlarged sexuality" (*Three Essays on the Theory of Sexuality*, vol.
7, p. 134). These deconstructive reversals, which give pride of
place to what had been thought marginal, are responsible for
much of the revolutionary impact of Freudian theory. To make
that unique monster Oedipus the model for normal maturation
or to study normal sexuality as perversion—a perversion of the
instinctual—is a procedure which even today has not lost the
force of scandal.

The most general instance of Freudian deconstruction is, of
course, the dislocation of the hierarchical opposition between
the conscious and the unconscious. Freud writes:

> It is essential to abandon the overvaluation of the property of
> being conscious, before it becomes possible to form any correct
> view of the origin of what is mental . . . the unconscious is the
> larger sphere, which includes within it the smaller sphere of the
> conscious. Everything conscious has an unconscious preliminary
> stage; whereas what is unconscious may remain at that stage and
> nevertheless claim to be regarded as having the full value of a
> psychical process. The unconscious is the true psychical reality.
> [*The Interpretation of Dreams*, vol. 5, pp. 612–13]

For a powerful humanistic tradition, of which Descartes is only
the most obvious representative, the human subject has been
defined in terms of consciousness: the "I" is that which thinks,
perceives, and feels. In revealing and describing the determining force of unconscious factors and structures in human life,
Freud inverts the traditional hierarchy and makes consciousness a particular derivative instance of unconscious processes.

But there are two ways of thinking about this Freudian operation. By the first, often preferred when discussing the psychoanalytic cure, we have an inversion that emphasizes the
superior power of the unconscious but still defines it in terms
of consciousness, as repressed or deferred consciousness. Experiences are repressed, relegated to the unconscious, where
they exercise a determining influence. During a psychoanalysis
their hidden presence is revealed; they are brought back to
consciousness and, as the humanist tradition would have it,

analysands free themselves from the control of these previously repressed ideas through this new self-consciousness, in which the self becomes maximally present to itself. By this way of thinking, the Freudian inversion privileges the unconscious, but it does so only by making it a hidden reality that can in principle be unveiled, reappropriated in and by a superior consciousness.

Freud's formulations are often open to this interpretation, but he also insists on a distinction between the psychoanalytic unconscious and what he calls the "preconscious," whose memories and experiences are not conscious at a given moment but can in principle be recovered by consciousness. The unconscious, on the other hand, is inaccessible to consciousness.[13] Moreover, particularly in the works that elaborate theories of primal repression, primal fantasies, and *Nachträglichkeit*, or deferred action, Freud emphasizes that the unconscious is by no means simply a layer of actual experiences that have been repressed, a hidden presence. It is both constituted by repression and the active agent of repression. Like *différance*, which designates the impossible origin of difference in differing and of differing in difference, the unconscious is a nonoriginary origin which Freud calls primary repression (*Urverdrängung*), in which the unconscious both initiates the first repression and is constituted as repression. If the discovery of the unconscious is a demonstration that nothing in the human subject is ever simple, that thoughts and desires are already doubled and divided, it turns out that the unconscious itself is not a simple hidden reality but always, in Freud's speculations, a complex and differential product. As Derrida writes,

> the unconscious is not, as we know, a hidden, virtual, potential self-presence. It differs/defers itself [Il se diffère], which no doubt means that it is woven of differences and also that it sends out or delegates representatives, mandates, but that there is no way the mandator could "exist," be present, be "itself" somewhere, much less become conscious. In this sense . . . the "unconscious" can no more be classed as a "thing" than as anything else; it is no more a thing than a virtual or concealed consciousness. This radical other-

[13]For discussion see Laplanche and Serge Leclaire, "The Unconscious: A Psychoanalytic Study," p. 127.

ness with respect to every possible mode of presence can be seen in the irreducible effects of deferred action. . . . In the otherness of the "unconscious" we are dealing not with a series of modified presents—presents that are past or still to come—but with a "past" that has never been nor ever will be present and whose future will never be its *production* or reproduction in the form of presence. [*Marges*, pp. 21–22/"Differance," p. 152]

Nachträglichkeit names a paradoxical situation that Freud frequently encounters in his case studies, in which the determining event in a neurosis never occurs as such, is never present as an event, but is constructed afterwards by what can only be described as a textual mechanism of the unconscious. In the case of the Wolfman, the analysis of key dreams leads Freud to the conclusion that the child had witnessed his parents copulating at age one-and-a-half. This "primal scene" had no meaning or impact at the time; it was inscribed in the unconscious like a text in an unknown language. When he was four, however, a dream linked to this scene by a chain of associations transformed it into a trauma, though it remained repressed except as a displaced symptom: a fear of wolves. The crucial experience, the determining event in the Wolfman's life, was one that never occurred. The "original" scene was not itself traumatic, and it may even have been, Freud allows, a scene of copulating animals transformed by deferred action into a primal scene. One cannot track down and make present the event or cause because it exists nowhere.

The case of "Emma" is another classic illustration of the textual, differential functioning of the unconscious. Emma traces her fear of shops to an incident at age twelve when she entered a store, saw two shop assistants laughing, and fled in fright. Freud traces it to a scene at age eight when a shopkeeper had fondled her genitals through her clothes. "Between the two scenes," writes Jean Laplanche, "an entirely new element has appeared—the possibility of a sexual reaction" (*Life and Death in Psychoanalysis*, p. 40). The sexual content is neither in the first scene, when she was aware of no sexual implications, nor in the second scene. "Here," Freud writes, "we have an instance of a memory exciting an affect which it did not excite as an experience, because in the meantime changes produced by puberty had made possible a different understanding of what was remembered . . . the memory is repressed which has only become a trauma *by deferred action* ("Project for a Scientific Psychology," vol. 1, p. 356).

"The irreducibility of the 'effect of deferral,'" writes Derrida, "such is no doubt Freud's discovery" (*L'Ecriture et la différence*, p. 303/203). "The unconscious text is already a weave of pure traces, differences in which meaning and force are united—a text nowhere present, consisting of archives which are always already transcriptions. Originary prints. Everything begins with reproduction. Always already: that is to say, repositories of a meaning which was never present, whose signified presence is always reconstituted by deferral, *nachträglich*, belatedly, *supplementarily*: for *nachträglich* also means *supplementary*" (p. 314/212). Further confirmation of the possibility of understanding Freudian theory in terms of *différance* comes from Freud's various differential models of the psyche, which Derrida discusses in "Freud et la scène de l'écriture," particularly the model of the mystic writing pad. In order to represent the paradoxical situation in which memories become inscribed or reproduced in the unconscious without ever having been perceived, Freud invokes a complex writing apparatus. Traces which never appeared on the perceptual surface are left beneath it, as reproductions without originals. In general, while emphasizing the heterogeneity of Freud's texts, deconstruction has found in his writings daring proposals that put in question the metaphysical assumptions with which he is ostensibly operating. As Derrida writes, "that the present in general is not primal but rather reconstituted, that it is not the full, living, absolute, and constitutive form of experience, that there is no purity of the living present—such is the theme, formidable indeed for the history of metaphysics, that Freud invites us to pursue, though in a conceptual framework inadequate to it" (p. 314/212).

A most striking instance of deconstructive speculation is the account in *Beyond the Pleasure Principle* of the death drive or death instinct. It might seem that if there is any clear binary opposition it ought to be *life* versus *death*: *life* is the positive term and *death* its negation. Yet Freud argues that the death instinct, the fundamental drive of every living thing to return to an inorganic state, is the most powerful life force; the organism "wishes only to die in its own fashion," and its life is a series of deferrals of its life goal (vol. 18, p. 39). The death drive, as manifested in the repetition compulsion, makes the activity of life instincts a special case within the general economy of repetition and expenditure. As Laplanche puts it, in this "carrying back of death into life . . . it is as though there were in Freud a more or less obscure perception of a necessity to refute every vitalistic interpretation, to shatter life in its very foundations" (*Life and Death in Psychoanalysis*, p. 123). The logic of Freud's argument effects a striking deconstructive reversal in which "the pleasure principle seems actually to serve the death instincts" (*Beyond the Pleasure Principle*, vol. 18, p. 63).

Readings of Freud have taken up a further opposition that is deeply sedimented in our thinking and the deconstruction of which may have more immediate social and political consequences: the hierarchical opposition of *man* and *woman*. Some writers have claimed that this is the primordial opposition on which all others are based and that, as Hélène Cixous puts it, the aim of logocentrism, though it could not admit it, has always been to found phallogocentrism, to assure a rationale for a masculine order ("Sorties," pp. 116–19). Whether or not it is the paradigm of metaphysical oppositions, man/woman is certainly a distinction whose hierarchical structure is marked in an endless number of ways, from the genetic account in the Bible, where woman is created from man's rib as a supplement or "helpmeet" to man, to the semantic, morphological, and etymological relations of *man* and *woman* in English.

This is a case where the effects of an imposed hierarchy are clear and the reasons for deconstructing that hierarchy palpable. We can also see here how right Derrida is to insist that it does not suffice to deny a hierarchical relation. It does little good simply to claim equality for writing against speech or for woman against man: even Reagan Republicans will pay lip service to equality. "I strongly and repeatedly insist," writes Derrida, "on the necessity of the phase of reversal, which people have perhaps too swiftly attempted to discredit. . . . To neglect this phase of reversal is to forget that the structure of the opposition is one of conflict and subordination and thus to pass too swiftly, without gaining any purchase against the former opposition, to a *neutralization* which *in practice* leaves things in their former state and deprives one of any way of *intervening* effectively" (*Positions*, pp. 56–7/41).[14] Affirmations of equality will not disrupt the hierarchy. Only if it includes an inversion or reversal does a deconstruction have a chance of dislocating the hierarchical structure.

The deconstruction of this opposition requires investigation of the ways in which various discourses—psychoanalytical, philosophical, literary, historical—have constituted a notion of man by characterizing the feminine in terms that permit it to be set aside. The analyst seeks to locate points at which these discourses undo themselves, revealing the interested, ideological nature of their hierarchical imposition and subverting the basis of the hierarchy they wish to establish. Derridean deconstruction might assist these investigations since many of the operations identified, for example, in Derrida's study of the treatment of writing also appear in discussions of woman. Like writing, woman is treated as a supplement: discussions of "man" can proceed without mention of woman because she is deemed to be automatically included as a special case; male pronouns exclude her without calling attention to her exclusion; and if she is considered separately she will still be defined in terms of man, as his other.

Celebrations of woman, which seem to contradict this structure, turn out to obey the logic Derrida has discerned in celebrations of writing. When a text seems to praise writing instead of treating it as a supplementary technique, the object of praise proves to be a metaphorical writing, distinguished from ordinary, literal writing. In the *Phaedrus*, for example, the writing or inscription of truth in the soul is distinguished from "sensible" writing "in space"; in the Middle Ages God's writing in the Book of Nature, which is praised, is scarcely the same as man's writing on parchment (*De la grammatologie*, pp. 26–27/15). Similarly, discussions of woman that appear to promote the feminine over the masculine—there are, of course, traditions of elaborate praise—celebrate the woman as goddess (the *Ewig-Weibliche*, Venus, Muse, Earth Mother) and invoke a metaphorical woman, in comparison with which actual women will be found wanting. Celebrations of woman or the identification of

[14]The first sentence of this quotation does not appear in the English translation of *Positions*.

woman with some powerful force or idea—truth as a woman, liberty as a woman, the muses as women—identify actual women as marginal. Woman can be a symbol of truth only if she is denied an effective relation to truth, only if one presumes that those seeking truth are men. The identification of woman with poetry through the figure of the muse also assumes that the poet will be a man. While appearing to celebrate the feminine, this model denies women an active role in the system of literary production and bars them from the literary tradition.[15]

Investigation of the place of women in various discourses will reveal the logic at work in these subtle and unsubtle oppressions, but nowhere are the results more interesting and suggestive than in the discourse of psychoanalysis, which has special importance since it has become our principal theory of sexuality and authority on sexual difference.

What does psychoanalysis have to say about the hierarchical opposition man/woman? Or rather, how is this opposition constituted in psychoanalytic theory? It is not difficult to show that in Freud's writings the feminine is treated as supplementary, parasitic. To define the feminine psyche in terms of penis envy is an indubitable instance of phallogocentrism: the male organ is the point of reference; its presence is the norm, and the feminine is a deviation, an accident or negative complication that has befallen the positive norm. Even Lacanians, who would confute this charge by arguing that the phallus is not the penis, reconfirm this structure by taking the male penis as the model for their purely symbolic phallus. Woman, as Luce Irigaray's title has it, is *Ce Sexe qui n'en est pas un*—"this sex which isn't one"—nothing but a negation of the masculine. Woman is not the creature with a vagina but the creature without a penis, who is essentially defined by that lack.

In his account of infant sexuality Freud quite explicitly presents the feminine as derivative. "We are now obliged to recognize," he writes, "that the little girl is a little man." Boys learn "how to derive pleasurable sensations from their small penis. . . . Little girls do the same thing with their still smaller

[15]For discussion and bibliographical leads, see chapters 1 and 2 of Gilbert and Gubar's *The Madwoman in the Attic*. Derrida's *Eperons*, in discussing "woman" in Nietzsche's writings, particularly explores those passages that identify truth as a woman.

clitoris. It seems that with them all their masturbatory acts are carried out on this penis-equivalent, and that the truly feminine vagina is still undiscovered by both sexes" ("Femininity," vol. 22, p. 118). Femininity begins as an attenuated version of male sexuality; sexual distinction arises when the female identifies herself as an inferior version of the male. Freud speaks of "a momentous discovery which little girls are destined to make. They notice the penis of a brother or playmate, strikingly visible and of large proportions, at once recognize it as the superior counterpart of their own small and inconspicuous organ, and from that time forward fall a victim to envy for the penis" ("Some Psychical Consequences of the Anatomical Distinction between the Sexes," vol. 19, p. 252). The girl is said to take the male as norm from the beginning. Without question she immediately defines herself as an aberration: "She makes her judgement and her decision in a flash," Freud continues. "She has seen it and knows that she is without it and wants to have it." From this recognition follow dire consequences. "She acknowledges the fact of her castration, and with it, too, the superiority of the male and her own inferiority" ("Female Sexuality," vol. 21, p. 229).

Later on, the discovery of the vagina will certainly have further consequences, but the vagina is something of an extra; it supplements her inadequate organ and does not, in Freud's account, give her an autonomous or independent sexuality. On the contrary, the structure of dependency and derivation is still operative. Mature feminine sexuality, focused on the vagina, is constituted by the repression of clitoral sexuality, which is essentially male. Woman is an inadequate male whose sexuality is defined as the repression of her original maleness, and the feminine psyche continues to be characterized above all by penis envy.

Much can be and has been written about Freud's masculine bias. His language suggests where he stands: he speaks of the woman "*acknowledging* the fact of her castration" and of her "*discovery* that she is castrated" and of her immediate "*recognition*" of "the boy's far superior equipment" ("Femininity," vol. 22, p. 126). In *Speculum, de l'autre femme* and *Ce Sexe qui n'en est pas un* Luce Irigaray launches a vigorous attack, arguing that this radical theorist, whose discoveries disrupt fundamental metaphysical schemes, is in his discussions of woman a prisoner of the most traditional philosophical and social assumptions. But rather than reject Freud one can, as Sarah Kofman does in *L'Enigme de la femme: La femme dans les textes de Freud*, take his writing seriously and see how this theory, which so clearly privileges male sexuality and defines woman as an incomplete man, deconstructs itself. To do this is not to trust Freud the man but to give oneself maximum opportunity to learn from Freud's writing by supposing that if this powerful and heterogeneous discourse is at one point operating with unjustified assumptions, these assumptions will be exposed and undermined by forces within the text that a reading can bring out.

A first line of enquiry is to determine what Freud's theories have to say about the construction of theories of sexuality. In "Spéculer—Sur 'Freud'" Derrida applies what Freud says about his grandson's play to Freud's own play with the Pleasure Principle, but in the case that now concerns us the situation is somewhat different, for Freud's theories explicitly discuss the formation of sexual theories. Interestingly, the theory of the castrated woman and of penis envy is first presented, in an article "On the Sexual Theories of Children," as a theory developed by the male child: one of three "false theories which the state of his own sexuality imposes on him" (vol. 9, p. 215). In his "ignorance of the vagina" the child assumes that everyone has a penis and that the girl's organ will grow bigger in time. "The woman's genitalia, when seen later on, are regarded as a mutilated organ" (p. 217). This infantile sexual theory later becomes Freud's own theory, and if one situates it within the psychic economy Freud describes, one can see, as Sarah Kofman argues, that the effect of a theory of woman's incomplete sexuality is not just to make male sexuality the norm by which everything is to be judged but specifically to make possible a certain "normal" male sexuality. Given Freud's emphasis on the inexorable force of the castration complex and castration anxiety, woman would either be an object of horror and revulsion, living proof of the possibility of castration, or else, as "On Narcissism" suggests, an altogether superior and autonomous being, complete in herself with nothing to lose or gain. Both possibilities are threatening to men. The theory of feminine sexuality and penis envy is a way of mastering woman: the more woman envies the male penis, the more certain it is that the male penis is intact, that it is indeed "superior equipment." Woman's penis envy reassures man of his sexuality and makes woman desirable both as the repository of this reassurance and as a sexual object. Freud argues that "the curb put upon love by civilization involves a universal tendency to debase sexual objects" and that therefore the woman who is to be an object of sexual attentions must be debased. "As soon as the condition of debasement is fulfilled, sensuality can be freely expressed, and important sexual capacities and a high degree of pleasure can develop" ("On the Universal Tendency to Debasement in the Sphere of Love," vol. 11, pp. 187, 183). As Kofman explains, the castrating operation which ascribes to woman an incomplete sexuality and hence penis envy is the "solution" Freud proposes for restoring to civilized man his full sexual power (L'Enigme de la femme, pp. 97–103).

One might argue, as Juliet Mitchell does in her pioneering Psychoanalysis and Feminism, that Freud is describing what is the case in relations between the sexes. "That Freud did not more emphatically denounce what he analysed is a pity. . . . However, I think we can only go further with analysis. That Freud's account of woman comes out pessimistic is not so much an index of his reactionary spirit as of the condition of women" (p. 362). But Freud's theory explicitly presents penis envy, the castration complex, and other elements of femininity as necessary rather than contingent, not as symptoms of the historical condition of women but as ineluctable aspects of the constitution of human beings; and in that way his theory works to validate, as an ahistorical necessity, the debasement of women and the authority of the male. Moreover, since Freud's own account shows that the male's own sexual situation gives him an interest in formulating theories with this sort of hierarchical structure, we have every reason to question the claim that Freud's account is a neutral description.

Freud's theory reveals itself as a male imposition motivated by forces within the economy of sexual drives and anxieties, but it also undoes itself in another way. In order to make woman's sexuality derivative and dependent, an attenuated version of male sexuality and then a repression of phallic sexuality, Freud posits for the woman an original bisexuality. If "the little girl is a little man" who has it in her to become a woman, she is from the beginning bisexual, and it is in these terms that Freud poses the question of femininity: psychoanalysis seeks to understand "how a woman develops out of a child with a bisexual disposition" ("Femininity," vol. 22, p. 116). Without this originary bisexuality, there would be simply two separate sexes, man and woman. Only by positing such bisexuality can Freud treat feminine sexuality as derivative and parasitic: first an inferior phallic sexuality, followed by the emergence of femininity through the repression of clitoral (masculine) sexuality. But the theory of bisexuality—one of the radical contributions of psychoanalysis—brings about a reversal of the hierarchical relation between *man* and *woman*, for it turns out that woman, with her combination of masculine and feminine modes and her two sexual organs, one "male" and one "female," is the general model of sexuality, and the male is only a particular variant of woman, a prolonged actualization of her phallic stage. Since woman has, as Freud says, a masculine and a feminine phase, instead of treating woman as a variant of "man," it would be more accurate, according to his theory, to treat man as a particular instance of woman. Or perhaps one should say, in keeping with the Derridean model, that man and woman are both variants of archi-woman.

It is thus possible to show, through a careful and resourceful reading of Freud, that the moves by which psychoanalysis establishes a hierarchical opposition between man and woman rely on premises that reverse this hierarchy. A deconstructive reading reveals that woman is not marginal but central and that the account of her "incomplete sexuality" is an attempt to construct a male plenitude by setting aside a complexity that proves to be a condition of sexuality in general. The hierarchical opposition implies the identity of each term, and particularly the coherent, unequivocal self-identity of the male; but, as Shoshana Felman argues, this male self-identity, and "the mastery to which it lays claim, turns out to be a sexual as well as a political fantasy, subverted by the dynamics of bisexuality and by the rhetorical reversibility of masculine and feminine" ("Rereading Femininity," p. 31). Whether one concentrates on the texts that conceal an archi- or protowoman or, as Sarah Kofman does elsewhere in *L'Enigme de la femme*, on those that reveal under exegetical pressure the determining role of the mother, Freud's writings can be shown to disrupt the sexual hierarchy of psychoanalysis.

In response to a question from Lucette Finas about "phallogocentrism" and its relation to the general project of deconstruction, Derrida replies that the term asserts the complicity between logocentrism and phallocentrism. "It is one and the same system: the erection of a paternal logos . . . and of the phallus as 'privileged signifier' (Lacan). The texts I published between 1964 and 1967 only prepared the way for an analysis of phallogocentrism" ("Avoir l'oreille de la philosophie," p. 311). In both cases there is a transcendental authority and point of reference: truth, reason, the phallus, "man." In combating the hierarchical oppositions of phallocentrism, feminists confront in immediately practical terms a problem endemic to deconstruction: the relationship between arguments conducted in logocentric terms and attempts to escape the system of logocentrism. For feminists this takes the form of an urgent question: to minimize or to exalt sexual differentiation? Does one concentrate on a range of attempts to challenge, neutralize, or transcend the opposition between "male" and "female," from demonstrating women's proficiency at "male" activities, to tracing the historical evolution of the distinction, to challenging the very notion of an oppositional sexual identity? Or does one, on the contrary, accept the opposition between male and female and celebrate the feminine, demonstrating its power and independence, its superiority to "male" modes of thought and behavior? To take a specific issue that American feminists have debated, when discussing women writers of the past and present should one seek to identify a distinctively feminine achievement, at the risk of contributing to the isolation of a ghetto of "women's writing" within the city of literature, or should one insist on the undesirability of categorizing authors by sex and describe the magnificent *general* achievements of particular women authors? For women writers the question has been whether to adopt "male" modes of writing and prove themselves "masters" of it or whether to develop a specifically feminine mode of discourse, whose superior virtues they might hope to demonstrate. Disagreements within feminist movements have often reached the point of hostility, as is perhaps inevitable, since choices must be made; but the example of deconstruction suggests the importance of working on two fronts at once, even though the result is a contradictory rather than unified movement. Analytical writings that attempt to neutralize the male/female opposition are extremely important, but, as Derrida says, "the hierarchy of the binary opposition always reconstitutes itself," and therefore a movement that asserts the primacy of the oppressed term is strategically indispensable (*Positions*, p. 57/42).

Many theorists influenced by deconstruction have worked to invert the traditional hierarchy and assert the primacy of the feminine. In "Sorties" Hélène Cixous contrasts man's neurotic fixation on a phallic monosexuality with woman's bisexuality which, she argues, ought to give women a privileged relation to writing. Male sexuality denies and resists otherness, while bisexuality is an acceptance of otherness within the self, as is writing. "To man it is much more difficult to let oneself be traversed by the other; writing is the passage, entrance, exit, sojourn in me of the other that I am and am not" (p. 158). Women's writing should affirm this relation to otherness; it should take strength from its more immediate access to literariness and its ability to escape male desires for mastery and domination. Luce Irigaray urges women to recognize their power as "la terre-mère-nature (ré)productrice" [the "(re)productive earth-mother-nature"] and seeks to develop a new mythology linking these terms (*Ce Sexe qui n'en est pas un*, p. 99 and passim). Julia Kristeva promotes the combination of the maternal and the sexual in the figure of the orgasmic mother ("la mère qui jouit") and describes art as the language of *la jouissance maternelle* (*Polylogue*, pp. 409–35). The feminine is the space not only of art and writing but also of truth, "le vréel" [the "trureal" or "she-truth" (*vrai-elle*)]: the unrepresentable truth that lies beyond and subverts the male orders of logic, mastery, and verisimilitude (*Folle vérité*, p. 11). Sarah Kofman in *L'Enigme de la femme* demonstrates the primacy of the mother in Freudian theory: she is not only the enigma to be deciphered but the teacher of truth, and Freud's "science" is devoted to attributing a lack to woman, who is seen as dangerously self-sufficient. Taking up the Freudian and Nietzschean images of the woman as a narcissistic master-criminal or redoubtable bird of prey, she develops the notion of the affirmative woman, unwilling to accept castration as decided or decidable but asserting her own double, undecidable feminine sexuality.

Writers who celebrate the feminine in this way can always be accused of myth-making, of countering myths of the male with new myths of the female; and perhaps for this reason hierarchical reversals are likely to be most convincing when they emerge from critical readings of major texts, as in Kofman's demonstrations that Freud's misogynistic writings covertly identify the threatening potency and primacy of the feminine. But the promotion of the feminine should also be accompanied by the deconstructive attempt to displace the sexual opposition. "Femininity," concludes Shoshana Felman in a reading of Balzac's *La Fille aux yeux d'or*, "as real otherness, in Balzac's text, is uncanny in that it is not the opposite of masculinity but that which subverts the very opposition of masculinity and femininity" ("Rereading Femininity," p. 42). The novel reveals this as the distinctive threat of femininity. Other analyses show how the feminine, or "woman," is identified with radical otherness— whatever lies outside or escapes the control of male-centered narratives and their hierarchical categories. Though woman is strictly located and defined by the languages and ideological narratives of our culture, the coding of this radical otherness as feminine makes possible a new concept of "woman" that subverts the ideological distinction between man and woman, much as proto- or archi-writing displaces the ordinary distinction between speech and writing.

This new concept of "woman" has little direct relation to what feminists identify as the problems of "real" women. Julia Kristeva explains in an interview entitled "La Femme, ce n'est jamais ca" ["Woman is never that" or "can never be defined"]:

> The belief that "one is a woman" is almost as absurd and obscurantist as the belief that "one is a man." I say "almost" because there are still many goals that women can achieve: freedom of abortion and contraception, day-care centers for children, equality on the job, etc. Therefore we must use "we are women" as an advertisement or slogan for our demands. On a deeper level, however, a woman is not something one can "be"; it does not even belong in the order of *being*. . . . By "woman" I understand what cannot be represented, what is not said, what remains above and

beyond nomenclatures and ideologies. There are certain "men" who are familiar with this phenomenon; it is what some modern texts never stop signifying: testing the limits of language and sociality—the law and its transgression, mastery and (sexual) plea-sure—without reserving one for males and the other for females. . . . [Pp. 20–21/137–38]

Feminists are rightly disturbed that in this deconstructive pal-eonomy "woman" may no longer refer to actual human beings defined by historical representations of sexual identity but serves rather as the horizon of a critique identifying "sexual identity," "representation," and the "subject" as ideological im-positions. But this is the other front of a struggle that also in-volves celebration of the work and writing of women. In Chap-ter One we encountered much the same division in feminist criticism: between those interested in promoting the distinctive experiences women readers have or can have and those con-cerned to expose "male" or "female" readings as products of the ideology to be dismantled. The question, as Derrida says, is how to reduce the gap between these two unsynthesizable proj-ects without sacrificing one to the other; as far as one can tell, it will be necessary for some time to continue the struggle on both fronts at once.

A final hierarchical opposition with institutional implications is the distinction between reading and misreading or under-standing and misunderstanding. The morphological system of English makes the second term dependent on the first, a deriv-ative version in *mis-* of the primary term. Misunderstanding is an accident which sometimes befalls understanding, a deviation which is possible only because there is such a thing as under-standing. That accidents may befall reading or understanding is an empirical possibility which does not affect the essential nature of these activities. When Harold Bloom propounds a theory of "The Necessity of Misreading" and puts in circulation *A Map of Misreading*, his critics reply that a theory of necessary misreading—a claim that all readings are misreadings—is in-coherent, since the idea of misreading implies the possibility of a correct reading. A reading can only be a misreading if there is a true reading that it misses.

This seems eminently reasonable, but when we press further

another possibility emerges. When one attempts to formulate the distinction between reading and misreading, one inevitably relies on some notion of identity and difference. Reading and understanding preserve or reproduce a content or meaning, maintain its identity, while misunderstanding and misreading distort it; they produce or introduce a difference. But one can argue that in fact the transformation or modification of meaning that characterizes misunderstanding is also at work in what we call understanding. If a text can be understood, it can in principle be understood repeatedly, by different readers in different circumstances. These acts of reading or understanding are not, of course, identical. They involve modifications and differences, but differences which are deemed not to matter. We can thus say, in a formulation more valid than its converse, that understanding is a special case of misunderstanding, a particular deviation or determination of misunderstanding. It is misunderstanding whose misses do not matter. The interpretive operations at work in a generalized misunderstanding or misreading give rise both to what we call understanding and to what we call misunderstanding.

The claim that all readings are misreadings can also be justified by the most familiar aspects of critical and interpretive practice. Given the complexities of texts, the reversibility of tropes, the extendibility of context, and the necessity for a reading to select and organize, every reading can be shown to be partial. Interpreters are able to discover features and implications of a text that previous interpreters neglected or distorted. They can use the text to show that previous readings are in fact misreadings, but their own readings will be found wanting by later interpreters, who may astutely identify the dubious presuppositions or particular forms of blindness to which they testify. The history of readings is a history of misreadings, though under certain circumstances these misreadings can be and may have been accepted as readings.

The inversion that treats understanding as a version of misunderstanding allows one to preserve a variable distinction between two classes of misunderstandings, those whose *mis*-matters and those whose does not, but it nevertheless has significant effects. It contests the assumption that misunderstanding arises as a complication or negation of the act of understanding, that misunderstanding is an accident which in principle might be eliminated, much as we might in principle eliminate automobile accidents and allow every vehicle to reach its correct destination. Wayne Booth, the great contemporary champion of understanding, defines it as follows: "Understanding is the goal, process, and result whenever one mind succeeds in entering another mind or, what is the same thing, whenever one mind succeeds in incorporating any part of another mind" (*Critical Understanding*, p. 262). In Booth's terms, misunderstanding is simply negative, a failure to enter or to incorporate something which is there to be entered or incorporated. Misunderstanding is to understanding as negative to positive. Assertions of the necessity of misreading, on the other hand, suggest that the contrast is not of this sort but that both reading and misreading, understanding and misunderstanding are instances of incorporation and penetration. The question of which misreadings or misunderstandings will be treated as acts of understanding is a complex one, involving a host of circumstantial factors not reducible to rules. What is accepted as an "understanding" of a particular biblical parable, for example, will vary immensely from one situation to another.

Booth's own *Critical Understanding* provides an excellent illustration of reading as misreading. To show what pluralism might be, Booth attempts to espouse and expound the critical practice of Kenneth Burke, R. S. Crane, and M. H. Abrams. He has a considerable stake in demonstrating the possibility of correctly adopting these contrasting approaches, and he spares no pains to achieve a sympathetic, accurate understanding; but Burke and Abrams both reject various aspects of his account. "If we cannot prove that even one critic has fully understood *one* other," writes Booth, "what are we to make of the pluralist's claim that he has understood and embraced more than one?" (p. 200).

We might conclude, as Abrams and Burke suggest, that Booth's understanding is a form of misunderstanding: his reading is a misreading, albeit a generous and scrupulous one. In some circumstances, confronted with other misreadings, one might credit Booth with one of those misunderstandings that count as understanding, but whether this happens depends upon a host of complex and contingent factors. We need not conclude that understanding is impossible, for acts of interpretation that seem perfectly adequate to particular purposes and circumstances occur all the time; but these readings could also be shown to be misreadings, had we reason to do so. My own misreading of Derrida may in some contexts pass as sufficient understanding, but it will also be attacked as a misreading. "The work," de Man writes, "can be used repeatedly to show where and how the critic diverged from it" (*Blindness and Insight*, p. 109).

As Barbara Johnson puts it,

> The sentence "all readings are misreadings" does not *simply* deny the notion of truth. Truth is preserved in vestigial form in the notion of error. This does not mean that there is, somewhere out there, forever unattainable, the one true reading against which all others will be tried and found wanting. Rather, it implies 1) that the reasons a reading might consider itself *right* are motivated and undercut by its own interests, blindnesses, desires, and fatigue, and 2) that the *role* of truth cannot be so easily eliminated. Even if truth is but a fantasy of the will to power, *something* still marks the point from which the imperatives of the not-self make themselves felt. ["Nothing Fails like Success," p. 14]

According to the paleonymic strategy urged by Derrida, "misreading" retains the trace of truth, because noteworthy readings involve claims to truth and because interpretation is structured by the attempt to catch what other readings have missed and misconstrued. Since no reading can escape correction, all readings are misreadings; but this leaves not a monism but a double movement. Against the claim that, if there are only misreadings, then anything goes, one affirms that misreadings are errors; but against the positivist claim that they are errors because they strive toward but fail to attain a true reading, one maintains that true readings are only particular misreadings: misreadings whose misses have been missed. This account of misreading is not, perhaps, a coherent, consistent position, but, its advocates would claim, it resists metaphysical idealizations and captures the temporal dynamic of our interpretive situation.

Like other inversions, the reversal of relations between understanding and misunderstanding disrupts a structure on which institutions have relied. Attacks on deconstructionists and on other critics as diverse as Bloom, Hartman, and Fish frequently emphasize that if all reading is misreading, then the notions of meaning, value, and authority promoted by our institutions are threatened. Each reader's reading would be as valid or legitimate as another, and neither teachers nor texts could preserve their wonted authority. What such inversions do, though, is displace the question, leading one to consider what are the processes of legitimation, validation, or authorization that produce differences among readings and enable one reading to expose another as a misreading. In the same way, identification of the normal as a special case of the deviant helps one to question the institutional forces and practices that institute the normal by marking or excluding the deviant.

In general, inversions of hierarchical oppositions expose to debate the institutional arrangements that rely on the hierarchies and thus open possibilities of change—possibilities which may well come to little but which may also at some point prove critical. Richard Rorty notes that we have not yet worked out the consequences for culture and society of Freud's massive yet detailed redescription of the human psyche and human behavior but are living uneasily with "the still unassimilated effects of psychoanalysis upon our attempts to think in moral terms" ("Freud, Morality, and Hermeneutics," p. 185). Freud's deconstruction of strategic oppositions has created problems for the logic of moral evaluation that uses categories such as "generosity"/"selfishness," "courage"/"cowardice," or "love"/"hatred." It is not clear what adjustments in the language and institutions of morality will occur: "we are still in the stage of suspecting that *something* is going to have to change in our old ways of speaking, but not yet knowing *what*" (p. 177). With deconstruction what is at stake, Derrida says, in "l'ébranlement actuel" [the current disruption] is the reevaluation of the relation between the general text and that which might have been thought of as simply outside language, discourse, or writing, as realities of a different order (*Positions*, p. 126/91). The "apparently local" conceptual disruptions thus have a more general bearing, though the effects are not immediately calculable.

5. CRITICAL CONSEQUENCES

Despite the manifest relevance to literary studies of the relation between reading and misreading, the implications of deconstruction for the study of literature are far from clear. Derrida frequently writes about literary works but has not dealt
directly with topics such as the task of literary criticism, the
methods for analyzing literary language, or the nature of meaning in literature. The implications of deconstruction for literary
study must be inferred, but it is not clear how such inferences
are to be made. The argument that all readings are misreadings, for example, does not seem to have logical consequences
that would compel critics to proceed differently, yet it may well
affect the way critics think about reading and the questions
they pose about acts of interpretation. In this case as in others,
that is to say, the deconstruction of a hierarchical opposition
does not entail or compel changes in literary criticism, yet it
can have considerable impact on how critics proceed. In particular, through its questioning of the philosophical oppositions
on which critical thought has inevitably relied, deconstruction
raises theoretical issues that critics must either ignore or pursue. By disrupting the hierarchical relations on which critical
concepts and methods depend, it prevents concepts and methods from being taken for granted and treated as simply reliable
instruments. Critical categories are not just tools to be employed in producing sound interpretations but problems to be
explored through the interaction of text and concept. This is
one reason why criticism seems so theoretical these days: critics
more readily investigate how critical categories are affected by
the works they are used to analyze.

Before passing, in Chapter Three, to a discussion of the literary criticism indebted to Derridean deconstruction, we should
assess the consequences for literary theory and criticism of the
deconstructive practice we have been expounding. One can distinguish four levels or modes of relevance. The first and most
important is deconstruction's impact upon a series of critical
concepts, including the concept of literature itself; but deconstruction also has effects in three other ways: as a source of

themes, as an example of reading strategies, and as a repository of suggestions about the nature and goals of critical inquiry.

(1) The notion of literature or literary discourse is involved in several of the hierarchical oppositions on which deconstruction has focused: serious/nonserious, literal/metaphorical, truth/fiction. We have seen how philosophers, to develop a theory of speech acts, construct a notion of "ordinary language" and "ordinary circumstances" by setting aside as parasitic exceptions all nonserious utterances, of which literature is the paradigm case. Relegating problems of fictionality, rhetoricity, and nonseriousness to a marginal and dependent realm—a realm in which language can be as free, playful, and irresponsible as it likes—philosophy produces a purified language which it can hope to describe by rules that literature would disrupt if it had not been set aside. The notion of literature has thus been essential to the project of establishing serious, referential, verifiable discourse as the norm of language.

Deconstruction's demonstration that these hierarchies are undone by the workings of the texts that propose them alters the standing of literary language. If serious language is a special case of the nonserious, if truths are fictions whose fictionality has been forgotten, then literature is not a deviant, parasitical instance of language. On the contrary, other discourses can be seen as cases of a generalized literature, or archi-literature. In "Qual Quelle" Derrida quotes a remark of Valéry's: if we can free ourselves from our habitual assumptions, we will note that "philosophy, defined by its opus, which is a body of writing, is objectively a special literary genre . . . which we must situate not far from poetry." If philosophy is a species of writing, then, writes Derrida,

a task is prescribed: to study the philosophic text in its formal structure, its rhetorical organization, the specificity and diversity of its textual types, its models of exposition and production—beyond what were once called genres—and, further, the space of its stagings [*mises en scènes*] and its syntax, which is not just the articulation of its signifieds and its references to being or to truth but also the disposition of its procedures and of everything invested in them. In short, thus to consider philosophy as "a particular literary genre," which draws upon the reserves of a linguistic system, organizing, forcing, or diverting a set of tropological possibilities that are older than philosophy. [*Marges*, pp. 348–49]

Reading philosophy as a literary genre, Derrida has taught us to consider philosophical writings as texts with a performative as well as cognitive dimension, as heterogeneous constructs, organizing and organized by a variety of discursive forces, never simply present to themselves or in control of their implications, and related in complex ways to a variety of other texts, written and lived. If this constitutes treating philosophy as literature, it is only because, since romanticism, literature has been the potentially most comprehensive mode of discourse. There is nothing that might not be put into a literary work; there is no pattern or mode of determination that might not be found there. To read a text as philosophy is to ignore some of its aspects in favor of particular sorts of argument; to read it as literature is to remain attentive even to its apparently trivial features. A literary analysis is one that does not foreclose possibilities of structure and meaning in the name of the rules of some limited discursive practice.

We have, therefore, an asymmetrical structure in which "literature" contrasts with "philosophy" or "history" or "journalism" but can also include anything that is opposed to it. This corresponds to an experience of literature: we think we know what literature is but are always finding other elements in it, and it expands to include them; there is nothing so definitively unliterary that it may not turn up in a book of poems. This asymmetrical relation is also the general structure that emerges from Philippe Lacoue-Labarthe's and Jean-Luc Nancy's *L'Absolu littéraire*, an analysis of the origins of modern notions of literature in German romantic theory. "The Literary Absolute" of their title is a reference to the self-transcending movement repeatedly built into different accounts of literature. Literature is a mode of writing distinguished by its quest for its own identity; the questioning of the literary thus becomes the mark of the literary. The novel includes the parody of the novel and the theory of the novel. The essence of literature is to have no essence, to be protean, undefinable, to encompass whatever might be situated outside it. This strange relationship, in which literature transcends any account of it and can include what is opposed to it, is partly reproduced in the notion of a generalized literature which would have literature as one of its species.

One should not infer, however, that for deconstruction literature is a privileged or superior mode of discourse. Derrida notes that Valéry's project of treating philosophy as a literary genre is an excellent strategy but that unless it is adopted strategically, as a reaction and intervention, it will lead one back in a circle, to the "place in question" (*Marges*, p. 350). Any claim for the superiority of literature to philosophy would presumably be based on the argument that philosophy deludedly hopes to escape fiction, rhetoric, trope, while literature explicitly announces its fictional and rhetorical nature. But to support this claim by demonstrating the rhetorical nature of a philosophical text, one would have to know what was literal and what was figurative, what was fictional and what nonfictional, what was direct and what was oblique. One would thus need to be able to distinguish authoritatively between essence and accident, form and substance, language and thought. An attempt to demonstrate the superiority of literature would not be based on superior literary knowledge but would depend upon and lead back to these fundamental philosophical difficulties.

Treating philosophy as a literary genre does not, for Derrida, entail the superiority of literary discourse or of literary knowledge, neither of which can resolve or escape intractable philosophical problems. Moreover, it would be precipitous to claim that philosophical texts are ignorant of something—their own rhetoricity—which literary texts understand. Deconstructive readings that show philosophical texts deconstructing their own arguments and identifying their own strategies as rhetorical impositions in effect credit these texts with what is better called knowledge than ignorance. When Derrida argues that Rousseau's *Essai sur l'origine des langues* "declares what he wants to say" yet "describes what he does not want to say" or inscribes a declared intention "within a system that it no longer controls," he is not identifying some failing in this text that might be made good in a literary work (*De la grammatologie*, pp. 326, 345/229, 243). On the contrary, this very self-deconstructive structure, the text's difference from itself, can be called "literary," as Paul de Man does in arguing that in this text "Rousseau escapes from the logocentric fallacy precisely to the extent that his language is literary" (*Blindness and Insight*, p. 138). "Literary" seems to be a privileged category here, and such passages have led many theorists to assume that de Man and perhaps Derrida grant literature a special and authoritative epistemological status. But de Man applies the category "literary" to all language—philosophical, historical, critical, psychoanalytic, as well as poetic—that prefigures its own misunderstanding and is misread: "the criterion of literary specificity does not depend on the greater or lesser discursiveness of the mode but on the degree of consistent "rhetoricity" of the language" (p. 137). This scarcely helps one to recognize the literariness of a discourse, but it does help to indicate that deconstruction's production of an archi-literature provides no warrant for asserting the privileged status of poems, novels, and plays over other works.

Nor does the inversion of the hierarchical relation between literature and philosophy produce a monism that obliterates all distinctions. Instead of an opposition between a serious philosophical discourse and a marginal literary discourse that takes fictional detours in the hope of attaining seriousness, we have a variable and pragmatic distinction within an archi-literature or general textuality. Philosophy has its distinctive rhetorical strategies: "for example, the philosophical text includes, precisely as its philosophical specificity, the project of effacing itself in the face of the signified content it transports and in general teaches" (*De la grammatologie*, p. 229/160). "Valéry reminds the philosopher," Derrida notes, "that philosophy is written. And that the philosopher is a philosopher insofar as he forgets this" (*Marges*, p. 346). The distinctiveness of philosophy is thus maintained within the argument that seemed to obliterate distinctions by treating philosophy as literature. To interpret Kant's *Critique of Judgment* as if it were a work of art, as Derrida proposes to do in *La Vérité en peinture*, or to discuss philosophically the implications of Artaud's theatrical project, as he does in *L'Ecriture et la différence*, is to maintain a variable distinction. The effect of deconstruction is to disrupt the hierarchical relation that previously determined the concept of literature by reinscribing the distinction between literary and nonliterary works within a general literarity or textuality, and thus to encourage projects, such as the literary reading of philosophical texts and the philosophical reading of literary texts, that allow these discourses to communicate with one another.

In addition to the notion of literature itself, deconstruction has an impact on a host of critical concepts through its disruption of underlying philosophical hierarchies. For example, the deconstruction of the opposition between the literal and the metaphorical, as noted earlier, accords a greater importance to the study of figures, which become the norm rather than the exception, the basis of linguistic effects rather than a special case. But at the same time deconstruction makes such studies more difficult by putting in question any attempt to distinguish rigorously between the literal and the metaphorical. If, as Derrida writes, "before being a rhetorical procedure within language, metaphor were thus the emergence of language itself," then the critic cannot simply describe the functioning of figurative language within the text but must also reckon with the possibility of the figurality of all discourse and thus with the figural roots of "literal" statements (*L'Ecriture et la différence*, p. 166/112). As we shall see in the next chapter, this often involves reading literary works as implicit rhetorical treatises, which conduct in figurative terms an argument about the literal and the figural.

Among the particular figures that have been affected by the questioning of philosophical categories are *symbol* and *allegory*, which romantic aesthetics contrasted as organic to mechanical and motivated to arbitrary. Paul de Man's essay "The Rhetoric of Temporality," in describing the symbol as a mystification and associating allegory with an "authentic" understanding of language and temporality, initiated a reversal which made allegory a primary mode of signification and left "symbol" a special, problematical case.

Another concept affected by deconstructive theory is the notion of mimesis, which involves hierarchical oppositions between object and representation and between original and imitation. A long footnote in "La Double Séance" outlines an argument projected for an article on Plato's theory of mimesis and identifies a schema of two propositions and six possible consequences said to form "a kind of logical machine; it programs the prototypes of all the propositions inscribed in Plato's discourse and those of the tradition. This machine deals out all the clichés of criticism to come, according to a complex but implacable law" (*La Dissémination*, p. 213n/187n). Different values may be assigned to mimesis: it may be condemned as duplication that substitutes copies for originals, praised insofar as it accurately reproduces the original, or seen as neutral, with the value of the representation depending on the value of the original.

A later aesthetic tradition which Derrida analyzes in "Economimesis" even allows imitations to be superior to the objects imitated, if the artist in his freedom and creativity imitates the creativity of Nature or God. In all these cases, Derrida argues, "the absolute discernibility of the imitated and the imitation" is maintained. There is a metaphysical stake in maintaining the distinction between the representation and what is represented and the priority of what is represented to its representation. Mimesis and *mnémè* (memory) are closely associated—memory is a form of mimesis or representation—and mimesis is articulated upon the concept of truth. When truth is conceived as *aletheia*, the unveiling or making present of what has been hidden, then mimesis is the representation necessary to this process, the doubling which enables something to present itself. When truth is not *aletheia* but *homoiosis*, adequation or correspondence, then mimesis is the relation between an image or representation and that to which it may truly correspond. In both cases, Derrida writes, "mimesis must follow the process of truth. Its norm, its rule, its law, is the presence of the present" (*La Dissémination*, p. 220/193).

There is a certain instability to this logocentric system. First, in distinguishing an original from its mimetic presentation and in maintaining the connection with truth, presentations of mimesis get caught up in a proliferation of moments of mimesis. Jean-Luc Nancy in his reading of Plato's *Sophist* describes a series of six stages of mimesis, between which are produced effects of ventriloquism; every presentation is a representation whose voice comes in truth from elsewhere ("Le Ventriloque," pp. 314–32). A simple example would be the mimetic chain engendered by, for example, a painting of a bed; if it represents a bed made by a carpenter, that bed may prove in turn to be an imitation of a particular model, which can in turn be seen as the presentation or imitation of an ideal bed. The distinction between a representation and what it represents may have the effect of putting in question the status of any particular bed: every supposed original may be shown to be an imitation, in a process that is arrested only by positing a divine origin, an absolute original.

Moreover, texts such as Plato's, which insist on the derivative character of mimesis and set it aside as a supplementary activity, reintroduce mimesis in ways that make it central and essential. In the *Philebus*, for example, Socrates describes memory in specifically mimetic terms, as pictures painted in the soul. "If Plato often sets aside mimesis," writes Derrida, "and almost always the mimetic arts, he never separates the unveiling of truth, *aletheia*, from the movement of anamnesia [the return of memory]. There thus emerges a division within mimesis, a self-duplication of repetition itself" (*La Dissémination*, 217/191). Imitation divides into an essential mimesis, inseparable from the production of truth, and its inessential imitation; and this later mimesis, found for example in the arts, will again be divided into acceptable forms and their imitations. There is a doubling of imitations of imitation, "ad infinitum," concludes Derrida, "for this movement nourishes its own proliferation."

Just as Freud's account of *Nachträglichkeit* led to the notion of an originary reproduction, just as the work of supplementation in Rousseau revealed that there are only supplements, so the play of mimesis in theoretical texts suggests the (non)concept of an originary mimesis, which disrupts the hierarchy of original and imitation. Mimetic relations can be regarded as intertextual: relations between one representation and another rather than between a textual imitation and a nontextual original. Texts that assert the plenitude of an origin, the uniqueness of an original, the dependency of a manifestation or derivation of an imitation, may reveal that the original is already an imitation and that everything begins with reproduction.

A concept closely related to representation, which has been affected in a similar way by deconstruction, is that of the sign. Deconstruction is frequently seen as one of the language-oriented or semiotic theoretical movements that treat literature as a system of signs; but, as Derrida notes in his reading of Saussure, the notion of the sign, with its distinction between a content or signified and a signifier which presents that content, is fundamentally metaphysical. Despite Saussure's insistence on the purely differential nature of the sign,

> maintenance of the rigorous distinction—an essential and juridical distinction—between the *signans* [signifier] and the *signatum* [signified] and the equation between the *signatum* and the concept leaves open in principle the possibility of conceiving of a *signified concept in itself*, a concept simply present to thought, independent from the linguistic system, that is to say from a system of signifiers. In leaving this possibility open, and it is so left by the very principle of the opposition between signifier and signified and thus of the sign, Saussure contradicts the critical acquisition of which we have spoken. He accedes to the traditional demand for what I have proposed to call a "transcendental signified," which in itself or in its essence would not refer to any signifier, which would transcend the chain of signs and at a certain moment would no longer itself function as a signifier. On the contrary, though, from the moment one puts in question the possibility of such a transcendental signified and recognizes that every signified is also in the position of a signifier, the distinction between signifier and signified and thus the notion of sign becomes problematic at its root. [*Positions*, pp. 29–30/19–20]

This does not mean that the notion of sign could or should be scrapped; on the contrary, the distinction between what signifies and what is signified is essential to any thought whatever. But it follows from the purely differential, nonsubstantial nature of the sign that the difference between signifier and signified cannot be one of substance and that what we may at one point identify as a signified is also a signifier. There are no final meanings that arrest the movement of signification. Charles Sanders Peirce makes this structure of deferral and referral an aspect of his definition: a sign is "anything which determines something else (its *interpretant*) to refer to an object to which itself [sic] refers (its *object*) in the same way, the interpretant becoming in turn a sign, and so on *ad infinitum*. . . . If the series of successive interpretants comes to an end, the sign is thereby rendered imperfect, at least" (*Collected Papers*, vol. 2, p. 169).

This formulation captures the claim encountered in discussions of speech acts and of mimesis: that the possibility of endless replication is not an accident that befalls the sign but a constitutive element of its structure, an incompletion without which the sign would be incomplete. However, literary critics should exercise caution in drawing inferences from this principle. While it does enjoin skepticism about possibilities of arresting meaning, of discovering a meaning that lies outside of and governs the play of signs in a text, it does not propose indeterminacy of meaning in the usual sense: the impossibility or unjustifiability of choosing one meaning over another. On the contrary, it is only because there may be excellent reasons for choosing one meaning rather than another that there is any point in insisting that the meaning chosen is itself also a signifier that can be interpreted in turn. The fact that any signified is also in the position of signifier does not mean that there are no reasons to link a signifier with one signified rather than another; still less does it suggest, as both hostile and sympathetic critics have claimed, an absolute priority of the signifier or a definition of the text as a galaxy of signifiers. "The 'primacy' or 'priority' of the signifier," writes Derrida, "would be an absurd and untenable expression. . . . The signifier will never by rights precede the signified, since it would no longer be a signifier and the signifier 'signifier' would have no possible signified" (*De la grammatologie*, p. 32n/324). The structural redoubling of any signified as an interpretable signifier does suggest that the realm of signifiers acquires a certain autonomy, but this does not mean signifiers without signifieds, only the failure of signifieds to produce closure.

There is one respect, however, in which Derrida's work leads to emphasis on the signifier. In his reading of Saussure, in *De la grammatologie* but especially in *Glas*, Derrida shows that to establish his doctrine of the arbitrary nature of the sign, Saussure follows a procedure of exclusion that by now will be familiar. There are onomatopoeic signs in languages, Saussure allows, but they are "of secondary importance," not "organic elements of a linguistic system," and therefore need not be taken account of in formulating a theory of the linguistic sign. Besides, he argues, these supposedly motivated signs are never purely mimetic but always partly conventional. "Words such as *fouet* [whip] or *glas* [knell] may strike [*frapper*] some ears with suggestive sonority," but they do not originate as onomatopoeias: *Fouet* comes from *fagus*, "beech-tree," and *glas* from *classicum*, "sound of a trumpet," so that the mimetic quality attributed to them is not an essential property but "a *fortuitous* result of phonetic evolution" (quoted in *Glas*, p. 106). As Derrida notes, this passage carries out an exclusion of the fortuitous that Saussure's reader, attuned to the promotion of the arbitrary at the expense of motivation, might find strange, but in order to define the linguistic system as *essentially* fortuitous, i.e., arbitrary, Saussure needs to exclude fortuitous *motivation*.

If one granted Saussure's argument that onomatopoeias are never pure, never solidly grounded in resemblance, one might nevertheless still be interested in the contamination of arbitrariness by motivation, including motivation that is the fortuitous result of linguistic evolution. Saussure, however, excludes this as an accident that does not affect essence. From the perspective of the linguistic system, this may be justified; the claim is that the structure of French or of English is not affected by the potential mimetic suggestiveness of various signifiers. But Derrida asks whether this contamination of arbitrary signs by suggestions of motivation, by possibilities of remotivation, might be not accidental and excludable but inseparable from the working of language. "What if this *mimesis* meant that the internal system of the language does not exist or that one never uses it, or at least never uses it but in contaminating it, and that this contamination is inevitable and thus regular and 'normal,' belongs to the system and to its functioning, *en fasse partie*, that is to say, both is a part of it and also makes the system which is the whole, part of a whole larger than itself?" (*Glas*, p. 109). Arbitrary signs of the linguistic system may be elements of a larger literary or discursive system in which effects of motivation, demotivation, and remotivation are always occurring, and in which relations of resemblance between signifiers or between signifiers and signifieds can always produce effects, whether conscious or unconscious.

Literary critics have long been alert to this sort of motivation, which they have seen as a fundamental poetic or aesthetic device, but its effects can be traced elsewhere. In "Fors" Derrida presents the work of the psychoanalysts Nicolas Abraham and Maria Torok on the "Verbarium" of the Wolfman, the Joycean network of interlingual connections and mimetic relays of signifiers that structure and generate the text of his psychic experience: "The *Verbarium* shows how a sign, having become arbitrary, can re-motivate itself. And into what labyrinth, what multiplicity of heterogeneous places, one must enter in order to track down the cryptic motivation" ("Fors," pp. 70–71/114). In the dream from which the Wolfman gained his name, there were six wolves.

> Schematically: the *six* in the six wolves . . . is translated into Russian (*Chiest*, perch, mast, and perhaps sex, close to *Chiestero* and *Chiesterka*, "the six," the "lot of six people," close to *Siestra*, sister, and its diminutive *Siesterka*, sissy, toward which the influence of the German *Schwester* had oriented the decipherment): thus, within the mother tongue, through an essentially verbal relay this time, the sister is associated with the phobic image of the wolf. But the relay is nevertheless not semantic: it comes from a lexical contiguity or a formal consonance. If one passes through the virtual expression *Siesterka-Bouka* (sissy-wolf), deformed, in the nightmare of the star and the half moon, into *Zviezda-Louna*, one would perhaps begin to see a confirmation. [P. 60/106]

The account of the Wolfman throws up numerous examples in which, one might say, motive turns out to be a motivation of signs. Though the motivating of signs is in a sense extraneous to the internal system of a language and thus available as a specific poetic technique for making symbols more persuasive or increasing the solidity of important thematic connections, it functions powerfully and covertly within the system of language and now appears to be central to other textual constructs or discursive activities.[16]

The more pervasive the effects of motivation prove to be, the less it can be treated as a mastered or masterable technique and the more it must be analyzed as an uncanny feature of the

---

[16]In addition to Derrida's "Fors" and Freud's extensive work on the decisive role of connections between signifiers, one might consult two studies that employ Abraham and Torok's notion of *incorporation*: Nicolas Rand, "'Vous joyeuse melodie—nourrie de crasse': A propos d'une transposition des *Fleurs du Mal* par Stephan George," and Cynthia Chase, "Paragon, Parergon: Baudelaire Translates Rousseau." In *Saving the Text*, Geoffrey Hartman speculates on various surreptitious motivations of the sign and on the possibility that literature may be the elaboration and repetition of what he calls a "specular name" (pp. 97–117).

functioning of language and of the subject's investment in language. Take the case of the proper name, for instance. Derrida suggests in *Glas* that "the great stake of literary discourse—and I mean discourse—is the patient, stealthy, quasi-animal or vegetable, tireless, monumental, derisory transformation of one's name, a rebus, into a thing or name of a thing" (p. 11). And in his reading of the contemporary French poet Francis Ponge he focuses particularly on the movement of the sponge, the porous logic of the sign, the *signe "éponge,"* which is also an effect of signature, a *signé Ponge*, but a signature that disperses the subject in the text. Writing has frequently been treated as a process of appropriation, by which the author signs or signs for a world, making it his vision or his thing; but effects of signature, traces of the proper name/signature in the text, produce a disappropriation while they appropriate. The proper name becomes improprietary. "We encounter here the problem of the proper name as word, name, the question of its place in the system of a language. A proper name as mark ought to have no meaning, ought to be a pure reference; but since it is a word caught up in the network of a language, it always begins to signify. Sense contaminates this non-sense that is supposed to be kept aside; the name is not supposed to signify anything, yet it does begin to signify" ("Signéponge," part I, p. 146).

The work of concealed or fragmented proper names in producing a text problematizes the distinction between the rhetorical and the psychological (the name is also the name of the father) and shows "thought" determined by surprising exigencies, caught up in a play of language whose signifying ramifications it never masters: conventional linguistic signs may always be affected by motivation of various sorts. Andrew Parker suggests, for example, that Derrida's concern with *marques*, with the structure of marks, is an incorporation of Marx ("Of Politics and Limits: Derrida Re-Marx," pp. 95–97). But the inscription of the proper name in the text is above all a version of the signature. In theory signatures lie outside the work, to frame it, present it, authorize it, but it seems that truly to frame, to mark, or to sign a work the signature must lie within, at its very heart. A problematical relation between inside and outside is played out in the inscription of proper names and their attempt to frame from the inside.

This problem of the frame—of the distinction between inside and outside and of the structure of the border—is decisive for aesthetics in general. As Derrida writes in a work of great pertinence for the literary theorist, "Parergon," aesthetic theory has been structured by a persistent demand:

> we must know what we are talking about, what concerns the value of beauty intrinsically and what remains external to an immanent sense of beauty. This permanent demand—to distinguish between the internal or proper meaning and the circumstances of the object in question—organizes every philosophical discourse on art, the meaning of art, and meaning itself, from Plato to Hegel, Husserl, and Heidegger. It presupposes a discourse on the boundary between the inside and the outside of the art object, in this case, a discourse on the frame. Where do we find it? [*La Vérité en peinture*, p. 53/"The Parergon," p. 12]

Derrida finds it in Kant's *Critique of Judgment* and, since Kant says that reflective judgment begins with examples, in the examples of a section of the "Analytic of the Beautiful" entitled "Elucidation by Means of Examples." Kant is explaining that judgments of taste (judgments that something is beautiful) do not involve the purely empirical delight provoked by qualities or adornments which charm. In the visual arts the essential is what gratifies by its form. Other qualities such as color are important, Kant says, insofar as

> they make the form more clearly, definitely, and completely intuitable, and besides stimulate the representation by their charm, as they excite and sustain the attention directed to the object itself.
>
> Even what is called ornamentation (*parerga*), i.e. what is only an adjunct, and not an intrinsic constituent in the complete representation of an object, in augmenting the delight of taste does so solely by means of its form. Thus it is with the frames of pictures or the draperies on statues, or the colonnades of palaces. [*The Critique of Judgment*, p. 68]

The Greek *parergon* means "hors d'oeuvre," "accessory," "supplement." A *parergon* in Plato is something secondary. "Philosophical discourse is always *against* the *parergon*. . . . A *parergon* is *against*, beside, and above and beyond the *ergon*, the work accomplished, the accomplishment, the work, but it is not incidental; it is connected to and cooperates in its inside operation from the outside" (*La Vérité en peinture*, p. 63/"The Parergon," p. 20). Kant makes this clear when he uses the concept of parergon in *Religion within the Limits of Reason Alone* to describe four "adjuncts"—works of Grace, miracles, mysteries, and means of grace—which do not belong to a purely rational religion but border it and supplement it: they compensate for a lack within rational religion.

The examples offered in the *Critique of Judgment* are suggestive but strange. One can understand that garments or draperies on statues might be additions which enhanced the figures but were not intrinsic to them, but this example already poses a problem of delimitation: is everything that is detachable from the human body a *parergon*? And how much is detachable? What about limbs—*fragments* of antique sculpture thought beautiful in Kant's day as in ours? The example of columns makes it clear that detachability cannot be the decisive criterion, since the palace might well be supported by its columns. Rather, as the example of the picture frame suggests, the columns and drapery may be a boundary space between the work of art and its surroundings. "*Parerga* have a thickness, a surface which separates them not only, as Kant would have it, from the inside, from the body of the *ergon* itself, but also from the outside, from the wall on which the painting is hung, the space in which the statue or column stands, as well as from the entire historic, economic, and political field of inscription in which the drive of the signature arises" (p. 71/24). (To sign something is to attempt to detach it from a context and by so doing to give it a unity. The signature has, as Derrida suggests in *Glas* and in "Signéponge," the structure of a parergon, neither wholly inside nor outside the work.)

The problem, then, is this:

Every analytic of aesthetic judgment presupposes that we can rigorously distinguish between the intrinsic and the extrinsic. Aesthetic judgment *must* concern intrinsic beauty, and not the around and about. It is therefore necessary to know—and this is the fun-

damental presupposition, the presupposition of the fundamental—how to define the intrinsic, the framed, and what to exclude
as frame *and* as beyond the frame. . . . And since when we ask,
"what is a frame?" Kant responds, it is a *parergon*, a composite of
inside and outside, but a composite which is not an amalgam or
half-and-half but an outside which is called inside the inside to
constitute it as inside; and since he gives as examples of the *parergon*, alongside the frame, the drapery and the column, we can say
that there are indeed "considerable difficulties." [P. 74/26]

To understand the workings of the *parergon* one can investigate the framing structure at work in the *Critique of Judgment*
itself, which is engaged in an attempt to frame or delimit pure
judgments of taste, to separate them from what might sur-
round them or attach to them. In the "Analytic of the Beautiful" the judgment of taste is examined from four sides: according to quality, quantity, relation to ends, and modality.
This categorical frame, Derrida notes, comes from the analysis
of concepts in the *Critique of Pure Reason*, but since Kant insists
that aesthetic judgment is not cognitive judgment, to use this as
the frame of reference is something of a frame-up. This frame
is convoked by and "because of the lack—a certain 'internal'
indeterminacy—within that which it comes to frame," shall we
say, the lack of concepts within aesthetic judgment for a cognitive description of aesthetic judgment (p. 83/33). This lack which
produces the frame is also produced by the frame, in that it
appears only when aesthetic judgment is considered from a
conceptual perspective. Above all, the frame is what gives us an
object that can have an intrinsic content or structure. The possibility of determining what properly belongs to pure judgments of taste depends on a categorical framework. This framing analytic of judgment makes possible the distinctions of the
analytic of the beautiful, between formal and material, pure
and impure, intrinsic and extrinsic. It is what leads to the definition of the frame as *parergon*, thus defining its own subsidiary
externality. At the very moment that it is playing an essential,
constitutive, enshrining and protecting role—various aspects of
the Kantian *Einfassung* ("framing," etc.)—it undermines this role
by leading itself to be defined as subsidiary ornamentation.
The logic of the *parergon* is, as one can see, quite similar to the

logic of the supplement, in which the marginal becomes central by virtue of its very marginality.

If, Derrida continues, "the procedures initiated and criteria proposed by the analytic of the beautiful depend upon this parergonality, if all the oppositions which dominate the philosophy of art (before and after Kant) depend on it for their pertinence, their rigor, their purity, their propriety, then they will be affected by this logic of the parergon which is more powerful than the logic of the analytic" (p. 85/33). The consequence of this relation between frame and what it frames is a "certain repeated dislocation."

One example is the dislocation of the opposition between pleasure and cognition. "The analytic of the beautiful warps," writes Derrida, "continually undoing the work of the frame, insofar as, while allowing itself to be framed by the analytic of concepts and by the doctrine of judgment, it describes the absence of the concept in the activity of taste" (p. 87/35). Although the *Critique* is based on an absolute distinction between cognition and the pleasure or *aisthesis* accompanying the pure apprehension of the work of art, an analogy with the process of understanding is introduced at the moment when Kant is trying to describe the distinctiveness of *aisthesis*.

Another example might be what Derrida calls "the law of genre," or rather, "the law of the law of genre. . . . a principle of contamination, a law of impurity, a parasitical economy" ("La Loi du genre," p. 179/206). Though it always participates in genre, a text belongs to no genre, because the frame or trait that marks its belonging does not itself belong. The title "Ode" is not a part of the genre it designates, and when a text identifies itself as a *récit* by discussing its *récit*, this mark of genre is about, not of, the genre. The paradox of parergonality is that a framing device which asserts or manifests class membership is not itself a member of that class.

Framing can be regarded as a frame-up, an interpretive imposition that restricts an object by establishing boundaries: Kant's framing confines aesthetics within the frame of a theory of the beautiful, the beautiful within a theory of taste, and taste within a theory of judgment. But the framing process is unavoidable, and the notion of an aesthetic object, like the constitution of an aesthetics, depends upon it. The supplement is essential. Anything that is properly framed—displayed in a museum, hung in a gallery, printed in a book of poems— becomes an art object; but if framing is what creates the aesthetic object, this does not make the frame a determinable entity whose qualities could be isolated, giving us a theory of the literary frame or the painterly frame. "There is framing," asserts Derrida, "but the frame does not exist" (*La Vérité en peinture*, p. 93/"The Parergon," p. 39). "Il y a du cadre, mais le cadre n'existe pas."

> The *parergon* detaches itself both from the *ergon* and from the milieu; it detaches itself first as a figure against a background, but it does not set itself off in the same way as the work, which is also set off against a background. The parergonal frame detaches itself from two backgrounds, but in relation to each it backs into the other. In relation to the work, which serves as its background, it disappears into the wall and then by degrees into the general text [context]. In relation to the background of the general text, it backs into the work which is set off from the general background. Always a figure against a ground, the *parergon* is nevertheless a form that has traditionally been defined not as setting itself off but as disappearing, sinking in, effacing itself, dissolving just as it expends its greatest energy. The frame is never a background as the milieu or the work can be, but neither is its thickness of margin a figure, unless a self-razing figure [figure qui s'enlève d'elle-même]. [Pp. 71–73/24–26]

This disappearing figure, this marginal supplement, is nevertheless in certain ways the "essence" of art. In his purifying account of beauty Kant proceeds by stripping away possible qualities: the *pulchritudo vaga* or "free beauty" that is the object of judgments of pure taste is an organization "which signifies nothing, shows nothing, represents nothing." These structures can *also* represent, indicate, signify; but their beauty is independent of any such functions, based on what Derrida calls "le *sans* de la coupure pure," the *without* of the pure break or distinction that defines aesthetic objects, as in Kant's "purposiveness *without* purpose." If the object of judgments of pure taste is an organization which signifies nothing, refers to nothing, then the *parergon*, though Kant excludes it from the work itself, is in effect the very place of free beauty.

Take away from a painting all representation, signification, theme, text as intended meaning, take away also all the material (canvas, colored paint) which for Kant cannot be beautiful in itself, rub out any drawing oriented toward a determinable end, take away its background and its social, historical, political, and economic support, and what is left? The frame, the framing, a play of forms and lines which are structurally homogeneous with the structure of the frame. [P. 111]

In fact, one of Kant's examples of free beauty is "Laubwerk zu Einfassungen," frames worked with leafy patterns. If, as Derrida says, "the trace of the 'without' is the origin of beauty," the frame may be or bear that trace.

In "The Question Concerning Technology" Heidegger identifies the essence of technology as a process of Enframing (*Ge-Stell*), which is not itself technological but frames phenomena as a "standing-reserve" and which threatens to conceal the revealing or enframing he calls *poiesis* (pp. 301–9). The problem of framing is indeed a general one, but its technological character already emerges in the stakes and procedures of a theory of art or literature as that theory attempts to construct a discipline. Debates about critical method turn on what is inside literature or inside a literary work and what is outside it. Wellek and Warren's authoritative *Theory of Literature* organized itself and its field with a distinction between the inside and the outside: "The Extrinsic Approach to the Study of Literature," versus "The Intrinsic Study of Literature."

What Derrida's analysis shows is the convoluted structure of parergonal divisions. On several occasions he uses the term "invagination" for the complex relation between inside and outside ("Living On," p. 97). What we think of as the innermost spaces and places of the body—vagina, stomach, intestine—are in fact pockets of externality folded in. What makes them quintessentially inner is partly their difference from flesh and bone but especially the space they mark off and contain, the outside they make inner. An external frame may function as the most intrinsic element of a work, folding itself in; conversely, what seems the most inner or central aspect of a work will acquire this role through qualities that fold it back outside of and against the work. The secret center that appears to explain everything folds back on the work, incorporating an external position from which to elucidate the whole in which it also figures.

The distinction between criticism and literature opposes a framing discourse to what it frames, or divides an external metalanguage from the work it describes. But literary works themselves contain metalinguistic commentary: judgments of their own plots, characters, and procedures. Curiously, the authority of critics' metalinguistic position depends to a considerable extent on metalinguistic discourse within the work: they feel securely outside and in control when they can bring out of the work passages of apparently authoritative commentary that expound the views they are defending. When reading a work that apparently lacks an authoritative metalanguage or that ironically questions the interpretive discourses it contains, critics feel uneasy, as if they were just adding their voice to the polyphony of voices. They lack evidence that they are indeed in a metalinguistic position, above and outside of the text.

This is a paradoxical situation: they are outside when their discourse prolongs and develops a discourse authorized by the text, a pocket of externality folded in, whose external authority derives from its place inside. But if the best examples of metalinguistic discourse appear within the work, then their authority, which depends on a relation to externality, is highly questionable: they can always be read as part of the work rather than a description of it. In denying their externality we subvert the metalinguistic authority of the critic, whose externality had depended on the folds that created this internal metalanguage or pocket of externality. The distinction between language and metalanguage, like the distinction between inside and outside, evades precise formulation but is always at work, complicating itself in a variety of folds.

The problem of the frame has a bearing on another concept that has played a major role in critical thinking, the notion of unity. Theorists have frequently suggested that the "organic unity" of works of art is the product of framing, the effect of what de Man calls "the intent at totality of the interpretive process" (*Blindness and Insight*, p. 31). In recent critical analyses, the celebration of heterogeneity, the description of texts as grafts or intertextual constructs, the interest in teasing out incompatible strands of argument or logics of signification, and the linking of a text's power to its self-deconstructive efficacy have all worked to deny to the notion of organic unity its former role as the unquestioned telos of critical interpretation. However, the critical writings that most vigorously proclaim their celebration of heterogeneity are likely to reveal, under exegetical scrutiny, their reliance on notions of organic unity, which are not easy to banish. Deconstruction leads not to a brave new world in which unity never figures but to the identification of unity as a problematical figure.

Moreover, skepticism about organicist terms and categories is encouraged by analysis of the system in which such notions operate. In *The Mirror and the Lamp*, M. H. Abrams argued that contemporary organicist concepts belong to a system which is fundamentally a displaced theology. In "Economimesis" Derrida situates Kant's explicit rejection of a mimetic conception of art within an economy of mimesis. In this system, organicist descriptions of the aesthetic object work, paradoxically, to establish the absolute superiority of human art, freedom, and language to the natural activity of animals. Kantian theory makes a fundamental distinction between art and nature and is at pains to distinguish the mimetic activity of man from that of animals, the free creativity or productivity of man from the practical work of bees. It does so by stressing the freedom of art, which should be neither mechanical nor mercenary but as free as if it were a product of pure nature, a flower or tree. "Pure and free productivity," writes Derrida in a reproduction of Kant's argument, "should resemble that of nature. It does so precisely because, free and pure, it does not depend on natural laws. The less it depends on nature, the more it resembles her" ("Economimesis," p. 67/9). To establish the absolute privilege of free human creation or imitation, one renaturalizes it with organicist language, as something natural and proper to man, a function which cannot be contaminated by animality, as can other human activities.

Equally important but more frequently ignored is deconstruction's questioning of the association of self-referentiality with self-presence in discussions of the literary work's organic autonomy. For New Criticism an important feature of a good poem's organic unity was its embodiment or dramatization of the positions it asserts. By enacting or performing what it asserts or describes, the poem becomes complete in itself, accounts for itself, and stands free as a self-contained fusion of being and doing. "The poem is an instance of the doctrine which it asserts," writes Cleanth Brooks of his paradigm case, Donne's "The Canonization." "It is both the assertion and the realization of the assertion. The poet has actually before our eyes built within the song the 'pretty room' with which he says the lovers can be content. The poem itself is the well-wrought urn which can hold the lover's ashes and which will not suffer in comparison with the prince's 'halfe-acre tomb'" (*The Well Wrought Urn*, p. 17).

What the poem says about tombs, urns, and rooms is taken as self-reference, and this self-reflexivity is seen as self-knowledge, self-possession, a self-understanding or presence of the poem to itself. Derridean analyses that we have considered in this chapter also exploit potential self-reference, applying Freud's description of the *Fort/Da* game to Freud's own play with the Pleasure Principle or Kant's account of *parerga* to his own framing procedures in the "Analytic of the Beautiful." There is a neatness in the relations that deconstruction's exploitation of self-reference reveals which must seem similar to the coincidence of being and doing that Brooks and innumerable critics since have sought and valued. But the relation deconstruction reveals is not the transparency of the text to itself in an act of reflexive self-description or self-possession; it is rather an uncanny neatness that generates paradox, a self-reference that ultimately brings out the inability of any discourse to account for itself and the failure of performative and constative or doing and being to coincide. In the domain of logic, self-reference has long been recognized as the major source of paradoxes: Epimenides' Paradox, better known as the Paradox of the Cretan Liar, the paradox of the barber who shaves all the men in the village who do not shave themselves, Russell's paradox about sets which are not members of themselves, Grelling's paradox of "heterologicality."[17] When Russell and Whitehead attempted in *Principia Mathematica* to resolve or dispose of such paradoxes, which threaten the foundations of mathematics, they did so by outlawing self-reference. Their theory of

[17]The most extensive and fascinating recent exploration of paradoxes arising from self-reference is Douglas Hofstader's *Gödel, Escher, Bach*.

logical types makes it impossible for a statement to be about itself by placing any statement about an X in a higher logical category than X. An assertion about poems is decreed to be of a different logical type from the poems it is about. This may be an appropriate solution to the problems of set theory, but as a principle of discourse it simply begs the question of self-reference in language, treating even the most ordinary cases, such as "In this chapter I attempt to show . . ." as logical improprieties. Discourse is irredeemably, necessarily self-referential, but even "In this chapter I attempt to show . . . ," which situates itself both inside and outside what it frames, poses interesting problems of parergonality.

Under exegetical pressure, self-reference demonstrates the impossibility of self-possession. When poems denounce poetry as lies, self-referentiality is the source of undecidability, which is not ambiguity but a structure of logical irresolvability: if a poem speaks true in describing poetry as lies, then it lies; but if its claim that poems lie is a lie, then it must speak true. It is also possible to show that poems which the New Critics have analyzed as instances of the doctrine they proclaim are in fact more complex and problematic in their self-referentiality. "The Canonization," Brooks's canonical example, begins its self-referential conclusion thus:

> Wee can dye by it, if not live by love,
>   And if unfit for tombes and hearse
> Our legend bee, it will be fit for verse;
>   And if no peece of Chronicle wee prove,
>   We'll build in sonnets pretty roomes;
>   As well a well wrought urne becomes
> The greatest ashes, as halfe-acre tombes,
>   And by these hymnes, all shall approve
>   Us *Canoniz'd* for Love:

The narrator posits that the legend of his love will be fit for verse, sonnets if not chronicles, which will function as hymns for those who hear them. Moreover, listeners will be moved to speech upon hearing these verses:

> And by these hymnes, all shall approve
> Us *Canoniz'd* for Love:

And thus invoke us; You whom reverend love
  Made one anothers hermitage;
You, to whom love was peace, that now is rage;
  Who did the whole worlds soule contract, and drove
    Into the glasses of your eyes
    (So made such mirrors and such spies,
That they did all to you epitomize,)
    Countries, Townes, Courts: Beg from above
    A patterne of your love!

The speaker thus imagines that those who have heard the verse
legend of his love will invoke the lovers in idealizing descriptions that, more powerfully than anything in his own account,
portray the lovers as triumphantly gaining the whole world's
soul by seeking love alone. The response to the legend which
the speaker imagines and represents is an invocation and representation of the lovers that asks them to invoke God and to
ask Him for a further representation of their love which could
serve as pattern. We have, therefore, not so much a self-contained urn as a chain of discourses and representations: the
legend describing the lovers, the verse representation of this
legend, the celebratory portrayal of the lovers in the response
of those who have heard the legend, the request which the
lovers are asked to formulate, and the pattern from above that
will generate further versions of their love.

The chain of representations complicates the situation Brooks
describes, especially when one focuses on the question of self-
reference and asks what is the "pretty room," the "well wrought
urn," or the "hymn" to which the poem refers. Brooks answers,
the poem itself: "the poem itself is the well-wrought urn which
can hold the lovers' ashes." If this is so, if the poem is the urn,
then one of the principal features of this urn is that it portrays
people responding to the urn. If the urn or hymn is the poem
itself, then the predicted response to the hymn is a response to
the representation of a response to the hymn. This is confirmed by the fact that by far the most hymnlike element of the
poem is the invocation of the lovers by those who have heard
the hymn or verse legend of their love. The earlier stanzas of
the poem, in which the lover argues, as Brooks says, that "their
love, however absurd it may appear to the world, does no harm
to the world" (p. 13), can scarcely qualify as a hymn; so if the

poem refers to itself as a hymn it is including within itself its depiction of the hymnlike response—the response to the hymn it claims to be.

This may seem a perverse description of what is happening in the poem, an excessive exploitation of the skewed tightening that self-reference brings; but this account gives us a surprisingly apt description of what has happened. Brooks, after reading the verse legend of these lovers, invokes them, celebrates them as saints of love: "the lovers in rejecting life actually win to the most intense life. . . . The lovers, in becoming hermits, find that they have not lost the world but have gained the world in each other. . . . The tone with which the poem closes is one of triumphant achievement" (p. 15). He responds much as the poem predicts, praising their exemplary love, and asking for a pattern of their love, which he interprets as "the union which the creative imagination itself effects" (p. 18). His book invokes "The Canonization" as canonical example, as pattern: his project, as he describes it, is an attempt to see what happens when one reads other poems "as one has learned to read Donne and the moderns" (p. 193). The saintly yet worldly union celebrated in the poem—the union effected by the creative imagination—is taken as the pattern to be reproduced elsewhere. The phrase "well-wrought urn," which this exemplary example, "The Canonization," applies to poems and to itself, is taken up and applied by the book to other poems, and also to itself. Brooks's own book is called *The Well Wrought Urn*: the combination in his pages of Donne's urn and Brooks's response to it becomes itself an urn.

This self-referential element in Donne's poem does not produce or induce a closure in which the poem harmoniously is the thing it describes. In celebrating itself as urn the poem incorporates a celebration of the urn and thus becomes something other than the urn; and if the urn is taken to include the response to the urn, then the responses it anticipates, such as Brooks's, become a part of it and prevent it from closing. Self-reference does not close it in upon itself but leads to a proliferation of representations, a series of invocations and urns, including Brooks's *The Well Wrought Urn*. There is a neatness to this situation but it is the neatness of transference, in which the analyst finds himself caught up in and reenacting the drama he thought he was analyzing from the outside. The structure is one of repetition and proliferation rather than crystalline closure. The structure of self-reference works in effect to divide the poem against itself, creating an urn to which one responds and an urn which includes a response to the urn. If the urn is the combination of urn and response to the urn, then this structure of self-reference creates a situation in which responses such as Brooks's are part of the urn in question. This series of representations, invocations, and readings which, like moments of self-reference, are at once within the poem and outside it, can always be continued and has no end.

As Rodolphe Gasché has emphasized in an important article, though deconstruction explores self-referential structures in texts, these structures mount a critique of the notion of self-reflexivity or self-mastery through self-analysis ("Deconstruction as Criticism," pp. 181–85). The attempt to "know thyself," whether by a person or a poem, may produce powerful interpretive discourse, but something crucial will remain unknown or unnoticed, and the relation between a text and its self-description or self-interpretation will remain askew. As we noted when discussing *parerga*, the effect of self-reflexivity is produced by folds. When a text folds back upon itself it creates what Derrida calls an "invaginated pocket," in which an outside becomes an inside and an inner moment is granted a position of exteriority. Analyzing Blanchot's "La Folie du jour" in "La Loi du genre," Derrida investigates the way in which the work's self-designations, far from producing a transparency in which it accounts for itself, disrupt the very account they provide (pp. 190–91/217–18). A text's attempt to frame itself produces warps and strains, dislocations. Deconstruction emphasizes the self-referential moments of a text in order to reveal the surprising effects of employing a portion of a text to analyze the whole or the uncanny relationships between one textual level and another or one discourse and another. The notion of a text accounting for itself is another version of self-presence, another avatar of the system of *s'entendre parler*. Texts work in self-referential ways to provide concepts that are strategically important in reading them, but there is always, Derrida would say, a lag or a limp. "Ca boite et ça ferme mal" (*La Carte postale*, p. 418). Boxing itself in, a text does not produce closure.

(2) In its second mode or level of relevance to literary criticism, deconstruction makes itself felt not by disturbing critical concepts but by identifying a series of important topics on which critics may then focus in their interpretation of literary works: topics such as writing (or the relation between speech and writing), presence and absence, origin, marginality, representation, indeterminacy. In drawing attention to a numer of themes or issues, deconstruction works as do other theoretical projects. Existentialism, by its account of the human condition, encouraged critics to study what literary works had to say about choice, the relation between existence and essence, revolt, and the creation of meaning in an absurd universe. Such disparate theoretical enterprises as psychoanalysis, feminism, Marxism, and the Girardian account of mimetic desire and the scapegoating mechanism identify certain questions as especially important and lead critics to attend to their manifestation in literary works. It is not surprising that powerful theoretical discourses should have this effect nor that literature should prove to have subtle and revealing responses to the questions thus addressed to it.

There is, however, considerable disagreement about the status and value of thematic criticism. For many students of literature, the value of deconstruction, like the value of existentialism or Marxism before it, is determined by its ability to shed light on works that contain its privileged themes. Much of what is now thought of as deconstructive criticism is initially distinguished by the themes it discusses—speech and writing in Dante, indeterminacy of representation in Dickens, the absence of the referent in William Carlos Williams—and it is characteristically accused of neglecting the major concerns of a work to focus on themes that may be only minimally present. By these lights, deconstruction would be deemed useful for understanding works such as Edmond Jabès's *Le Livre des questions*, which Derrida interprets, thematically, as "the interminable song of absence and a book about the book" (*L'Ecriture et la différence*, p. 104/69). Feminist theory would be relevant when one was studying novels about the condition of women; psychoanalysis might clarify works of literature that were primarily psychological studies, and Marxism would help the critic understand books focused on the effects of class difference and economic forces on personal experience. Each theory sheds light on certain questions and the error would be to assume that these were the only questions.

Since critics prefer a strong case to a weak one and like to adduce evidence that the work they are studying explicitly addresses the theme they are discussing, most criticism appears to operate on the assumption that the theme of the work studied does indeed determine the relevance of a theoretical discourse. However, the major theoretical and critical enterprises of our day have, in discovering their most powerful and revealing applications, rejected this assumption of thematic criticism which, in Derrida's words, "makes the text into a form of expression and reduces it to its signified theme" (*La Dissémination*, p. 279/248). Some critics versed in psychoanalysis have attempted to transform a criticism devoted to the study of psychoanalytic themes, such as Oedipus complexes, into an exploration through psychoanalytic theory of the working of texts, such as their ability to provoke in readers and critics an uncanny transferential repetition of their most fundamental dramas. Feminist criticism, as we noted in Chapter One, has not restricted itself to the question of the depiction of women—woman as theme—but has addressed more generally the issue of sexual difference in relation to literature. Works not specifically about the condition of women nevertheless pose the question of the relation of the female reader to sexual codes and offer the feminist critic an occasion to investigate the implications for literature and the role in the text of sexually-marked models of creativity. Marxist critics too have insisted that, as Terry Eagleton puts it, Marxism is not a tool for interpreting novels with an explicit social content or theme but an attempt "to understand the complex, indirect relations between [literary] works and the ideological worlds they inhabit—relations which emerge not just in 'themes' and 'preoccupations' but in style, rhythm, image, quality, and *form*" (*Marxism and Literary Criticism*, p. 6). In each case the theory claims to be able to study with profit works other than those with a specific and suitable theme. What may often appear to be an insistence on posing inappropriate questions and searching a work for themes that are not evident may be a shift to another level of analysis where a theoretical discourse that makes claims about the fundamental organization of language and experience attempts to provide insights into the structure and meaning of texts, whatever their ostensible themes.

Since this move to another level of investigation may result in interpretations that treat the work as an allegory of Marxist, psychoanalytic, feminist, or deconstructive concerns, it may not always be easy to distinguish from the thematic criticism it aims to transcend; but the failure to grasp this distinction leads to misunderstandings. When considered at the first level, literature is remarkable for the diversity of its themes, and the critic generally seeks to articulate the distinctiveness of a particular work's concerns or to describe a common theme that distinguishes a group of works. At the second level, a powerful theory with literary implications seeks to analyze those structures which it takes to be most fundamental or characteristic and thus emphasizes repetition, the return of the same, rather than diversity. Themes that appear at both levels often have the same names, a fact which produces confusion but which also, as Derrida's earlier remarks on paleonomy suggest, marks a crucial relationship.

Derrida's own procedure in the *Grammatology* provides an excellent example. Chapter 1, "The End of the Book and the Beginning of Writing," could be described as an investigation of writing as a *theme* in works of the philosophical tradition; but Derrida moves from a discussion of what various works say about writing when they raise it as an issue to an analysis of a larger structure from which the theme of writing derives and which can be identified in texts that do not specifically discuss writing. At this second level *writing* is the name for a generalized writing, the condition both of speech and of writing. This *archi-écriture* is not a theme in the ordinary sense, certainly not a theme of the same order as the *writing* with which Derrida began. Although deconstructive readings work to reveal how a given text elucidates or allegorically thematizes this ubiquitous structure, they are not thereby promoting one theme and denying others but attempting at another level to describe the logic of texts.

We return to this issue when discussing deconstructive criticism in Chapter Three. What I emphasize here is that deconstruction inevitably gives rise to thematic criticism of different sorts even though it announces its suspicion of the notion of theme and on occasion attempts to define its procedures and preoccupations against those of thematic criticism. In "La Double Séance" Derrida takes issue with Jean-Pierre Richard's analysis of *blanc* and *pli* as themes in Mallarmé. Richard himself notes that the diacritical nature of meaning prevents one from simply treating *blanc* or *pli* as a nuclear unit with a particular Mallarmean meaning, but while stressing their particularly rich and prolific plurivalency, he nevertheless assumes that "the multiplicity of lateral relations" creates "an essence" and that there emerges a theme which "is nothing other than the sum, or rather the arrangement [mise en perspective] of its diverse modulations" (quoted, *La Dissémination*, p. 282/250). Derrida suggests, on the contrary, that the inexhaustibility identified here is not that of richness, depth, complexity of an essence, but rather the inexhaustibility of a certain poverty. One aspect of this is the phenomenon which Nicolas Abraham calls "anasemia": a condition of "de-signification" produced, for example, in Freud's writings, where metapsychological concepts such as the Unconscious, Death instinct, Pleasure, or Drive, connect with the signs from which they derive but empty them of their meaning and oppose further semantic actualization. "Take any term introduced by Freud," writes Abraham, "whether he coined it or simply borrowed it from scientific or colloquial language. Unless one is deaf to its meaning, one is struck by the vigor with which, as soon as it is related to the unconscious Kernel, it literally rips itself away from the dictionary and from language" (*L'Ecorce et le noyau*, p. 209/20). The *Pleasure Principle* for example, evokes and is linked to *pleasure*, yet the syntax of Freudian theory empties it of that content when it posits pleasure experienced as pain. "Pleasure, Id, Ego, Economic, Dynamic," Abraham continues, "are not metaphors, metonymies, synecdoches, catachreses; they are, through the action of the discourse, products of de-signification and constitute new figures, absent from rhetorical treatises. These figures of an anti-semantics, inasmuch as they signify nothing more than a going back to the [nonexperiential] source of their customary meaning, require a denomination properly indicative of their status and which—for want of something better—we shall propose to designate by the coined name of *anasemia*." Freud's discourse does not produce a new and richer concept of pleasure that could be grasped as a theme; his theory develops syntactic resources that produce accounts of a Pleasure experienced as suffering, displacing "pleasure" from a thematic level to an anasemic level.

Another textual logic that undermines thematic organization and produces complexity through a semantic impoverishment is identified in Derrida's reading of Genet. Working as a "dredge"—Derrida's term (*Glas*, p. 229)—which sucks up rocks, sludge, and algae, leaving the water behind, he takes up various elements and explores their semantic, phonetic, and morphological connections in the text: "Each word cited yields a key or grid that you can move through the text. . . . the difficulty is that there is no *unit* of occurrence: fixed form, identifiable theme, element determinable as such. [No themes but] Only anthems [*anthèmes*], scattered throughout, collecting everywhere" (p. 233). He strategically chooses to pursue elements that can function as "greffes du nom propre," grafts of the proper name. Genet's "*Le Miracle de la Rose* cultivates grafts of the proper name. . . . By breaking it up, fragmenting it, making it hard to recognize through splintering blows, . . . one makes it gain ground like a clandestine occupationary force. At the extreme limit—of the text, of the world—nothing would be left but an enormous signature, swelled up with everything it had previously swallowed up but pregnant only with itself" (p. 48). Derrida posits here as the logic of Genet's text, not an anasemic operation, but a different process of de-signifying which one should call *anathematic*.

In one of those movements in *ana*, Genet has thus, whether knowingly or not—I have my own guess, but what matter—silently, laboriously, painstakingly, obsessionally, compulsively, with the stealth of a thief in the night, set his signatures in the place of all the missing objects. In the morning, expecting to recognize all the usual objects, you find his name everywhere, in huge letters, in little letters, whole or in pieces, deformed or recomposed. He is gone, but you are living in his mausoleum or outhouse. You had thought you were deciphering, detecting, pursuing; you are taken (in). He has attached his signature to everything. He has simulated/made great use of his signature. He has affected himself with it (and will even, later on, have bedecked himself with a

circumflex). He has tried to write, properly, what happens between the affect and the signature. [P. 51]

Derrida's account identifies meaning of a sort—a perverse if
quintessentially literary project—but it does so in pursuing *anti*
or *ana*thematic connections.

Thematic interpretation of Mallarmé is troubled by anasemic
and anathematic displacements, but what Derrida calls the
"poverty" of *blanc* and *pli*'s plurivalency also results, as he says,
from syntactic connections with forms such as *aile, plume, éventail, page, frôlement, voile, papier*: one can see *fold* fanning out,
scattering itself among these figures and recomposing itself, or
one may see any of these other elements opening into and
expressing itself in *fold*. This structure Derrida describes as
a fanning or folding movement: "la polysémie des 'blancs' et
des 'plis' se déploie et se reploie en éventail" [the polysemy of
"blanks" and "folds" both fans out and snaps shut, ceaselessly]
(*La Dissémination*, p. 283/251). *Blanc* too becomes not just a
theme but a textual structure or process: "To a phenomenological or thematic reading *blanc* appears first as the inexhaustible
totality of the semantic valences that have some tropological
affinity with it (but what is 'it'?). But, in a repeatedly represented replication, *blanc* inserts (names, designates, marks, enun-
ciates, however you wish to put it, and we need here another
'word') *blanc* as a blank *between* valences, as the hymen that
unites them and distinguishes them in the series, the spacing of
the '*blancs*' which 'take on importance.'" (pp. 283–84/252). The
blank of a white space, spacing, empty paper is part of the
Mallarmean thematic series of *blanc*, but it is also the condition
of textual series, so that what one sought to describe as a theme
exceeds the thematic; it folds back on it as it names it.

Le blanc se plie, est (marqué d'un) pli. Il ne s'expose jamais à plate
couture. Car le pli n'est pas plus un thème (signifié) que le blanc
et si l'on tient compte des effets de chaîne et de rupture qu'ils
propagent dans le texte, rien n'a plus simplement la valeur d'un
thème. [P. 285]

The blank is folded (yields), is (marked with) a fold. It is never
available for flat sewing. For *fold* is no more a (signified) theme
than is *white* (blank), and if one takes account of the linkages and

rifts they propagate in the text, then nothing can simply have the value of a theme any more. [P. 253]

This general critique of theme results from the strategic and temporary identification of a theme and the subsequent discovery that it is also something other than—more or less than—a theme. The thematic figure, such as *pli*, comes to describe the general series to which it belongs, or the logic of thematic connection, or the condition of textuality. The *pli* is not a theme when it articulates, at another level, a general textual structure, just as writing is no longer a theme when it paleonymically becomes an *archi-écriture* behind all thematic effects. Derrida writes:

> In certain respects the theme of supplementarity is doubtless no more than one theme among others. It is in a chain, carried by it. Perhaps one could substitute something else for it. *But it happens that this theme describes the chain itself, the being-chain of a textual chain, the structure of substitution, the articulation of desire and of language, the logic of all conceptual oppositions taken over by Rousseau*, and in particular the role and the function, in his system, of the concept of Nature. It tells us in the text what a text is; it tells us in writing what writing is; in Rousseau's writing it tells us Jean-Jacques' desire, etc. [*De la grammatologie*, p. 233/163]

The theme of supplementarity thus emerges as an archi-theme or fundamental structure that no longer belongs to a thematic criticism.

Like any theoretical enterprise, deconstruction privileges various concepts which can be and are treated as themes, studied in literary works, but it is more distinctive in its critique of thematics and its interest in the parergonal process by which certain themes define a figural or textual logic that produces them. It is not easy to distinguish the study of themes from the study of structures or textual logics, especially since both may claim to reveal what the work is "really about," but an account of deconstruction must distinguish this second relation to literary criticism—deconstruction as a source of themes—from the third, in which deconstruction encourages the study of particular structures.

(3) Derrida's own discussions of literary works draw attention to important problems, but they are not *deconstructions* as we have been using the term, and a deconstructive literary criticism will be primarily influenced by his readings of philosophical works. Beyond the modification of critical concepts and the identification of special themes, deconstruction practices a style of reading, encouraging critics to identify or produce certain types of structure. This aspect of deconstruction is what we have been describing in our analyses of deconstructive readings—of Saussure, Rousseau, Plato, Austin, Kant, Freud—but it may be useful to sum up briefly what is involved, risking reductiveness for the sake of explicitness.

If deconstruction is, in Barbara Johnson's happy phrase, "the careful teasing out of warring forces of signification within the text" (*The Critical Difference*, p. 5), the critic will be on the lookout for different sorts of conflict. The first, and the most obvious from our earlier discussions in this chapter, is the asymmetrical opposition or value-laden hierarchy, in which one term is promoted at the expense of the other. The question for the critic is whether the second term, treated as a negative, marginal, or supplementary version of the first, does not prove to be the condition of possibility of the first. Along with the logic that asserts the preeminence of the first term, is there a contrary logic, covertly at work but emerging at some crucial moment or figure in the text, which identifies the second term as the enabling condition of the first? The relation between speech and writing, as Derrida has expounded it, is the best known version of this structure, but it can appear in numerous unpredictable guises that may be difficult to detect and dissect.

Second, the example of Derrida's readings leads the critic to look for points of condensation, where a single term brings together different lines of argument or sets of values. Such terms as *parergon, pharmakon, supplement, hymen* figure in oppositions that are essential to a text's argument, but they also function in ways that subvert those oppositions. These terms are the points at which the strains of an attempt to sustain or impose logocentric conclusions make themselves felt in a text, moments of uncanny opacity that can lead to rewarding commentary.

Third, the critic will be alert to other forms of the text's *écart de soi* or difference from itself. At its simplest and least specifically deconstructive, this involves an interest in anything in the text that counters an authoritative interpretation, including interpretations that the work appears most emphatically to encourage. Whatever themes, arguments, or patterns are cited in defining the identity of a particular work, there will be ways in which it differs from the self so defined, systematically or obliquely putting in question the decisions at work in that definition. Interpretations or definitions of identity involve the representation of a text within the experience of a person who writes or reads it, but says Derrida, "the text constantly goes beyond this representation by the entire system of its resources and its own rules" (*De la grammatologie*, p. 149/101). Any reading involves presuppositions, and the text itself, Derrida suggests, will provide images and arguments to subvert those presuppositions. The text will carry signs of that difference from itself which makes explication interminable.

Particularly important are the structures described in our discussions of parergonality and self-reference, when the text applies to something else a description, image, or figure that can be read as self-description, as a representation of its own operations. In treating such figures as moments of self-reference, one is often reading against the grain: the Freudian model that Derrida applies to the procedure of Freud's text is one Freud develops for the activities of a child, and the framing operations at work in Kant's text are identified by *The Critique of Judgment* as a specifically artistic process. A deconstructive reading of theoretical texts often demonstrates the return in a displaced or disguised form of a procedure that work claimed to criticize in others—as Austin is shown repeating the act of exclusion he had decried in his predecessors. In other cases, emphasis will fall on ways in which the devices that fold a text back on itself paradoxically dislocate its attempts at self-possession.

Fifth, there is an interest in the way conflicts or dramas within the text are reproduced as conflicts in and between readings of the text. De Man's adage that literary language prefigures its own misunderstandings is in part a claim that texts demonstrate allegorically the inadequacy of possible interpretive moves—the moves that their readers will make. Texts thematize, with varying degrees of explicitness, interpretive operations and their consequences and thus represent in advance the dramas that will give life to the tradition of their interpretation. Critical disputes about a text can frequently be identified as a displaced reenactment of conflicts dramatized in the text, so that while the text assays the consequences and implications of various forces it contains, critical readings transform this difference within into a difference between mutually exclusive positions. What is deconstructed in deconstructive analyses attuned to this problem is not the text itself but the text as it is read, the combination of text and the readings that articulate it. What is put in question are the presuppositions and decisions that convert a complex pattern of internal differences into alternative positions or interpretations.

Finally, deconstruction involves attention to the marginal. We have already noted Derrida's concentration on elements in a work or a corpus that previous critics had thought unimportant. This is an identification of the exclusions on which hierarchies may depend and by which they might be disrupted but it is also the beginning of an encounter with previous readings which, in separating a text into the essential and marginal elements, have created for the text an identity that the text itself, through the power of its marginal elements, can subvert. Since concentration on the marginal is an identification of what in a text resists the identity established for it by other readings, it is part of an attempt to prevent the work one is studying from being governed or determined by other, less rich or complex texts. Contextualist readings or historical interpretations generally rely on supposedly simple and unambiguous texts to determine the meaning of passages in more complex and evasive texts. We have already noted Derrida's insistence on the unsaturability of context and the concomitant possibility of extending context in ways that allow further complexities of the text one is studying to emerge. One could, therefore, identify deconstruction with the twin principles of the contextual determination of meaning and the infinite extendability of context. Derrida exploits the force of contextual determination whenever he reads a work in relation to the system of metaphysical values from which it cannot succeed in escaping.

However, to describe deconstruction in this way begs certain questions about the status of "marginal" elements. When deconstructive readings attack contextualists' attempts to decide the meaning of a complex work by referring to simpler and less ambiguous texts and when they continue to concentrate on elements that contextualists say are marginal in relation to a postulated authorial intention, are they denying the relevance of authorial intention to textual interpretation or are they adopting some other position? Since this is an issue that arises repeatedly in assessments of Derrida, we should not conclude a sketch of the reading strategies encouraged by deconstruction without facing it, especially since it provides a convenient way of reviewing the methodological import of Derrida's readings of Austin, Plato, and Rousseau.

In the case of Austin, a careful analysis of his procedure— one that does not, as is usual, skip over or ignore particular formulations in the name of an intention—shows him repeating the exclusionary move he criticized in his predecessors—a move which, one can argue, he is led to make for the same reason as they. But while refusing to discount formulations on the grounds that they are tangential to Austin's intentions, Derrida's analysis does not dispense with the category of intention or ignore textual marks of an intention. On the contrary, it is important for Derrida's account that Austin is attempting to remedy and avoid the failing he had identified in others, and it is significant that Austin presents or intends his exclusion of the nonserious as provisional and inessential. Austin's case is interesting, as Derrida says, precisely because by his refusal to take true and false propositions as the defining norm of discourse, he is attempting—intending—to break with a certain logocentric conception of language in "an analysis which is patient, open, aporetical, in constant transformation, often more fruitful in the acknowledgement of its impasses than in its positions" (*Marges*, p. 383/SEC, p. 187). That an analysis with these intentions should end by reintroducing the premises it has sought to put in question reveals more about the inescapability of logocentrism and the difficulties of a theory of language than would the failure of a discourse that implied different intentions. Austin's intention is not something that determines the meaning of his discourse, but there is in his writing an intention-effect, which can play an important role in one's account of the drama of this text.

The role of such effects emerges more clearly in Derrida's reading of Rousseau, where he does not hesitate to label a certain insistent thematic pattern in Rousseau's writings "what Rousseau wants to say": "He *declares* what he *intends to say,* namely, that articulation and writing are a post-originary malady of language; he says or *describes* what he *does not want to say*: articulation and therefore the space of writing operate at the origin of language" (*De la grammatologie*, p. 326/229). Rousseau intends to define culture as the negation of a positive state of nature, with unhappiness replacing happiness, writing speech, harmony melody, prose poetry; but at the same time he characterizes cultural supplementation in such a way as to reveal that the supposed negative complication has always already been at work in that upon which it is said to follow. This division of Rousseau's text into what Rousseau intends and what he does not intend is, of course, an artifice of reading (intention is always a textual construct of this sort). De Man would call this an example of a misreading prefigured by the text—the text's insistence on these themes induces the reader to identify them as the intended meaning and to treat the subversion or complication as an unintended residue. But this operative notion of intention is important to Derrida's analysis, both for the story he tells about Rousseau and for his account, in the section "Question of Method," of the writer's relation to language:

This brings up the question of the usage of the word "supplement": of Rousseau's situation within the language and the logic that assures this word or this concept sufficiently *surprising* resources that the presumed subject of the utterance always says, when using "supplement," more, less, or something other than what he means [*voudrait dire*]. This is not only therefore a question of Rousseau's writing but also of our reading. We should begin by taking rigorous account of this *being held* or this *surprise* [*de cette prise ou de cette surprise*]; the writer writes *in* a language and *in* a logic whose own system, laws, and life his discourse by definition cannot dominate absolutely. He uses them only by letting himself, after a fashion and up to a certain point, be governed by the system. And reading must always aim at a certain relationship, unperceived by the writer, between what he commands and what he does not command in the patterns of the language that he uses. This relationship is not a certain quantitative distribution of light and darkness, of weakness and force, but a signifying structure that critical reading must *produce*. [*De la grammatologie*, pp. 226–27/157–58]

The New Criticism rejected appeals to intention because the particular intentions of poets, as indicated by the documents apparently most relevant to this study, would prove narrow and limited in comparison with the rich and surprising resources of the works poets had composed. If New Critics outlawed a concern with discoverable intentions, it was in order to appeal to an abstract and comprehensive intention. Cleanth Brooks rejects the suggestion that he is revealing complexities not intended by the poet, on the principle that "the poet knows precisely what he is doing" (*The Well Wrought Urn*, p. 159). The poet, like God the creator, is held to intend all that he makes. For Derrida, on the contrary, intention may be viewed as a particular textual product or effect, distilled by critical readings but always exceeded by the text. Intention, as indicated in section 2 of this chapter, is not something prior to the text that determines its meaning but is an important organizing structure identified in readings that distinguish an explicit line of argumentation from its subversive other. The critic need not call one textual stratum the author's intention—the greater the author the less one may be inclined to limit authorial intention to one strand of the text—but to do this is a striking way of dramatizing the claim about the subject's relation to language and textuality—a relation of *prise* and *surprise*.

In his reading of Rousseau Derrida posits an intended argument in order to identify the text's subversion of its explicit declarations, but in his reading of Plato he notes the derivative nature of this notion of conscious intention and its excessive simplification of textual relations. In Plato's text the word *pharmakon*

> is situated [*pris*] in a chain of significations. The play of this chain seems systematic. But the system here is not simply that of the intentions of the author known by the name of Plato. This system is not primarily that of an intended meaning. Finely regulated connections are established, by the play of the language, among different functions of the word and, within it, among diverse strata or regions of culture. Sometimes Plato may seem to declare

these connections, these channels of meaning, bringing them to light in playing on them "deliberately". . . . Then again, in other cases, he may not see these links, may leave them in darkness or even interrupt them. And yet these links go on working by themselves. Despite him? Thanks to him? In *his* text? *Outside* his text? But then where? Between his text and the linguistic system? For what reader? At what moment? [*La Dissémination*, p. 108/96]

One cannot, Derrida continues, give a general and principled reply to these questions, for they assume that there is a place where these relations and connections either are established or are not established and thus invalidated. One might, of course, argue that these connections were all established in Plato's unconsicous or linguistic competence, but that would beg the question at issue, which Derrida seeks not to beg but to pose and not answer. He is not, for example, championing a principle or rule that any word in a text has all the meanings ever recorded for it or for any signifier differing from it by no more than one phoneme. When he argues in "La Pharmacie de Platon" for the potentially powerful relations between words "present" in a discourse and all the other words of a lexical system, he is denying that there are principles by which signifying possibilities can be excluded in advance and opening the way to the identification of relationships of uncanny pertinence, as between the play of *pharmakon* and *pharmakeus* in Plato's text and the fundamental cultural institution of the *pharmakos* (see above, pp. 142–44). Who is to say where this relation occurs, except that it must be produced by the critical reading? The relations deemed worth pursuing and producing are those which turn out to function in a parergonal way and to describe the structures of textuality and the strategies of reading.

(4) Finally, deconstruction has a bearing on literary criticism because, as a prominent theoretical movement in the humanities, it affects one's notion of the nature of critical inquiry and the goals appropriate to it. If we identify deconstruction as a leading form of post-structuralism and thus oppose it to structuralism, we may reach the conclusions outlined by J. Hillis Miller in the article quoted in the Introduction: deconstruction arrives in the wake of structuralism to frustrate its systematic projects. The scientific ambitions of structuralists are exposed

as impossible dreams by deconstructive analyses, which put in question the binary oppositions through which structuralists describe and master cultural productions. Deconstruction shatters their "faith in reason" by revealing the uncanny irrationality of texts and their ability to confute or subvert every system or position they are thought to manifest. Deconstruction, by these lights, reveals the impossibility of any science of literature or science of discourse and returns critical inquiry to the task of interpretation. Instead of using literary works to develop a poetics of narrative, for example, the critic will study individual novels to see how they resist or subvert the logic of narrative. Research in the humanities, which structuralism attempted to enlist in broad, systematic projects, is now urged to return to close reading, to "the careful teasing out of warring forces of signification within the text."

One can certainly argue that American criticism has found in deconstruction reasons to deem interpretation the supreme task of critical inquiry and thus to preserve some measure of continuity between the goals of the New Criticism and those of the newer criticism. In the next chapter we will consider the practice of deconstructive criticism and its varied relations to so-called "close reading." However, if one were to accept the view that deconstruction teaches critics to reject systematic enterprises and devote their efforts to elucidating individual texts, one would be puzzled by Derrida's example. Readers who have assumed, on the American model of critical inquiry, that the goal of deconstruction is to illuminate individual works, have found it wanting in numerous ways. They complain, for example, of a certain monotony: deconstruction makes everything sound the same. Derrida and his cohorts do not, indeed, seem committed to identifying the distinctiveness of each work (or even its distinctive uncanniness), as becomes an interpreter. They seem preoccupied instead with questions about signatures, tropes, frames, reading or misreading, or the difficulty of escaping some system of assumptions. Moreover, deconstructive readings show scant respect for the wholeness or integrity of individual works. They concentrate on parts, relating them to material of diverse sorts, and may not even consider the relation of any part to the whole. Interpreters are allowed to argue that a work lacks unity, but to ignore the question of unity is to flout the obligations of their task. Third, Derrida's choice of works to discuss is hard to comprehend. Feminist critics write about noncanonical works in an attempt to change the canon; but when Derrida treats Warburton and Condillac instead of Leibniz and Hume, he does not seek promotions and demotions. His choice of texts seems determined by issues they can illuminate, as when he spends time, in *Glas* and "L'Age de Hegel," on a number of Hegel's letters. He is patently not primarily engaged in reinterpreting or reforming the canon. Finally, the conclusions deconstructive readings reach are frequently claims about structures of language, operations of rhetoric, and convolutions of thought, rather than conclusions about what a particular work means. For readings reputedly based on a renunciation of general theoretical projects, they seem suspiciously interested in theoretical questions of the most general sort.

The notion that deconstruction rejects systematic enquiry in order to elucidate individual works is based on an assumed opposition that itself requires deconstruction. One cannot conclude that because Derrida identifies the difficulties or aporias in structuralist projects— Saussure's, Lévi-Strauss's, Austin's, Foucault's—his own writings escape systematic and theoretical pursuits. In a similar way, he is critical of Marxism, especially of Marxism as a science attempting to ground itself on "history," but he is nevertheless engaged in the kinds of investigation Marxism encourages: a systematic, expanding analysis of the overt and covert relations between base and superstructure or institutions and thought. As may by now be evident, Derrida's works are particularly concerned with regularities: structures that reappear in discourses of various sorts, whatever their ostensible preoccupations. In analyzing the way diverse writings are inextricably implicated in logocentrism, for example, he is investigating the structural determinants of discourse—a topic pursued in other ways by many structuralists.

The notion that the goal of analysis is to produce enriching elucidations of individual works is a deep presupposition of American criticism. Its power appears in resistance to the systematic projects of structuralism, Marxism, and psychoanalysis, which are labeled "reductive," and in the assimilation of deconstruction to interpretation, despite the evidence that this is not its goal. If interpretation *were* its goal, then opponents might be right to complain that deconstruction's stress on the indeterminacy of meaning makes its work pointless. "If all interpretation is misinterpretation," writes M. H. Abrams, "and if all criticism (like all history) of texts can engage only with a critic's own misconstruction, why bother to carry on the activities of interpretation and criticism?" ("The Deconstructive Angel," p. 434). Assuming that the goal of criticism is interpretation, he judges deconstruction to have made its own activity pointless by precluding the possibility of interpretive conclusions.

To see that there might nonetheless be a point, one needs to dispute the assumption that opposes science to interpretation, and generality to particularity, as the two alternative possibilities, and assimilates any critique of science to the interpretive celebration of particularity. To escape this opposition and this assimilation, we need a different description of the relation of structuralism to deconstruction.

If structuralist writings repeatedly appeal to linguistic models, it is because structuralism shifts the focus of critical thinking from subjects to discourse. Structural explanation appeals not to the consciousness of subjects but to structures and systems of conventions operating within the discursive field of a social practice. Meaning is the effect of codes and conventions—often the result of foregrounding, parodying, flouting, or otherwise subverting the relevant conventions. To describe these conventions, one posits various sciences—a science of literature, a science of mythology, a general science of signs—which serve as the methodological horizon of a range of analytical projects. Within each project interest often focuses on marginal or problematical phenomena, which serve to indicate the conventions that exclude them and whose force is a function of those conventions. Structuralist literary criticism, for example, shows more interest in avant-garde literature that violates convention than in well-formed examples of traditional literary genres. Structuralists celebrate the *nouveau roman*, the literature of surrealism, and earlier artists deemed revolutionary—Mallarmé, Flaubert, Sade, Rabelais—and when they do turn to classic writers, who might be supposed to comply with conventions, they discover an unsuspected radical force, as in Barthes's studies of Racine and Balzac.

Much the same happens in other structuralist writings: the notion of a science or complete "grammar" of forms serves as a methodological horizon for research that often stresses the ungrammatical or deviant, as in anthropological studies of pollution and taboo or Foucault's structuralist history of madness and recent work on prisons. One might argue that the notion of a science or grammar plays much the same role for structuralism as the notion of a systematic and comprehensive putting in question plays for deconstruction. Neither is a possible accomplishment but an imperative that brings into being projects which also accomplish something different. The deconstructive questioning of categories and assumptions leads back repeatedly to a small group of problems and gives conclusions that function as knowledge. Just as the structuralist study of rules and codes may focus on irregularities, so the deconstructive undoing of codes reveals certain regularities. And just as structuralists argue that ungrammaticalities will prove grammatical at another level or by another code, so denizens of deconstruction note that the mastery implied by the regularities of deconstructive results must be put in question by further analyses. If, as seems to be the case, structuralist science unearths surprising anomalies, while deconstructive interpretation brings out inexorable regularities, one cannot rely on the oppositions between structuralism and deconstruction, science and interpretation, or generality and particularity, except as guides to practices that subvert them.

In focusing on language or discourse, structuralism makes consciousness or the subject an effect of systems operating through it. Foucault advised that "man" is but a fold in our knowledge—a pronouncement that is complicated by Derrida's work on *folds* and *invagination*. But to get its analytical projects underway, structuralism must provide a new center, a given that can serve as point of reference. This given is *meaning*. Barthes notes perspicaciously in *Critique et vérité* that a poetics or science of literature is founded not on literary works themselves but on their intelligibility, the fact that they have been understood (p. 62). Taking meanings as given, poetics tries to identify the system of codes responsible for these accepted and acceptable meanings. Saussure's project of a scientific linguistics also depends on meaning—specifically, difference of meaning—as a given point of reference. To determine what are the signifying contrasts and thus the signs of a linguistic system one employs the commutation test: *p* and *b* are different phonemes and *pat* and *bat* different signs in English because the passage from *b* to *p* in the context *-at* produces a change in meaning. Reliance on this possibility of treating meaning of some kind as given creates a connection between structuralism and reader-response criticism, which does not just treat meanings as given social facts but explicitly identifies them with the experience of the reader. The critic's task, then, is to describe and elucidate the meanings given in the reader's experience.

Deconstruction attempts to show how this treatment of meaning is undermined by the theory that relies on it. "The possibility of reading," de Man writes, "can never be taken for granted. It is an act of understanding that can never be observed, nor in any way prescribed or verified." The work gives rise to "no transcendental perception, intuition, or knowledge" that could serve as the secure foundation for a science (*Blindness and Insight*, p. 107). As we saw in Chapter One, the reader's experience, which must function as a given for reader-response criticism to get underway, proves to be not a given but a construct—the product of forces and factors it was supposed to help elucidate. Structuralism, like New Criticism, trying to link the poem's meaning directly to its structures, invariably discovers that it cannot rely on a given meaning but confronts problems of ambiguity, irony, and dissemination. Given meanings—from the identification of Balzac as a traditionally intelligible novelist to the usual interpretation of a rhetorical figure—are indispensable points of departure, but they are displaced by the analyses that they make possible, as happens also in deconstructive readings.

"The aspect of deconstructive practice that is best known in the United States," writes Gayatri Spivak,

is its tendency towards infinite regression. The aspect that interests me most, however, is the recognition, within deconstructive practice, of provisional and intractable starting points in any investigative effort; its disclosure of complicities where a will to knowledge would create oppositions; its insistence that in disclosing complicities the critic-as-subject is herself complicit with the object of her critique; its emphasis upon "history" and upon the ethico-political as the "trace" of that complicity—the proof that we do not inhabit a clearly defined critical space free of such traces; and, finally, the acknowledgment that its own discourse can never be adequate to its example. ["'Draupadi,'" pp. 382–83]

The demonstration that structuralist "givens" are not foundations but provisional starting points which the analysis must question is a powerful critique of structuralist projects, but it does not mean that deconstruction has other than provisional and intractable starting points. It appeals, for example, to attested meanings and to the fundamental assumptions of the discourse to be deconstructed. The demonstration that critics attempting to stand above or outside a literary domain in order to master it are caught up in the play of forces of the object they seek to describe—its tropological and transferential ruses—does not imply that deconstructive readings can escape these intractable forces. Demonstrations of complicities between language and metalanguage, observed and observer, question the possibility of attaining a principled mastery of a domain but do not suggest that deconstruction has either achieved a mastery of its own or can ignore the whole problem of mastery from a secure position of externality. The effect of deconstructive analyses, as numerous readers can attest, is knowledge and feelings of mastery. In reading particular works and readings of those works, deconstruction attempts to understand these phenomena of textuality— the relations of language and metalanguage, for example, or effects of externality and internality, or the possible interaction of conflicting logics. And if the formulations produced by these analyses are themselves open to question because of their involvement with the forces and ruses they claim to understand, this acknowledgment of inadequacy is also an opening to criticism, analysis, and displacement.

Chapter Three

DECONSTRUCTIVE CRITICISM

DISCUSSION of the implications of deconstruction for literary criticism has identified a range of possible strategies and concerns, from the austere investigation of philosophical hierarchies as they are subverted in literary discourse to the pursuit of connections established by relays of signifiers in the manner of the Wolfman's cryptonyms. Since deconstructive criticism is not the application of philosophical lessons to literary studies but an exploration of textual logic in texts called literary, its possibilities vary, and commentators are irresistibly tempted to draw lines to separate orthodox deconstructive criticism from its distortions or illicit imitations and derivations. Taking Derrida and de Man as different but authoritative exemplars of true deconstruction, commentators can charge other critics either with diluting original deconstructive insights or with mechanically copying the procedures of these two masters. On the one hand, the opponents of deconstruction, writing in *Newsweek* or the *New York Review of Books*, pluralistically allow de Man and Derrida a perverse originality but reproach graduate students for mechanically imitating what lies beyond their reach; on the other hand, defenders of deconstruction, writing in *Glyph* or *Diacritics*, reproach American deconstructive critics for distorting and weakening the original formulations of Derrida and de Man.[1]

[1]*Newsweek* praises the original "professorial practitioners of deconstruction" as "formidable men of letters who have bent deconstruction to their own individual—and practical—purposes," but warns of its influence on graduate students who may commit "the pedagogic error of allowing one theory of

This combination of reproaches is familiar: it is in these terms that writing is described as it is set aside—as a distortion of speech and mechanical repetition of speech. A concern for purity is understandable among defenders of deconstruction, who are dismayed at the reception accorded ideas they admire, but to set up Derrida's or de Man's writings as the original word and treat other deconstructive writing as a fallen imitation is precisely to forget what deconstruction has taught one about the relation between meaning and iteration and the internal role of misfires and infelicities. Deconstruction is created by repetitions, deviations, disfigurations. It emerges from the writings of Derrida and de Man only by dint of iteration: imitation, citation, distortion, parody. It persists not as a univocal set of instructions but as a series of differences that can be charted on various axes, such as the degree to which the work analyzed is treated as a unit, the role accorded to prior readings of the text, the interest in pursuing relations among signifiers, and the source of the metalinguistic categories employed in analysis. The liveliness of any intellectual enterprise largely depends on differences which make argument possible while preventing any definitive distinction between what lies within and what without this enterprise.[2]

---

language to determine their response to great literature" (22 June 1981, p. 83). *The New York Review of Books*, through Denis Donoghue, complains of graduate students mechanically producing deconstructive readings "for the sake of the theory they are supposed to endorse" ("Deconstructing Deconstruction," p. 41). At the Colloque de Cérisy on Derrida in 1980, there were many complaints, especially by Americans, about the mechanical application of Derridean deconstruction, in America, to literary studies—an institutionalization that deprives it of its original radical force (see, for example, *Les Fins de l'homme*, ed. Lacoue-Labarthe and Nancy, pp. 278–81). The theme has become a familiar one: American deconstructive criticism is presented as repetition or application, a mechanical operation that distorts and destroys the force of the original it repeats. Rodolphe Gasché's "Deconstruction as Criticism," complaining of distortions of Derrida's original philosophical projects, speaks of "the all too often naive and sometimes even, in its uncontrolled and unwanted side effects, *ridiculous* application of the *results* of philosophical debates to the literary field" (p. 178). The convergence of opponents and supporters in this intense concern to distinguish the original from the derivative is an intriguing symptom of the play and forces within critical institutions.

[2]In addition to writings of critics discussed in this chapter, one might with profit consult works listed in the bibliography by the following: Timothy Bahti, Cynthia Chase, Eugenio Donato, Rodolphe Gasché, Carol Jacobs, Sarah Kofman, Richard Rand, Joseph Riddel, Michael Ryan, Henry Sussman, and Andrzej Warminski.

Not only does repetition produce what can then be regarded as a method, but critical writings that are said to imitate or deviate often provide clearer or fuller examples of a method than the supposed originals. De Man's own writings, for example, frequently assert, with authoritative confidence, claims that require demonstration but instead are simply adduced in order to move on to more "advanced" reflections. His essays often assure the reader that demonstration of these points would not be difficult, only cumbersome, and they do provide much detailed argument and exegesis, but these gaps in argumentation may be quite striking. Frank Lentricchia, reading de Man as an existentialist, complains that his essays are "marred at every point by the suggestion that he is in undisputed, authoritative, and truthful possession of the texts he reads," a position Lentricchia believes only a "historian" can occupy (*After the New Criticism*, p. 299). Though most critical prose seeks to suggest such authority, de Man's writing is special—and often especially annoying—in its strategy of omitting crucial demonstrations in order to put readers in a position where they cannot profit from his analyses without according belief to what seems implausible or at least unproven. As de Man says of Michael Riffaterre's "dogmatic assertions," "by stating them as he does, in the blandest and most apodictic of terms, he makes their heuristic function evident" ("Hypogram and Inscription," p. 19).

An account of deconstructive criticism cannot, of course, neglect de Man's writings, but his "rhetoric of authority" often makes them less exemplary than those of younger critics who must still try to demonstrate what they wish to assert and who therefore may provide a clearer view of important issues and procedures. A good point of departure is an elegant, relatively simple analysis by a critic whose practice is more insightful than his theory. Walter Michaels's "*Walden*'s False Bottoms" gives a deconstructive inflection to New Critical procedures and will thus help us to situate deconstructive criticism in a tradition of literary interpretation.

Emerson complained of Thoreau's "trick of unlimited contradiction. . . . It makes me nervous and wretched to read it." Michaels addresses *Walden*'s contradictions and the strategies readers adopt to avoid feeling wretched and nervous. *Walden* is usually read as a quest for foundations, an attempt to strip away the superfluous and find hard bottom. In his *Journal* Thoreau records an emblematic project, whose results are later reported in *Walden*: "To find the bottom of Walden Pond and what inlet and outlet it may have." A famous passage of *Walden* urges us to find hard bottom:

> Let us settle ourselves, and work and wedge our feet downward through the mud and slush of opinion, and prejudice, and tradition, and delusion, and appearance, that alluvion which covers the globe, . . . through church and state, through poetry and philosophy and religion, till we come to a hard bottom and rocks in place, which we can call *reality*, and say, This is, and no mistake; and then begin, having a *point d'appui*, below freshet and frost and fire, a place where you might found a wall or a state, or set a lamp-post safely, or perhaps a gauge, not a Nilometer, but a Realometer, that future ages might know how deep a freshet of shams and appearances had gathered from time to time. [Chap. 2]

This hard bottom is natural ground, a foundation in nature prior to or outside of human institutions, the reality we must attempt to grasp. But there is another hard bottom in *Walden*: "It affords me no satisfaction," Thoreau begins, "to commence to spring an arch before I have got a solid foundation. Let us not play at kittlybenders. There is solid bottom every where." And he proceeds with an illustrative anecdote, about a traveler who asked a boy "if the swamp before him had a hard bottom. The boy replied that it had. But presently the traveller's horse sank in up to the girths, and he observed to the boy, 'I thought you said that this bog had a hard bottom.' 'So it has,' answered the latter, 'but you have not got halfway to it yet.' So it is with the bogs and quicksands of society;" Thoreau concludes, "but he is an old boy that knows it" (chap. 18).

As Michaels observes, although the theme of the two passages is similar—"the explorer in search of a solid foundation—the point has been rather dramatically changed" ("*Walden*'s False Bottoms," p. 136). Both passages contrast the hard bottom with the mud and slush above it, but the structure of values shifts: in the first passage the sage works through mud and slush to get to the bottom; in the second the sage is one who knows enough to stay clear, and the heroic quester of the first passage is transformed into the foolish, sinking traveler. A further complication occurs in Thoreau's account of the quest for the bottom of Walden Pond.

> As I was desirous to recover the long lost bottom of Walden Pond, I surveyed it carefully, before the ice broke up, early in '46, with compass and chain and sounding line. There have been many stories told about the bottom, or rather no bottom of this pond, which certainly had no foundation for themselves. It is remarkable how long men will believe in the bottomlessness of a pond without taking the trouble to sound it. I have visited two such Bottomless Ponds in one walk in this neighborhood. Many have believed that Walden reached quite through to the other side of the globe. . . . Others have gone down from the village with a "fifty-six" and a wagon load of inch rope, but yet have failed to find any bottom; for while the "fifty-six" was resting by the way, they were paying out the rope in the vain attempt to fathom their truly immeasurable capacity for marvellousness. But I can assure my readers that Walden has a reasonably tight bottom at a not unreasonable, though at an unusual, depth. I fathomed it easily with a cod-line. . . . The greatest depth was exactly one hundred and two feet. . . . [Chap. 16]

So far, the pattern is clear: Thoreau gives us the mud and slush of opinion (the foolish belief in bottomlessness, which is without foundation) and his own tough-minded determination to get to the bottom of things, to produce a fact and say, This is, and no mistake. But he immediately continues: "This is a remarkable depth for so small an area; yet not an inch of it can be spared by the imagination. What if all ponds were shallow? Would it not react on the minds of men? I am thankful that this pond was made pure and deep for a symbol. While men believe in the infinite some ponds will be thought to be bottomless." The opposition between the reality of a tight bottom and a deluded belief in bottomlessness is transformed into an opposition between a shallowness associated with bottoms and an infinity associated with bottomlessness. The depth of the pond is celebrated for the suggestion of bottomlessness that might be eliminated by discovery of an actual bottom.

Michaels does not attempt to dispel these contradictions but explores the way they are reproduced in Thoreau's further discussions of natural foundations and of Nature as foundation. The same movement that here eliminates bottom as a value as soon as it is found occurs when Thoreau repudiates any actual "tokens of natural value which his society provides." The attraction of Nature as a firm bottom or bottom line depends on its otherness, so that any particular bottom must prove shallow and prompt a wish for further depth. "The category of the natural becomes an empty one," writes Michaels. But this doesn't mean that the distinction between the natural and the conventional is abandoned. "Quite the contrary: the more difficult it becomes to identify natural principles, the more privilege attaches to a position which can be defined only in theoretical opposition to the conventional or institutional" (pp. 140–41). This play of the bottom is confirmed in a passage Michaels does not quote. In the paragraph following the exhortation to work and wedge our feet downward to a *point d'appui*, Thoreau continues, "Time is but the stream I go a-fishing in. I drink at it; but while I drink I see the sandy bottom and detect how shallow it is. Its thin current slides away, but eternity remains. I would drink deeper; fish in the sky, whose bottom is pebbly with stars" (chap. 2). The bottom one can see is too shallow. The figure of the sky as pond combines the desire for a bottom with depth of bottomlessness. The blackness of the sky is the best natural bottom.

In the series of passages Michaels explores—about nature and foundations—"the desire for the solid bottom is made clear, but the attempt to locate it or specify its characteristics involves the writer in a tangle of contradictions." "What I have tried to describe thus far," he continues,

> is a series of relationships in the text of *Walden*—between nature and culture, the finite and the infinite, and (still to come) literal and figurative language—each of which is imagined at all times hierarchically, that is, the terms don't simply coexist, one is always thought of as more basic or more important than the other. The catch is that the hierarchies are always breaking down. Sometimes nature is the ground which authorizes culture, sometimes it is merely another of culture's creations. Sometimes the search for a hard bottom is presented as the central activity of a moral life, sometimes that same search will only make a Keystone-cop martyr out of the searcher. These unresolved contradictions are, I think, what makes us nervous reading *Walden*, and the urge to resolve

them seems to me a major motivating factor in most *Walden* criticism. ["*Walden*'s False Bottoms," p. 142]

If the attempt to resolve the contradictions distorts *Walden*, one might be tempted to leave them unresolved in an aesthetic suspension and to appreciate the rich ambiguity of Thoreau's work. This is not, however, an innocent choice, for the pattern of contradictory valorization is extended in the work from bottoms and nature to reading. A chapter entitled "Reading" contrasts the epic (particularly the *Iliad*) with what Thoreau calls "shallow books of travel" (chap. 3). The epic is deep. Its words are "a reserved and select expression, too significant to be heard by the ear," and in describing them Thoreau takes up again the image used a few paragraphs earlier of "the sky whose bottom is pebbly with stars": "The noblest written words are commonly as far behind or above the fleeting spoken language as the firmament with its stars is behind the clouds. *There* are the stars, and they who can may read them." In contrast with shallow books of travel, the epic requires a figurative reading: the reader must be prepared to conjecture "a larger sense than common use permits." Thus, Michaels says,

> the opposition between the epic and the travelogue has modulated into an opposition between the figurative and the literal and then between the written and the oral. In each case the first term of the opposition is privileged, and if we turn again to the attempt to sound the depths of Walden Pond, we can see that these are all values of what I have called "bottomlessness." A shallow pond would be like a shallow book, that is, a travel book, one meant to be read literally. *Walden* is written "deep and pure for a symbol."
> But this pattern of valorization, although convincing, is by no means ubiquitous or final. The chapter on "Reading" is followed by one called "Sounds," which systematically reconsiders the categories already introduced and which reasserts the values of the hard bottom. [P. 144]

The figurative language of books is contrasted unfavorably with the literal sounds of nature, "the language," Thoreau writes, "which all things and events speak without metaphor" (chap. 4), and whose reality, solidity, and literality the reader is enjoined to prefer, just as the earlier chapter extolled figurative reading.

The reader cannot simply accept this contradiction, because to read at all is to choose, to choose between literal and metaphorical readings, for example, or between the quest for a hard bottom and the appreciation of bottomlessness. "Our whole life," Thoreau writes, "is startlingly moral. There is never an instant's truce between virtue and vice" (chap. 11). He inveighs in particular against those who think they have no choice. *Walden* attempts, Michaels says, "to show us that we do have choices left and, by breaking down hierarchies into contradictory alternatives, to insist upon our making them. But this breakdown, which creates the opportunity or rather the necessity for choosing, serves at the same time to undermine the rationale we might give for any particular choice" (pp. 146–47). This is no less true of reading than of other choices. "If our reading claims to find a solid bottom, it can only do so according to principles which the text has both authorized and repudiated; thus we run the risk of drowning in our own certainties. If it doesn't, if we embrace the idea of bottomlessness . . . , we've failed *Walden*'s first test, the acceptance of our moral responsibility as deliberate readers. It's heads I win, tails you lose. No wonder the game makes us nervous" (p. 148).

Michaels's reading investigates *Walden*'s treatment of several central and related issues and discovers, as critical interpretation usually does, complex ambiguities; but the ambiguities discovered are of a more troubling kind than usual: not just divisions between alternative meanings but divisions between two attitudes toward meaning and toward difference of meaning. In insisting on the hortatory, ethical dimensions of the text, Michaels identifies the work's production of a double bind, in which one is urged to choose while the possibility of correct choice is eliminated. His analysis also dissents from customary critical notions of unity. "The essential structure of a poem," writes Cleanth Brooks in *The Well Wrought Urn*, "is a pattern of resolved stresses. . . . The characteristic unity of a poem lies in the unification of attitudes into a hierarchy subordinated to a total and governing attitude" (pp. 203, 207). Here, though, hierarchies are undone, and though the structure of contradictions has a certain unifying effect, it produces not a total and governing attitude but the division of any possible attitude. Finally, this analysis raises the stakes of the reading by concentrating on elements in the text with metalinguistic bearing, which provide matter and vocabulary—"hard bottom" and "bottomlessness"—for a discussion of meaning and interpretation. Instead of looking for symbols of poetry and the literary imagination, the critic investigates what the work says, implicitly and explicitly, about reading.

Many would argue, with some justification, that Michaels's reading, though interested in the breakdown of hierarchical oppositions, is not genuinely deconstructive but an exploration that leaves contradictions aesthetically unresolved and shows no effects of the nervousness it claims *Walden* creates. Though investigating the relations between what the work says about reading and the readings it elicits, Michaels's essay does not pursue the implications of language and rhetoric in ways characteristic of much deconstructive criticism. Moreover, one might think *Walden* too easy a case for the seeker of contradictions. Its narrative line is relatively weak and critics have often thought it a series of spectacular fragments. For a deconstructive reading of a more tightly woven text that seems fully in control of its narrative and thematic structures, we can consider Barbara Johnson's discussion of *Billy Budd*, "Melville's Fist: The Execution of *Billy Budd*," in her book *The Critical Difference*.

Billy Budd is the story of a beautiful, innocent young sailor on a British man-of-war. Falsely accused of mutinous plotting by Claggart, the devious master-at-arms, Billy, his speech impeded by a stutter, strikes Claggart dead in front of Captain Vere. The captain, an honest, well-read, serious man, has much sympathy for Billy but convinces his fellow officers that under the circumstances—Britain is at war and there have been other mutinies—Billy must hang, which he does, uttering as his last words, "God bless Captain Vere!" Each character is explicitly assigned moral qualities, but, Johnson notes, "the fate of each of the characters is the direct reverse of what one is led to expect from his 'nature.' Billy is sweet, innocent, and harmless, yet he kills. Claggart is evil, perverted, and mendacious, yet he dies a victim. Vere is sagacious and responsible, yet he allows a man whom he feels to be blameless to hang" (*The Critical Difference*, p. 82).

The issue in the story is thus not just the relation between good and evil but rather between characters' natures and what they do, between being and doing. "Curiously enough," writes Johnson,

> it is precisely this question of being versus doing that is brought up by the only sentence we ever see Claggart directly address to Billy Budd. When Billy accidentally spills his soup across the path of the master-at-arms, Claggart playfully replies, "Handsomely done, my lad! And handsome *is* as handsome *did* it too!" The proverbial expression "handsome is as handsome does," from which this exclamation springs, posits the possibility of a continuous, predictable, transparent relationship between being and doing. ... But it is this very continuity between the physical and the moral, between appearance and action, or between being and doing, that Claggart questions in Billy Budd. He warns Captain Vere not to be taken in by Billy's physical beauty: "You have but noted his fair cheek. A mantrap may be under the ruddy-tipped daises." [Pp. 83–84]

His suspicions are confirmed when he repeats his accusation before Billy and the ruddy-cheeked lad strikes him dead.

To investigate what is at stake in this drama, Johnson gathers the evidence Melville provides that the opposition between Billy and Claggart is an opposition "between two conceptions of language, or between two types of reading." Billy is a simple literalist, a believer in the transparency of signification. "To deal in double meanings and insinuations of any sort," writes Melville, "was quite foreign to his nature." To him "the occasional frank air and pleasant word went for what they purported to be, the young sailor never having heard as yet of the 'too fair-spoken man.'" He cannot believe that there might be a discrepancy between form and meaning. Claggart, on the other hand, is not only a personification of ambiguity and duplicity but a believer in the discrepancy between form and meaning. He has learned, Melville writes, "to exercize a distrust keen in proportion to the fairness of the appearance." Claggart accuses Billy of duplicity, of a discrepancy between appearance and reality; Billy denies this by striking a blow, which in fact illustrates the very discrepancy he denies, revealing a fatal mantrap beneath the daises. He demonstrates the truth of Claggart's accusation by the act of denying it.

The story thus takes place between the postulate of continuity between signifier and signified ("handsome is as handsome does") and the postulate of their discontinuity ("a mantrap may be under the ruddy-tipped daises"). Claggart, whose accusations of incipient mutiny are apparently false and therefore illustrate the very double-facedness they attribute to Billy, is negated for proclaiming the lie about Billy which Billy's act of negation paradoxically proves to be the truth. [P. 86]

This account of the opposition between the two characters and its articulation of contradictory models of signification and interpretation also identifies the two modes of reading involved in critical quarrels about the story. Some critics are suspicious interpreters, like Claggart, unwilling to accept Billy's goodness at face value. They may infer Claggart's latent homosexuality, interpreting his treatment of Billy as a repressed form of love. They frequently propose psychoanalytic descriptions of Billy's innocence as a pseudoinnocence and of his goodness as a repression of his own destructiveness, which comes to the surface in the fatal blow. Indeed, in the confrontation scene Claggart is portrayed as a psychoanalyst, moving toward Billy "with the measured step and calm collected air of an asylum physician approaching in the public hall some patient beginning to show indications of a coming paroxysm." Other critics side with Billy as believers in the continuity between being and doing and accept the characters' moral designations: Claggart is evil, Billy is good, Vere is wise. Both groups have persuasive interpretations of the crucial event of the story, the fatal blow: "If Billy represents pure goodness, then his act is unintentional but symbolically righteous, since it results in the destruction of the 'evil' Claggart. If Billy is a case of neurotic repression, then his act is determined by his unconscious desires, and reveals the destructiveness of the attempt to repress one's own destructiveness. In the first case, the murder is accidental; in the second, it is the fulfillment of a wish" (pp. 90–91).

The crucial point here is that in each case the interpretation of the blow is based on premises that undermine the claim the interpretation supports: Billy and the literalists, believers in continuity and motivation, must treat the blow as accidental and unmotivated in order to preserve Billy's goodness and the blow's symbolic righteousness. For Claggart and other suspicious interpreters, believers in the discrepancy between appearance and reality, the blow is proof of Billy's evil duplicity only if it is motivated and thus an instance of continuity between being and doing. Thus, the coherence of each interpretive scheme is undone by the principle of signification to which it must appeal in order to incorporate the blow into its account. The blow destroys each position—Billy's and Claggart's as well as the readings of literalists and ironists. It disrupts any interpretive account because *what* it means is undone by *the way* it means.

If the critic attempts to adjudicate the dispute between Billy and Claggart or between literalists and ironists, she finds herself in the position of Captain Vere, who is described as a learned and judicious reader. His "task is precisely to read the *relation* between naiveté and paranoia, acceptance and irony, murder and error," and he reads in a different way from Billy and Claggart. They are without pasts and futures, which play no role in their readings: they read for motive and meaning. Vere focuses instead on precedent and conseqence: "Budd's intent or non-intent·is nothing to the purpose," he declares. He reads in relation to political and historical circumstance and in relation to prior texts, the Bible and the Mutiny Law. Joining power and knowledge, Vere determines the relationships between other interpretations and acts by that judgment. And for him to judge Billy guilty is to kill him. Vere's reading is a political act that works by converting

> an ambiguous situation into a decidable one. But it does so by converting a difference *within* (Billy as divided between conscious submissiveness and unconscious hostility, Vere as divided between understanding father and military authority) into a difference *between* (between Claggart and Billy, between Nature and the King, between authority and criminality). . . . The political context in *Billy Budd* is such that on all levels the differences *within* (mutiny on the warship, the French Revolution as a threat to "lasting institutions," Billy's unconscious hostility) are subordinated to differences *between* (the *Bellipotent* vs. the *Athée*, England vs. France, murderer vs. victim). [Pp. 105–6]

Readers and critics disagree violently in their judgments of this reader, Vere, who seems compelled by circumstance to err in one way or another, and who is a partial reader precisely because he must in his judgment take account of the consequences of his judgment. Cannot we, as readers of a literary work, do better? Cannot we pass a more accurate and disinterested judgment than Vere? "If law is the forcible transformation of ambiguity into decidability, is it possible," Johnson asks, "to read ambiguity *as such*, without that reading functioning as a political act?" (p. 107). Even about this, she concludes, Melville has something to say, "for there is a fourth reader in *Billy Budd*, one who 'never interferes in aught and never gives advice': the old Dansker. A man of 'few words, many wrinkles' and 'the complexion of an antique parchment'" (p. 107). He sees and knows. Pressed by Billy for advice, he offers only the observation that Claggart is "down on" him; but this, along with his refusal to say more, has traceable consequences and contributes to the tragedy. The Dansker "dramatizes a reading that attempts to be as cognitively accurate and as performatively neutral as possible," but "the attempt to know without doing can itself function as a deed." The Dansker, like Vere, illustrates both the inseparability of knowledge and action and the impossibility of their harmonious fusion, for in each case, as Johnson writes, "authority consists precisely in the impossibility of containing the effects of its own application." Neither character can prevent unforeseen consequences that complicate and vitiate the acts of cognition and judgment.

Billy Budd, Johnson concludes, is

> much more than a study of good and evil, justice and injustice. It is a dramatization of the twisted relations between knowing and doing, speaking and killing, reading and judging, which make political understanding and action so problematic. . . . The "deadly space" or "difference" that runs through *Billy Budd* is not located between knowledge and action, performance and cognition. It is that which, within cognition, functions as an act; it is that which, within action, prevents us from ever knowing whether what we hit coincides with what we understand. And this is what makes the meaning of Melville's last work so *striking*. [Pp. 108–9]

This last phrase, from the concluding sentence of the article, illustrates a feature of this criticism not well represented in the passages I have cited: the use of expressions from the text, often punningly, to connect events of the narrative with events of reading and writing. Billy's blow is a striking event in the story, a complex structure of meaning and an act of compelling consequences; the meaning of the work, as it has been elucidated, also has a performative quality with consequences it is not easy to escape. A similar connection is made by the chapter's title, "Melville's Fist: The Execution of *Billy Budd*," which relates three performative speech acts: Melville's act of writing ("His [Claggart's] portrait I shall essay, but shall never hit it," he writes), Billy's pugilistic denial, and Vere's deadly judgment. In employing the language of the text as a metalanguage, critics continue a process that the text has already begun, but deconstructive readings vary considerably in their exploitation of this possibility. Derrida aggressively deploys signifiers from the text to describe a textual logic. De Man, on the contrary, avoids the categories offered by the text and swiftly relates the moments that interest him to metalinguistic terms from rhetoric and philosophy. Johnson's restrained exploitation of this textual resource produces what look like puns.

The second aspect of deconstruction this example illustrates is a suspicion of critics' willingness to celebrate ambiguity as an aesthetic richness. When confronted with two interpretations or two possibilities, Johnson asks about the premises on which each relies and investigates the relation between premises and conclusions, discovering that frequently the readings are undermined by the very assumptions that make them possible. Such discoveries then provide points of departure for an investigation of the frameworks within which such readings are elicited. Deconstructive readings may thus refuse to make aesthetic richness an end. Whenever one comes to what might seem a stopping point—a nice paradox or symmetrical formulation— one feeds this position back into the text, asking what the work has to say about the conclusion reached. After analyzing Vere's judgment, Johnson asks what the text has to say about the act of judgment itself, and after drawing conclusions about judgment as an act of violence that attempts, impossibly, to master its own consequences, she asks what the text might have to say about the aesthetic critique of political judgment that seems to be emerging from her reading. She then analyzes the predicament of the old Dansker as a further framing of the question of interpretation. With its "invaginated pockets," the text has something to say about any conclusion one is tempted to draw from it.

Third, Johnson's essay raises the stakes of "reading" by attending to the impossibility of separating action and judgment from the question of reading. In one sense, *Billy Budd* demonstrates that "il n'y a pas de hors texte": political action is revealed here as a particular type of reading, which vainly tries to make the consequences of a reading the grounds for it. Exploring the connection between the violence of means and the positing of meanings (or between the assumption of continuity between means and ends and the assumption that everything must have a meaning), *Billy Budd* produces a critique of authority as such—of law, for example, including the law of signification—and illustrates the textuality of judgment, much as de Man does in other terms in his reading of Nietzsche (*Allegories of Reading*, pp. 119–31).

Finally, Johnson's essay shows us deconstructive criticism pursuing structures that seem to become progressively tighter and often prove to be double binds. In the opening essay of *The Critical Difference* she comments on Barthes's decision in *S/Z* to break up the text, to treat it as a "galaxy of signifiers" rather than a structure of signifieds: "The question to ask is whether this 'anti-constructionist' (as opposed to 'de-constructionist') fidelity to the fragmented signifier succeeds in laying bare the functional plurality of Balzac's text, or whether in the final analysis a certain systematic level of textual difference is not also lost and flattened by Barthes's refusal to reorder or reconstruct the text" (p. 7). Summarizing her own procedure in the "Opening Remarks" to her book, Johnson writes:

> Reading, here, proceeds by identifying and dismantling differences by means of other differences that cannot be fully identified or dismantled. The starting point is often a binary difference that is subsequently shown to be an illusion created by the workings of differences much harder to pin down. The differences *between* entities (prose and poetry, man and woman, literature and theory, guilt and innocence) are shown to be based on a repression of differences *within* entities, ways in which an entity differs from itself. But the way in which a text thus differs from itself is never simple: it has a certain rigorous, contradictory logic whose effects

can, up to a certain point, be read. The "deconstruction" of a binary opposition is thus not an annihilation of all values or differences; it is an attempt to follow the subtle, powerful effects of differences already at work within the illusion of a binary opposition. [Pp. x–xi]

If deconstructive criticism is a pursuit of differences—differences whose suppression is the condition of any particular entity or position—then it can never reach final conclusions but stops when it can no longer identify and dismantle the differences that work to dismantle other differences.

Johnson's reading of *Billy Budd* is distinctive in deconstructive criticism for its comprehensiveness—a virtue easily overvalued—but she does not here explore, as she does in her *Défigurations du langage poétique*, the detailed implications of rhetorical figures. Introducing the collection on "The Rhetoric of Romanticism" in which her essay on *Billy Budd* first appeared, Paul de Man writes, "it is a common and productive gesture of all these papers to outdo the closeness of reading that has been held up to them and to show, by reading the close readings more closely, that they were not nearly close enough" ("Introduction," p. 498). We can characterize deconstructive criticism further by pursuing two questions this comment suggests: what makes a reading close? and what is the role of prior readings for deconstructive criticism? Johnson reads most closely when detailing the logic of signification at certain key moments of the text. What more might closeness involve?

Close reading, for de Man, entails scrupulous attention to what seems ancillary or resistant to understanding. In his foreword to Carol Jacobs's *The Dissimulating Harmony* he speaks of paraphrase as "a synonym for understanding": an act which converts the strange into the familiar, "facing up to apparent difficulties (be they of syntax, of figuration, or of experience) and . . . coping with them exhaustively and convincingly," but subtly eliding, concealing, and diverting what stands in the way of meaning. "What would happen," he asks, "if, for once, one were to reverse the ethos of explication and try to be really precise," attempting "a reading that would no longer blindly submit to the teleology of controlled meaning" (pp. ix–x)? What would happen, that is, if instead of assuming that elements of the text were subservient instruments of a controlling meaning or total and governing attitude, readers were to explore every resistance to meaning? Primary points of resistance might be what we call rhetorical figures, since to identify a passage or sequence as figurative is to recommend transformation of a literal difficulty, which may have interesting possibilities, into a paraphrase that fits the meaning assumed to govern the message as a whole. As we have seen in our discussion of Derrida, rhetorical reading—attention to the implications of figurality in a discourse—is one of the principal resources of deconstruction.

Consider, for example, de Man's dealing with a passage in Proust's *A la recherche du temps perdu*, where Marcel resists his grandmother's request that he go out to play and remains in his room reading. The narrator claims that through reading he can have truer access to people and passions, just as by remaining indoors he can grasp the essence of summer more intimately and effectively than if he were actually outside: "The dark coolness of my room . . . gave my imagination the total spectacle of summer, whereas my senses, if I had been on a walk, could only have enjoyed it in fragments." The sensation of summer is conveyed to him "by the flies who were performing before me, in their little concert, the chamber music of summer: evocative not in the manner of a human tune which, heard perchance during the summer, afterwards reminds us of it, but united to summer by a more necessary link: born from beautiful days, resurrecting only when they return, containing something of their essence, it not only awakens their image in our memory, it guarantees their return, their actual, persistent, immediately accessible presence." Proust's passage is metafigural, de Man argues, in that it comments on figural relations.

It contrasts two ways of evoking the natural experience of summer and unambiguously states its preference for one of these ways over the other: the "necessary link" that unites the buzzing of the flies to the summer makes it a much more effective symbol than the tune heard "perchance" during the summer. The preference is expressed by means of a distinction that corresponds to the difference between metaphor and metonymy, necessity and chance being a legitimate way to distinguish between analogy and contiguity. The inference of identity and totality that is constitutive of metaphor is lacking in the purely relational metonymic contact. . . . The passage is *about* the aesthetic superiority of metaphor over metonymy. . . . Yet, it takes little perspicacity to show that the text does not practice what it preaches. A rhetorical reading of the passage reveals that the figural praxis and the metafigural theory do not converge and that the assertion of the mastery of metaphor over metonymy owes its persuasive power to the use of metonymic structures. [*Allegories of Reading*, pp. 14–15]

To demonstrate that he can experience "the total spectacle of summer" through a metaphorical transfer of essence, Marcel must explain how the heat and activity characteristic of the scene outside are brought inside. The dark coolness of my room, he writes, "s'accordait bien à mon repos qui (grâce aux aventures racontées par mes livres et qui venaient l'émouvoir) supportait, pareil au repos d'une main immobile au milieu d'une eau courante, le choc et l'animation d'un torrent d'activité" [suited my repose which (thanks to the adventures narrated in my books and which had stirred my tranquility) supported, like the quiet of a hand held motionless in the middle of a running stream, the shock and animation of a torrent of activity]. The expression "torrent d'activité," which brings in the heated activity of summer, works metonymically, not metaphorically, de Man argues. It exploits contiguity, or accidental as opposed to essential connections, in three ways: first, the image relies on the contingent association of the words *torrent* and *activité* in a cliché or idiomatic expression (the literal and essential qualities of "torrent" are not important to the idiom); second, the juxtaposition of the cliché *torrent d'activité* with the image of the hand in the water awakens, as an effect of contiguity, the association of *torrent* with water; and third, *torrent* helps to bring heat into the passage through its contingent association with the signifier *torride*. "Heat is therefore inscribed in the text," de Man writes, "in an underhand, secretive manner. . . . In a passage that abounds in successful and seductive metaphors and which, moreover, explicitly asserts the superior efficacy of metaphor over that of metonymy, persuasion is achieved by a figural play in which contingent figures of chance masquerade deceptively as figures of necessity" (pp. 66–67).[3] A rhetorical reading shows

[3] One might argue that the figure opposed to metonymy in the passage is not metaphor (substitution on the basis of a similarity) but synecdoche (substitution

how the text relies on the contingent relations it claims to reject: "precisely when the highest claims are being made for the unifying power of metaphor, these very images rely in fact on the deceptive use of semi-automatic grammatical patterns" (p. 16). In a similar discussion of *The Birth of Tragedy,* de Man remarks that "the deconstruction does not occur between statements, as in a logical refutation or in a dialectic, but happens instead between, on the one hand, metalinguistic statements [in the text] about the rhetorical nature of language and, on the other hand, a rhetorical praxis that puts these statements into question" (p. 98).

Close reading here involves attention to the rhetorical mode or status of important details. A thematic reading of the passage from Proust would most likely comment on the splendid fusion of cool and heat in "torrent d'activité," without enquiring into the rhetorical basis of that effect or its philosophical implications. De Man does not, of course, attempt to show that every thematic statement is undermined by its means of expression; his close readings concentrate on crucial rhetorical structures in passages with a metalinguistic function or metacritical implications: passages which comment directly on symbolic relations, textual structures, or interpretive processes, or which by their discussion of philosophical oppositions on which rhetorical structures depend (such as essence/accident, inside/outside, cause/effect) have an indirect bearing on problems of rhetoric and reading. Many of de Man's analyses are directed against metaphorical totalization: the claim to master a domain or a phenomenon through a substitution that presents its essence. Such moments can be shown to depend upon the suppression of contingent relations, just as, in the terms of de Man's earlier book, critical insights result from critical blindness. "Metaphor," he writes, "becomes a blind metonymy" (*Allegories of Reading,* p. 102). But de Man's demonstrations of

---

of part for whole): the flies evoke summer not because they resemble it but because they are deemed an essential part of it. What prevents such considerations from invalidating de Man's argument is the passage's insistent contrast between essential figures of substitution and contingent figures of substitution, a contrast generally identified, in the *Recherche* as elsewhere, with the opposition between metaphor and metonymy. That is to say, this passage assimilates a synecdoche to the model of metaphor (as the figure based on the capture of essences) that the work elaborates elsewhere.

the role of the mechanical processes of grammar, chance, and contiguity do not, he insists, yield knowledge that arrests the process of deconstruction. When we read this passage of the *Recherche* as deconstructing the hierarchical opposition of metaphor and metonymy, we must then note that "the narrator who tells us about the impossibility of metaphor is himself, or itself, a metaphor, the metaphor of a grammatical syntagm whose meaning is the denial of metaphor stated, by antiphrasis, as its priority" (p. 18). The assertion of the priority of metaphor (which proved on analysis to demonstrate its dependency on metonymy) is attributed to a narrator that is a metaphorical construct, a grammatical subject whose properties are transferred from contiguous predicates. The ultimate result, de Man concludes, with great assurance, is "a state of suspended ignorance" (p. 19).

These readings move with unusual rapidity from textual details to the most abstract categories of rhetoric or metaphysics. Their "closeness" seems to depend on their investigation of possibilities that would be neglected or eliminated by other readings, and that are neglected precisely because they would disrupt the focus or continuity of readings which their elimination makes possible. The concluding lines of Yeats's "Among School Children," for example, are generally read as a rhetorical question that asserts the impossibility of telling the dancer from the dance.

> O chestnut-tree, great-rooted blossomer,
> Are you the leaf, the blossom or the bole?
> O body swayed to music, O brightening glance,
> How can we know the dancer from the dance?

"It is equally possible," de Man writes, "to read the last line literally rather than figuratively, as asking with some urgency the question . . . how can we possibly make the distinctions that would shelter us from the error of identifying what cannot be identified? . . . The figural reading, which assumes the question to be rhetorical, is perhaps naive, whereas the literal reading leads to greater complication of theme and statement" (p. 11).

Faced with this suggestion, a critic may be inclined to ask which reading better accords with the rest of the poem, but it is precisely this move that is in question: our inclination to use notions of unity and thematic coherence to exclude possibilities that are manifestly awakened by the language and that pose a problem. If a reader heard "bowl" in "bole," that might not engage with the interpretation that was developing, but the literal reading of Yeats's concluding question cannot be dismissed as irrelevant. "The two readings have to engage each other in direct confrontation," de Man notes, "for the one reading is precisely the error denounced by the other and has to be undone by it . . . the authority of the meaning engendered by the grammatical structure is fully obscured by the duplicity of a figure that cries out for the differentiation that it conceals" (p. 12). The problem of the relation between the dancer and the dance, or between the chestnut tree and its manifestations, is similar to and entangled with the problem of the relation between the literal, grammatical structure and its rhetorical use. To interpret "How can we know the dancer from the dance?" as a rhetorical question is to take for granted the possibility of distinguishing accurately between the form of an utterance (the grammatical structure of the question) and the rhetorical performance of that structure here; it is to assume that we can tell the question itself from its rhetorical performance. But to read the question as a rhetorical question is precisely to assume the *impossibility* of distinguishing between an entity (the dancer) and its performance (the dance). The claim that the poem has been interpreted as making—the affirmation of fusion or continuity—is subverted by the discontinuity that must be assumed in order to infer that claim.

"Deconstruction," Derrida declares parenthetically in an interview, "is not a critical operation. The critical is its object; the deconstruction always bears, at one mement or another, on the confidence invested in the critical or critico-theoretical process, that is to say, in the act of decision, in the ultimate possibility of the decidable" ("Ja, ou le faux bond," p. 103). Decisions about meaning—necessary and inevitable—eliminate possibilities in the name of the principle of decidability. "A deconstruction," writes de Man, "always has for its target to reveal the existence of hidden articulations and fragmentations within assumedly monadic totalities" (*Allegories of Reading*, p. 249).

In the preceding chapter we identified some totalizing notions that deconstructive readings work to undo. Deconstructive literary criticism, often focused on the literature of the romantic period, has posed particular challenges to the genetic patterns of literary history and the totalizations required by the organic models that genetic narratives usually employ. Critics make sense of literature by employing historical narratives, grouping works together in sequences through which something—a genre, a mode, a theme, a particular type of understanding—can be said to develop. Thus Rousseau's *Julie, ou La Nouvelle Héloise* is assimilated to the *Confessions* and the *Rêveries du promeneur solitaire* and read as a novel of reflective inwardness, in order that it may function as the inauguration of an important novelistic type. "The historical investment in this interpretation of Rousseau is considerable, and one of the more intriguing possibilities inherent in a rereading of *Julie* is a parallel rereading of the texts assumed to belong to the genealogical line that is said to start with Rousseau. The existence of historical 'lines' may well be the first casualty of such a reading, which goes a long way to explaining why it is being resisted" (*Allegories of Reading*, p. 190).

One of the principal effects of deconstructive criticism has been to disrupt the historical scheme that contrasts romantic with post-romantic literature and sees the latter as a sophisticated or ironical demystification of the excesses and delusions of the former. Like so many historical patterns, this scheme is seductive, especially since, while providing a principle of intelligibility that seems to insure access to the literature of the past, it associates temporal progression with the advance of understanding and puts us and our literature in the position of greatest awareness and self-awareness. The strategy of many deconstructive readings has been to show that the ironic demystification supposedly distinctive of post-romantic literature is already to be found in the works of the greatest romantics— particularly Wordsworth and Rousseau—whose very force leads them to be consistently misread.[4] The critical tradition

[4]See de Man's six essays on Rousseau in *Allegories of Reading*, Ellen Burt's "Rousseau the Scribe," Frances Ferguson's *Wordsworth: Language as Counter-Spirit*, and Cynthia Chase's "Accidents of Disfiguration," as examples of this reevaluation.

has worked by transforming a difference within into a difference between, construing as distinctions between modes and periods a heterogeneity at work within texts. Within an organicist, periodizing literary history, for example, romanticism has been seen as the passage from a mimetic to a genetic or organic concept of art. If, as de Man suggests, romantic literature works to undermine the system of conceptual categories associated with organicism and geneticism, "one may well wonder what kind of historiography could do justice to the phenomenon of Romanticism, since Romanticism (itself a period concept) would then be the movement that challenges the genetic principle which necessarily underlies all historical narrative" (p. 82). Deconstructive readings characteristically undo narrative schemes by focusing instead on internal difference.

Deconstructive readings also engage the simplifications effected by decisions about referentiality. The opposition between referential and rhetorical functions of language is persistent and fundamental, always at issue in the act of reading, which requires decisions about what is referential and what is rhetorical. In novels, J. Hillis Miller argues in *Fiction and Repetition*, powerful thematic assertions of the mimetic function of language urge readers to interpret details as representations of a world, but at the same time there are other indications, which vary in kind from one novel to another, that one cannot rely on the referentiality of any particular linguistic instance. The illusions and delusions of characters, for example, are frequently presented by novels as the result of taking figures literally or of mistaking rhetorical fictions for reality. Miller analyzes *Middlemarch* in these terms as a case of "the self-defeating turning back of the novel to undermine its own grounds" by exposing the representational presumption on which it relies as an unreliable fiction ("Narrative and History," p. 462).

"To understand primarily means to determine the referential mode of a text," de Man writes, "and we tend to take for granted that this can be done. . . . As long as we can distinguish between literal and figural meaning, we can translate the figure back to its proper referent." To identify something as a figure is to assume the possibility of making it referential at another level and thus to "postulate the possibility of referential meaning as the *telos* of all language. It would be quite foolish to

assume that one can lightheartedly move away from the constraint of referential meaning" (*Allegories of Reading*, p. 201). De
Man's reading of *La Nouvelle Héloïse* explores the complexity of
this problem, showing how the novel undermines any particular determination of referentiality, and thus puts in question
the possibility of distinguishing the referential from the rhetorical, but does not by any means enable reading to dispense with
referentiality, which always reappears. The Preface, for example, debates the novel's referential status: is it a representation
of real life—a series of actual letters, for instance—or is it a
construction of fictional letters that works referentially at another level, to describe love? Though the Preface leaves the
question unresolved, readers are inclined to opt for the second
solution, treating the characters, for example, as figures for
love. But the account of love given in the Preface and in the
work, de Man argues, undercuts this referentiality. "Like 'man'
[in Rousseau's *Discours sur l'origine de l'inégalité* and *Essai sur
l'origine des langues*], 'love' is a figure that disfigures, a metaphor
that confers the illusion of proper meaning upon a suspended,
open semantic structure" (p. 198). The novel says, for example,
that "Love is a mere illusion: it fashions, so to speak, another
Universe for itself; it surrounds itself with objects that do not
exist or that have received their being from love alone; and
since it states its feelings by means of images, its language is
always figural."

"It is not only possible but necessary," de Man writes, "to
read *Julie* in this way, as putting in question the referential
possibility of 'love' and as revealing its figural status" (p. 200)
(which makes this another of Rousseau's "deconstructive narratives aimed at metaphorical seductions"). But as the work
undermines the referential status of love, treating it as a trope,
it lends an impressive pathos to desire and makes the pathos of
love and the pathos of the author's desire to represent it into a
referent. "The very pathos of the desire (regardless of whether
it is valorized positively or negatively) indicates that the presence of desire replaces the absence of identity and that, the
more the text denies the actual existence of a referent, real or
ideal, and the more fantastically fictional it becomes, the more
it becomes the representation of its own pathos" (p. 198).

In the dialogue of Rousseau's Preface, one of the interlocu-

tors seeks to arrest the deferral and reappearance of referentiality by finding "some statement in the text that establishes a
margin between text and external referent" and determines the
text's referential mode. "Don't you see," says N., "that your
epigraph gives it all away?" This decisive evidence is a quotation from Petrarch, which is itself a free adaptation of the
Bible, and whose mode is as problematic as any question it is
used to resolve. It can be employed to establish intelligibility
but possesses no special authority. De Man concludes:

> The innumerable writings that dominate our lives are made intel-
> ligible by a preordained agreement as to their referential author-
> ity; this agreement however is merely contractual, never constitu-
> tive. It can be broken at all times and every piece of writing can be
> questioned as to its rhetorical mode, just as *Julie* is being ques-
> tioned in the Preface. Whenever this happens, what originally ap-
> peared to be a document or an instrument becomes a text and, as
> a consequence, its readability is put in question. The questioning
> points back to earlier texts and engenders, in its turn, other texts
> which claim (and fail) to close off the textual field. For each of
> these statements can in its turn become a text, just as the citation
> from Petrarch or Rousseau's assertion that the letters were "col-
> lected and published" by him can be made into texts—not by
> simply claiming that they are lies whose opposites could be true,
> but by revealing their dependence on a referential agreement that
> uncritically took their truth or falsehood for granted. [Pp. 204–5]

The contrast is not between believing or denying something a
text says but between granting this moment a referential function, so that it can be true or false, and treating it as figure, so
that the inevitable moment of referentiality is postponed.

Finally, deconstructive criticism attends to structures that resist a text's unifying narrative scheme. This is the project of
many of J. Hillis Miller's essays: after describing novels' reliance
on narrative "lines" that connect origins and ends by revealing
retrospectively a law that ties all together in a unified sequence,
Miller goes on to explore the different ways in which novels
adumbrate contrary narrative logics or expose their organizing
figures as unwarranted impositions.[5] We might take as our ex-

---

[5]See "Ariadne's Thread: Repetition and the Narrative Line." A collection of
Miller's essays on this topic is scheduled for publication as *Ariadne's Thread*.

ample, however, John Brenkman's "Narcissus in the Text," an analysis of the disruption of narrative schemes in the Narcissus story of Ovid's *Metamorphoses*. Ovid first presents a beautiful and proud Narcissus, then tells how the nymph Echo was restricted to echoing other people's words—a punishment imposed by Juno. Echo is spurned by Narcissus and her body wastes away, leaving only her consciousness and voice; but Narcissus meets his downfall when he falls in love with his own reflection. Realizing the impossibility of his desire, "he laid down his weary head and death closed the eyes which so admired their owner's beauty."

We think of a successful literary form as a synthesis of *mythos*, *dianoia*, and *ethos*; thus critical interpretation seeks a unified totality in which plot, character, and meaning inform one another. "It is clear," Brenkman writes,

> that describing the narrative organization (*mythos*) and its thematic unity (*dianoia*) will entail specifying the relation between Echo and Narcissus. Taken separately, their stories are related to one another through a displaced parallelism—a parallelism in that each character is pushed toward death when desire is not reciprocated by another, a displaced parallelism in that for Echo the other is another like herself, while for Narcissus the other is his mirror image. In both instances sexual union fails to occur, first because Narcissus withholds it and then because it is impossible. Their stories intersect in a way that gives meaning to this difference. Narcissus's imaginary capture is presented as the "punishment" for his refusal to reciprocate the desire of others, and his encounter with Echo is obviously the narrative's most developed example of such a refusal. In short, the refusal to reciprocate desire is answered by the impossibility of having desire reciprocated. [P. 297]

The narrative is quite explicit in designating Narcissus's fate as a structurally appropriate punishment. After interpreting the echoes of his own voice as expression of Echo's sexual desire, he rejects her. "Thereafter someone who had been shunned, raising his hands to heaven, said, 'So may he himself love and

---

Meanwhile, *Fiction and Repetition* analyzes seven English novels as unravelings of their own continuities.

not possess what is loved!' Nemesis agreed with his just prayers. There was a pool. . . ."

The task of interpretation is to understand the displaced parallelism that the narrative establishes between Echo and Narcissus. There are two punishments, Echo's and Narcissus's, two forms of repetition, the vocal repetition of Echo's speech and the visual repetition of Narcissus's reflection; two delusions, Narcissus's mistaking the echoes of his own voice for Echo's voice and his mistaking of his own reflection for another body; and two representations of death, the death of Echo's body, which leaves behind voice and consciousness, and the death of Narcissus, which removes him to the underworld.

How does the narrative structure exploit the differences in these parallels, and what significance does it assign them? Consider first the case of Echo. In condemning Echo to repetition, Juno's punishment might have destroyed the relation between self and language, made Echo unable to speak her desires, and made her wholly unintelligible as a character. By devising a set of utterances such that in echoing them Echo does in fact express her desires, Ovid's narrative intervenes to restore the relation between language and self. (For example, when Narcissus cries "May I die first before my abundance is yours!" Echo repeats the final words, *sit tibi copia nostri*, "let my abundance be yours!") "We can say," writes Brenkman, "that the story of Echo emerges within the larger narrative as the drama of the self's identity and integrity restored. What could have been the mere play of significations left unattached to a speaker, a character, a consciousness, becomes the other side of an actual dialogue between autonomous speakers, between two equally realized characters" (p. 301).

Though Echo's "voice" is only an empty, echoing repetition of Narcissus's words, which he mistakes for another voice, it is crucial to the thematic and structural unity of the narrative to suppress the fact of delusion and empty repetition by telling us that Echo's echoes *do* express her desire, thus restoring her voice, selfhood, and intelligibility. It is crucial, for if Narcissus's fate is to be an appropriate punishment, Echo must be a character who has expressed her desire and been rejected.

The suppression of the threat to selfhood posed by mere repetition depends on the contrast between the types of repetition involved in the two punishments. In Echo's case, where voice repeats voice, the narrative can treat the second voice as independent (as of the same status as the first) and present the vocal repetition as a dialogue of independent subjects. When Narcissus's image is repeated in the pool, however, "it is by means of a delusion that the other appears as another like the self . . . the reflected image and what it reflects are divided by an absolute difference." Echo's repetition is *vox* like the *vox* it repeats, while in Narcissus's case "the original is *corpus*, its reflection is but *umbra* or *imago* [Ovid's terms]. The other is not another like the self but the other of the self" (p. 306). The opposition between speech and visual reproduction, well established by a tradition that Brenkman succinctly outlines, is essential to the story's structural and thematic unity. "It regulates the narrative system and seals the unity of *mythos, dianoia, ethos*. Every aspect of the narrative depends on the possibility of the echo becoming speech: Echo's stability as a character or consciousness; the determination of each element of the *dianoia*—self and other, justice and the law, sexuality, death; the meaning of Narcissus's imaginary capture; and the hierarchy voice-consciousness/body/reflection" (p. 308).

The decisive narrative intervention that makes Echo's echoes the expression of her thoughts suppresses, as we have said, the empty repetition of signifiers and transforms Narcissus's delusion into correct understanding.

> These suppressions are integral to the narrative and thematic system that prepares for Narcissus's encounter at the pool by *designating* it as a punishment. That designation serves to prescribe the episode's meaning—that is, to orient its multiple significations toward a meaning that will remain consistent with the thematic constructs of the narrative. Does that gesture too entail a suppression designed to secure the stability and values of the narrative system? . . . If the Narcissus scene produces significations that the narrative system must suppress, they can be triggered only if we actively ignore the designation and the prescription which orient that scene. [P. 310]

If we do actively ignore the orienting designation, "what we do read is a text that exceeds the limits prescribed for it by the overt thematic system of the narrative."

There are two aspects to this further reading: the elaboration of what must be suppressed in order for the text to achieve its narrative and thematic unity, and the investigation of how these secondary or marginal elements disrupt the hierarchy on which the thematic structure depends by reinscribing the drama in displaced terms. "In designating the Narcissus scene as a punishment, the narrative would restrict it to being a secondary or even false drama of the self, a drama of mere entrapment, futility, and death" (pp. 316–17). But when we look at what is presented as the moment of recognition, we find that Narcissus recognizes the reflection as an image of himself because he sees the movement of its lips but does not hear speech: Narcissus says, "you return words that are not reaching my ears. I am that one."

> "*Iste ego sum*"—marking the moment in which Narcissus not only recognizes the image as image but also *recognizes himself* (as image), opening the way to the fulfillment of Tiresias' prophecy that he would live to an old age "si *se* non *noverit*" ["if he does not know himself"]—that articulation entangles the self with the other and with the spatial. This entanglement is here irreducible since self-recognition does not occur except in relation to the other and to the spatial.
>
> It is precisely this moment in Narcissus's drama of the self that the metaphysical description of the self must exclude. [P. 316]

However, Ovid's text not only tells us that the self is known as other in a mirror stage but also presents this cognition as depending on the silent, spatial, visible repetition of the voice. "Grouped around the reflected image is an entire cluster of predicates that have traditionally been assigned to writing. . . . As the non-living representation of the voice, writing installs a relation to death within the processes of language" (p. 317). Thus, "the drama of Narcissus—if deprived of its designation as a punishment, as the ironic reenactment of a crime that abolishes itself, and read as a drama of the self—puts the self in primordial relation to its other, to spatiality, to death, to 'writing'" (p. 320). The other that Narcissus discovers "is a nonsubject that affects the self, a nonsubject without which the self could not appear to itself or recognize itself" (p. 321). This account of the self, which the narrative and thematic structure suppresses in determining the meaning of the final episode, is not simply an interesting complication that inhabits the margins of the text; it reactivates the suppressed elements of the earlier episode and shows that for Echo too, *Iste ego sum*: the self is constituted by a purely mechanical repetition (here, of sound) in which Echo knows or recognizes herself.

Brenkman explores further consequences—moments of the narrative that are reinscribed with a different force by this transgression of the narrative and thematic structure. His reading shows the text deconstructing the model of dialogue which the narrative promotes, a model "which would protect the identity of the self and the primacy of voice"; but the result is not a new unified reading or an alternative unity. Brenkman writes, "the Narcissus episode ruptures the self-enclosure of the narrative system—*mythos, dianoia, ethos*—which then becomes, not the formal unity that masters all the significations of the text, but the limit perpetually transgressed by them" (p. 326).

This reading confirms what we have seen earlier: the "closeness" of deconstructive readings lies not in word-by-word or line-by-line commentary but in attention to what resists other modes of understanding. We find, for example, an emphasis on the literal formulations employed at points in a text where unifying understanding encourages paraphrase or figurative interpretation. De Man takes literally the question that concludes "Among School Children"; Brenkman emphasizes the letter of Narcissus's exclamation: *Iste ego sum*, rather than "That's not another person" or "That is my reflection," both of which would suffice for the unifying thematic interpretation. Ovid's literal formulation, irrelevant to the interpretation the work seems to encourage, is exploited by deconstructive criticism because it engages with the hierarchical oppositions on which the unifying understanding depends. To calculate the nature and consequences of that engagement, the critic must bring out the philosophical oppositions on which the work relies, and the exegetical labor this involves will vary considerably. As it happens, *vox* is prominent in Ovid's text, but the hierarchies in which it figures and the stakes of those hierarchies are brought out by following various strands of the text and drawing upon the philosophical tradition. (Brenkman provides a succinct account of relevant moments in Kant, Husserl, Heidegger, and Derrida.)

In having Narcissus punished for self-love, the story of Narcissus presupposes the self, but, as Brenkman shows, it identifies the self as a tropological construct, a substitutive denomination based on resemblance: *Iste ego sum*. Ovid's text would thus be what de Man calls a "parable of denomination" or tropological narrative (*Allegories of Reading*, p. 188). "The paradigm for all texts consists of a figure (or a system of figures) and its deconstruction." "Primary deconstructive narratives centered on figures, and ultimately always on metaphor," are tropological narratives which tell the story of denomination and its undoing (p. 205). The passage from Proust analyzed earlier is a story of metaphor and its subversion. *Billy Budd* uses Billy's blow to narrate the deconstruction of a logic of signification. The story of Narcissus portrays self-recognition as a deluded denomination. "A narrative," writes de Man, "endlessly tells the story of its own denominational aberration" (p. 162).

Such deconstructive narratives seem "to reach a truth, albeit by the negative road of exposing an error, a false pretense. . . . We seem to end up in a mood of negative assurance that is highly productive of critical discourse" (p. 16). In fact, however, this model of a figure and its deconstruction "cannot be closed off by a final reading" and "engenders, in its turn, a supplementary figural superposition which narrates the unreadability of the prior narration." Such narratives to the second degree are allegories of reading—in fact, allegories of unreadability. "Allegorical narratives tell the story of the failure to read, whereas tropological narratives, such as [Rousseau's] *Second Discourse*, tell the story of the failure to denominate" (p. 205). Primary deconstructive narratives cannot be closed off at a point of negative assurance as the exposure of a trope because, de Man suggests in remarks on Proust and on *Julie* cited above, the story of the deconstruction—the deconstruction of metaphor or of "love"—is produced by the work's narrator, and this narrator is the metaphorical product of a grammatical system. The story unmasking a tropological construct thus depends on a trope, leaving not negative assurance but unwarrantable involvement or, as de Man calls it, perhaps less happily, "suspended ignorance" before an allegory of unreadability.

De Man claims that the move from the deconstruction of figure to allegories of reading is inherent in the logic of figures but that some texts, such as Rousseau's, actively and brilliantly provide allegories of their unreadability. *Julie* is a good example. Halfway through the book, Julie writes a decisive letter to Saint-Preux rejecting love and adumbrating the deconstruction of love as a figure, a mystified exchange of properties between inside and outside, body and soul, self and other. The first half of the narrative has rung the changes on possible substitutions within a system of specular oppositions, and Julie announces that all these substitutions were grounded on an aberration now past. She writes, for example, "I thought I recognized in your face the traces of a soul which was necessary to my own. It seemed to me my senses acted only as the organs of nobler sentiments, and I loved you, not so much for what I thought I saw in you as for what I felt in myself." This language of exalted sentiment offers in fact a precise analysis of the figural logic of love, elucidates the process of substitution on which the story has so far depended, and thematizes the work's deconstructive unmasking of a figure.

The narrative also draws conclusions from this discovery of aberration. "In the place of 'love,' based on the resemblances and substitutions of body and soul or self and other, appears the contractual agreement of marriage, set up as a defense against the passions and as the basis of social and political order" (p. 216). But, as de Man also argues in his reading of Proust, the lucidity of the deconstruction of figure produces greater problems. "At the moment when Julie acquires a maximum of insight, the control over the rhetoric of her own discourse is lost, for us as well as for her" (p. 216).

The result is an unreadability that emerges in several ways: thematically for characters, linguistically and allegorically for readers and "authors." First, there is Julie's inability to understand her own deconstruction. She immediately begins to repeat the same deluded figural involvement she has so lucidly exposed, this time substituting God for Saint-Preux. "Julie's language at once repeats the notions she has just denounced as errors. . . . she is unable to 'read' her own text, unable to recognize how its rhetorical mode relates to its meaning" (p. 217). Second, there is an insistent ethical discourse that readers and critics have found hard to read: the moralizing tone of portions of *Julie* and R's lengthy discussion in the second Preface of the good his book will do readers are indications of the allegory of reading. "Allegories are always ethical," de Man writes. "The passage to an ethical tonality does not result from a transcendental imperative but is the referential (and therefore unreliable) version of a linguistic confusion," the inability to read and calculate the force of a deconstructive narrative (p. 206). Third, R's claim in the Preface not to know whether he wrote the work or not allegorizes, de Man claims, "the rigorous gesture . . . by which the writer severs himself from the intelligibility of his own text" (p. 207). "R's statement of helplessness before the opacity of his own text is similar to Julie's relapse into metaphorical models of interpretation at her moments of insight" (p. 217n). The aspects of *Julie* that readers have often found tediously unreadable function in an allegory of· unreadability, a combination of epistemological refinement and utilitarian naiveté that is itself hard to read and results from characters' and author's inability to read their own discourses.

One might say, more generally and more crudely, that works that turn boring and sentimental or moralistic in their second halves, such as *Julie, Either/Or,* or *Daniel Deronda,* and seem to regress from the insights they have attained, are allegories of reading which, through ultimately incoherent ethical moves, display the inability of deconstructive narratives to produce settled knowledge. "Deconstructions of figural texts engender lucid narratives which produce, in their turn and as it were within their own texture, a darkness more redoubtable than the error they dispel" (p. 217). The problem, it seems, is "that a totally enlightened language . . . is unable to control the recurrence, in its readers as well as in itself, of the errors it exposes" (p. 219n).

My account of de Man's criticism, like all accounts of deconstruction, is misleading, not because it misses some *je ne sais quoi* of deconstructive criticism or heretically commits paraphrase of complex writings but because the logic of summary and exposition leads one to focus on conclusions, points of arrival—and thus on self-subversion, or aporia, or suspended ignorance—as if they were the payoff. Since deconstruction treats any position, theme, origin, or end as a construction and analyzes the discursive forces that produce it, deconstructive writings will try to put in question anything that might seem a positive conclusion and will try to make their own stopping points distinctively divided, paradoxical, arbitrary, or indeterminate. This is to say that these stopping points are not the payoff, though they may be emphasized by a summary exposition, whose logic leads one to reconstruct a reading *in view of* its end. The achievements of deconstructive criticism, as most appreciative readers have seen, lie in the delineation of the logic of texts rather than in the postures with which or in which critical essays conclude.

It is easy to take critical conclusions as statements of the meaning of a work when, as in the examples so far considered, the essay addresses a particular work, drawing occasionally on theoretical discourses to identify the stakes of certain hierarchical oppositions, but exploring how, in a particular text, elements that a unifying understanding has repressed work to undo the structures to which they seem marginal. But deconstructive readings can be conducted in an intertextual space, and there it becomes clearer that the goal is not to reveal the meaning of a particular work but to explore forces and structures that recur in reading and writing.

Thus deconstructive criticism can analyze one work as a reading of another—in Derrida's words, as "a machine with multiple reading heads for other texts" ("Living On," p. 107)— pursuing the logic of a signifier or signifying complex as it operates through a number of works or using the structures of one work to reveal a radical energy in apparently stultifying passages of another. "We would suggest," writes Jeffrey Mehlman in *Revolution and Repetition*, "that a reading of a text be valued above all in terms of its capacity to 'read' other texts, to liberate energies otherwise *contained* elsewhere. Moreover, to the extent that a reading is radical, the quality of that energy should be determinable as a multiplicity of entirely *local* surprises" (p. 69). In an analysis that he calls "resolutely and perversely superficial" (p. 117), Mehlman plays surface against surface to produce a convergence of the revolutionary Marx and the reactionary Hugo in their writings on revolution. Elements such as *tocsin* (warning bell) and its homophones and the imagery of moles and subterranean tunnels establish connections between the two discourses that prove surprisingly productive in awakening or identifying comparable logics, by which the fundamental oppositions and the movement of dialectical synthesis in each work are subverted. The application of these surfaces to one another releases a bizarre yet comparable affirmation of heterogeneity from each of two works that seem resolutely devoted to totalization.

Reading Marx with Kant as Mehlman reads Marx with Hugo, Richard Klein uses Marx's analysis of gold and of "equivalent form" to discover that the most prominent moment of bad taste in Kant's aesthetic theory, the sycophantic celebration of the sublime beauty of a poem by Frederick the Great, in which the king compares himself to the sun, has the same structure as the "sublime infinity of equivalent form" in Marx, and thus is not an unfortunate lapse to be disregarded but the key to the economy that aesthetics presupposes ("Kant's Sunshine"). Shoshana Felman's *Le Scandale du corps parlant: Don Juan avec Austin ou la séduction en deux langues* sets up a complex interplay of texts, reading Molière's *Don Juan* as a more perspicacious theory of speech acts than J. L. Austin's and exposing Austin as an archseducer. But if Austin seduces, Lacan captivates, as Felman finds Austin saying "à peu près la même chose" as Lacan and inscribing the projects his followers attempt to complete within a general economy that prevents their completion.

Addressing a different sort of problem by studying closely related works whose relations have been reductively defined, Barbara Johnson reads Baudelaire's prose poems against their verse equivalents. Her *Défigurations du langage poétique* investigates how the prose poems internalize and problematize the supposed differences between prose and poetry. The "code struggle" between verse and prose is staged within the prose poems themselves in a series of complex movements that she expertly traces.

But rather than summarize such discussions one might consider a different sort of essay, remarkable for its tact—no declarations that this deconstructs that—and for its success in including in the textual series some fascinating biographical material and a network of human relations. Neil Hertz's intertextual reading of "Freud and the Sandman" takes as its point of departure the section of "The Uncanny" where Freud analyzes Hoffmann's novella, linking its literary power to the repetition compulsion he has recently posited and thus establishing a relation between the sorts of parallelisms and repetitions commonly at work in literary compositions and a powerful, mobile psychic force. Hertz's materials for exploring the conjunction of the literary and the psychological include Hoffmann's novella, which becomes an agent of illumination as well as an object of study, Freud's essay, the metapsychological account of the repetition compulsion in *Beyond the Pleasure Principle*, and the biographical evidence that tells the story of Freud's relations with his disciple Victor Tausk and two women: first, Freud's admirer and Tausk's sometime lover, Lou Andreas-Salomé, and then Tausk's analyst and Freud's analysand, Helene Deutsch.

The opening paragraph of Freud's essay identifies the subject of the uncanny as a remote province of aesthetics, of the sort that a psychoanalyst may on rare occasions feel impelled to investigate. Since Hoffmann is the "unrivalled master of the uncanny in literature," his stories offer the material for a psychoanalytic investigation of the basis of certain literary effects. Freud's reading focuses on a pattern of repetition in which a father-figure (the Sandman/Coppelius/Coppola) blocks Nathanael's attempts at love (with Klara and Olympia). Nathanael's sense that he is "the horrible plaything of the dark powers," and the reader's sense of the uncanny, are identified as effects of the veiled but insistent castration complex. "The feeling of something uncanny," Freud writes, "is directly attached to the figure of the Sand-Man, that is, to the idea of being robbed of one's eyes"; and elements of repetition that otherwise seem "arbitrary and meaningless" become intelligible as soon as we connect the Sandman with "the dreaded father at whose hands castration is expected" ("The Uncanny," vol. 17, pp. 230, 232).

The writing of "The Uncanny" is itself entangled with the problem of repetition. In May 1919, Freud reports, he returned to and rewrote an earlier draft, and he is thought to have done so as a result of the new understanding of the repetition compulsion he gained in March or April of 1919 while working on a draft of *Beyond the Pleasure Principle*. Moreover, Freud's identification in "The Sandman" of a repeated triangle based on castration anxiety (Coppelius/Nathanael/Klara and Coppola/Nathanael/Olympia) suggests a tantalizing parallel to a triangular repetition that emerges in Freud's own relations to his disciple Tausk, where there seem to be powerful feelings of oedipal rivalry at work. In the first triangle (Freud/Tausk/ Salomé), Salomé and Freud had long talks about Tausk's feeling of rivalry and Freud's uneasiness about originality and discipleship. In the second (Freud/Tausk/Deutsch), Freud refused to take Tausk for a training analysis (lest Tausk imagine that the ideas he had picked up in his sessions with Freud were his own) and sent him to Helene Deutsch, who was herself in analysis with Freud. Tausk talked about Freud in his sessions with Deutsch and Deutsch talked about Tausk in her sessions with Freud, until Freud demanded that she break off Tausk's analysis. Three months later, on the eve of his marriage, Tausk killed himself, leaving a note for Freud full of expressions of respect and gratitude.

Three points which tempt one to superimpose these triangles are, first, the combination of Freud's anxiety about originality and plagiarism with his effective intervention in Tausk's relations with women; second, the "coincidence" whereby Freud, as he put it, "stumbled upon" a new theory of the death instinct just at the time of Tausk's suicide; and third, the fact that "Freud's removing himself from a triangular relation with Tausk and Deutsch coincides with his beginning work on the first draft of *Beyond the Pleasure Principle*, that is, on the text in which he first formulates a puzzling theory of repetition" ("Freud and the Sandman," pp. 316–17). Freud then turns back to his work on the uncanny and rewrites it, proposing "the discovery that whatever reminds us of this inner repetition-compulsion is perceived as uncanny" and citing, as an instance of this sort of compulsion, the sequence of triangular relations in "The Sandman." Here, Hertz continues, "one may begin to feel the pull of the interpreter's temptation": can we superimpose these two series of triangles?

> And if we think we can—or wish we could—what then? Can we make a story out of it? Might we not feel "most strongly compelled" to do so [as the narrator of "The Sandman" says of his impulsion to tell Nathanael's story], to arrange these elements in temporal and causal sequences? For example, could we say that the theory of repetition Freud worked out in March 1919 followed close upon—was a consequence of—his realization that he was once again caught in a certain relationship to Tausk? Could we add that Freud was bound to perceive that relation as un-

canny—not quite literary but no longer quite real, either, the workings of the compulsion glimpsed "through" an awareness of some-
thing-being-repeated? [P. 317]

Hertz's formulation alludes to Freud's claim that the uncanny
results not from being reminded of whatever it is that is being
repeated but from glimpsing or being reminded of this repetition compulsion, which would be most likely to happen in cases
where whatever is repeated appears particularly gratuitous or
excessive, the result of no cause but a bizarre manifestation of
repetition itself, as if for the sake of literary or rhetorical effect.
Part of the uncanniness of the case before us—the relations of
repetition between the structures of the novella, the processes
and conclusions of Freud's writing, and the patterns of his
relations with others—may come from the fact that it feels
like a literary pattern that would be violated by a quest for a
psychological cause, for an original of which these repetitions
were repetitions. To the degree that this pattern still solicits us
and still resists solution, Hertz writes, "we are kept in a state
somewhere between 'emotional seriousness' and literary fore-
pleasure, conscious of vacillating between literature and 'non-
fiction,' our sense of repetition-at-work colored in with the lurid
shades of aggression, madness, and violent death" (pp. 317–18).

The interpreter's temptation, in such situations, is to master
these effects of repetition by casting them into a story, determining origins and causes, and giving it dramatic, significant
coloring. Thus Freud had spoken of Tausk making an "uncanny" impression on him; for us to define and explain this as,
specifically, a fear of plagiarism—a fear that Tausk would steal
and repeat his ideas—is to focus and control repetition with a
lurid tale. One might expect, then, that an interpreter of the
uncanny in "The Sandman," such as Freud, would also find a
way of controlling repetitions that through their rhetoricity
provide glimpses of repetition itself.

What Hertz shows, in fact, is that Freud's neglect of the
narrator and narrative frame in his reading of "The Sandman"
is a significant evasion, for the self-conscious acrobatics of the
narrator at the beginning of the story establish a puzzling parallelism between "the forces driving Nathanael and whatever is
impelling the narrator" to try to repeat or represent the story.

264

The activities of the characters and of the narrator, including those of Nathanael when he tries to write about or represent his condition, are linked by a series of images involving the transmission of energy. "As a result of Hoffmann's manipulations," Hertz writes, "a reader is made to feel, confusedly, that Nathanael's life, his writings, the narrator's storytelling, Hoffmann's writing, and the reader's own fascinated acquiescence in it, are all impelled by the same energy, and impelled precisely, to represent that energy, to color in its barely discerned outlines" (pp. 309–10). The story, in short, presents a tantalizing range of repetitions, situating Nathanael's plight in the context of a generalized repetition; but that which is repeated here, and which thus represents or colors in repetition, is precisely the impulse to represent energy, to color in its outlines. In turning aside from the "literary" repetitions within the work to concentrate on repetitions within Nathanael's story—repetitions that he ascribes to the castration complex—Freud is following a pattern repeated in the story: representing energy, coloring it in a lurid way (as fear of castration). Avoiding the most puzzling and evasive repetition—which may provide glimpses of repetition itself—and adducing fear of castration to lend a powerful emotional coloring to the repetition he analyzes, Freud focuses and circumscribes repetition, thus "domesticating the story precisely by emphasizing its dark, daemonic side" (p. 313).

In each of these cases we encounter the notion of *coloring*—that which lends visibility, definiteness, or intensity to the indefinite, much as figurative language is said to color, make visible, and intensify concepts that are difficult to grasp.[6] Freud notes, for example, that the fundamental drives he posits, such as the death instinct, are visible only when "tinged or colored" by sexuality. Similarly, what is repeated works to color in and make visible (and give affective coloring to) the repetition compulsion. Freud also identifies his theoretical categories, such as the notion of the repetition compulsion itself, as figurative language which makes visible what it names. Apologizing in *Beyond*

[6]Readers may deem my stress on coloring an attempt to make Hertz's admirable essay my own by signing its most decisive moments. I will doubtless do nothing to dispel this belief by reporting that it took me an extraordinarily long time to discover that coloring was in fact the key to Hertz's subtle and elusive argument.

the Pleasure Principle for "being obliged to operate with the scientific terms, that is to say with the figurative language peculiar to psychology," he notes that "we could not otherwise describe the processes in question at all, and indeed we could not have become aware of them" (vol. 18, p. 60). The most striking reference to coloring—conferring visibility, intensity, and definiteness—comes in the conclusion of Freud's analysis of "The Sandman." We may try to deny that fears about loss of an eye are fears about castration, Freud writes, but rational argument about the value of sight does not account for the substitutive relation between the eye and the penis in dreams and myths; "nor can it dispel the impression that the threat of being castrated in especial excites a particularly violent and obscure emotion, and that this emotion is what first gives the idea of losing other organs its intense coloring" (vol. 17, p. 231). Just as fear of castration provides intense coloring, so the invocation of castration provides intense coloring and drama for a story of repetition.

It seems that in the different sorts of material Hertz has assembled we have a series of colorings that represent or give definiteness and intensity to forces that might otherwise be indefinite, or at least less intense and graspable. Elsewhere, Hertz has written of the way in which, when confronted with proliferation of any sort, we are tempted to dramatize and exacerbate our predicament so as to produce a moment of blockage—what Kant in his account of the mathematical sublime calls "a momentary checking of the vital powers"—so that proliferation or repetition or an indefinite sequence is resolved into an obstacle that produces something like a one-to-one confrontation—a confrontation that assures the identity and integrity of the self that experiences blockage. Indefiniteness, proliferation, repetition, become less threatening if they are concentrated into a threatening adversary or powerful force, such as the castrating father; for this concentration makes possible a specular confrontation which, even though it bring terror or defeat, confirms the status of the self that repetition and proliferation threatened. "The goal in each case," Hertz writes, "is the oedipal moment. . . . when an indefinite and disarrayed sequence is resolved (at whatever sacrifice) into a one-to-one confrontation, when numerical excess is converted into that supererogatory identification with the blocking agent that is the guarantor of the self's integrity as an agent. . . . A passage to the limit may seem lurid, but it has its ethical and metaphysical uses" ("The Notion of Blockage in the Literature of the Sublime," p. 76). The demonic or the oedipal—the coloring of castration, for example—can in fact be reassuring through its focusing and domesticating (bringing back to the father) of repetition that otherwise might seem indefinite, rhetorical, uncanny, gratuitous. For example, Freud's interpretation of Tausk's uncanniness as a threat of plagiarism, when taken with other passages where Freud claims or modestly disclaims originality, suggests

> that more fundamental "doubts" and "uncertainties"—doubts about the grasp any figurative language has on first principles, especially when the first principles include a principle of repetition—may be at work generating the anxiety that is then acted out in the register of literary priority. The specificity of that range of wishes and fears—the wish to be original, the fear of plagiarizing or of being plagiarized—would act to structure and render more manageable, in however melodramatic a fashion, the more indeterminate affect associated with repetition, marking or coloring it, conferring "visibility" on the forces of repetition and at the same time disguising the activity of those forces from the subject himself. ["Freud and the Sandman," p. 320]

In the case of the repetitions linking Freud's relations with Tausk, his writings, and his reading of "The Sandman," we would be domesticating the curiously threatening, quasi-literary character of these patterns if we were to make them into a story of a deadly oedipal rivalry, much as Freud sets aside the literary repetitions of "The Sandman" to attribute its effect to castration anxiety. The more intense the coloring of these dramas, the more successfully they avoid the problem of repetition, whose uncanniness may make itself felt better in less motivated, more "rhetorical" moments: what seems "merely" literary may bring one in touch with repetition more profoundly. But what is most wishful in the dramatic colorings of repetition, Hertz argues, is the attempt "to isolate the *question* of repetition from the question of figurative language itself" (p. 320). Freud's discussions, which treat sexuality, what is repeated, castration anxiety, and his own technical terms as coloring, suggest the impossibility of disentangling these two questions: "in trying to come to terms with the repetition-compulsion one discovers that the irreducible figurativeness of one's language is indistinguishable from the ungrounded and apparently inexplicable notion of the compulsion itself. At such moments the wish to put aside the question of figurative language might assert itself as a counterforce to one's most powerful apprehension of the compulsion to repeat, and it might take the form it does in Freud's reading of 'The Sandman,' the form of a wish to find 'no literature' there" (p. 321). Hertz reads this neglect of the literary and ultimately of the intertextual aspects of repetition (the repetition brought out by inscribing Freud's personal relations and his own acts of writing within this peculiar textual series) as a defense against or compensation for the adumbration of such relations by Freud's theory of repetition. His essay is a subtle example of the way deconstructive criticism can explore the stakes of intertextual repetition.

The final axis on which to plot versions of deconstructive criticism is the use of prior readings. De Man speaks of his followers reading previous close readings to show that they were not nearly close enough, and we have seen how deconstructive analyses undo positions or conclusions apparently asserted by a work and conveniently manifested in prior readings of it. Yet most criticism does something similar, contrasting a work with prior readings to show where they erred and seeking to correct or complete. How is deconstruction different, if it is different?

Some of the examples we have discussed suggest that the attempt to correct prior readings is a version of the general tendency to convert a difference within to a difference between: a problem within the text is transformed into a difference between the text and the critical interpretation of it. Though deconstructive analyses draw heavily upon prior readings and may diverge strikingly from those readings, they may treat these readings less as external accidents or deviations to be rejected than as manifestations or displacements of important forces within the work. Essays such as Barbara Johnson's "The Frame of Reference" suggest the infinite regress of correction and make critics more inclined to situate readings than to correct them. Derrida and de Man make considerable use of prior readings of Rousseau so as to identify inescapable strands or problems within Rousseau's writings.

Nevertheless, the way in which prior readings are situated by deconstructive essays varies considerably. J. Hillis Miller, for example, often speaks of the relation between the deconstructive reading and what he sometimes calls the "metaphysical" reading or, following M. H. Abrams, "the obvious or univocal reading," as a relation of tense coexistence. Shelley's *The Triumph of Life*, he writes, "contains within itself, jostling irreconcilably with one another, both logocentric metaphysics and nihilism. It is no accident critics have disagreed about it. The meaning of *The Triumph of Life* can never be reduced to any 'univocal' reading, neither the "obvious" one nor a single-minded deconstructionist one, if there could be such a thing, which there cannot" ("The Critic as Host," p. 226). "Great works of literature," Miller writes in another essay, "are likely to be ahead of their critics. They are there already. They have anticipated explicitly any deconstruction the critic can achieve. A critic may hope, with great effort, and with the indispensable help of the writers themselves, to raise himself to the level of linguistic sophistication where Chaucer, Spenser, Shakespeare, Milton, Wordsworth, George Eliot, Stevens, or even Williams are already. They are there already, however, necessarily in such a way that their works are open to mystified readings" ("Deconstructing the Deconstructors," p. 31). The critic's task, then, is "to identify an act of deconstruction which has always already, in each case differently, been performed by the text on itself." Prior readings and deconstructive readings·both focus on meanings and operations "thematized in the text itself in the form of metalinguistic statements" which wait there, in tense coexistence, for acts of identification that will bring them out.

In his reading of *Die Wahlverwandtschaften*, for example, Miller outlines a traditional "religio-aesthetic-metaphysical interpretation of the novel," which Goethe himself seems to have authorized, but then argues that certain "features of the text lead to an entirely different reading of it" and produce an irreducible heterogeneity, as these readings, both of which are thematized in the work, articulate "two entirely incompatible notions in our tradition" about selves and personal relations ("A 'Buchstäbliches' Reading of *The Elective Affinities*," p. 11). What he calls the "ontological reading" and the "semiotic reading" are both "woven into the text, articulated there, a black thread intertwined with the red one. The text is heterogeneous. The novel's lines of self-interpretation contradict one another. The meaning of the novel lies in the necessity of this contradiction, in the way each of these readings generates its subversive counterpart and is unable to appear alone" (p. 13). This relation of tense coexistence makes "*Die Wahlverwandtschaften* another demonstration of the self-subverting heterogeneity of each great work of Western literature. This heterogeneity of our great literary texts is one important manifestation of the equivocity of the Western tradition generally" (p. 11). Here the meaning of the work is seen as the unsynthesizable combination of prior readings and the new reading Miller offers—a combination that represents the heterogeneous combinations of our tradition.

Other deconstructive analyses situate these prior readings somewhat differently. Shoshana Felman's discussion of James's *The Turn of the Screw* undertakes to show, for example, that when critics claim to be interpreting the story, standing outside it and telling us its true meaning, they are in fact caught up in it, playing an interpretive role that is already dramatized in the story. Quarrels between critics about the story are in fact an uncanny transferential repetition of the drama of the story, so that the most powerful structures of the work emerge not in what the critics say about the work but in their repetition of or implication in the story. The reader of *The Turn of the Screw*, writes Felman, "can choose either to *believe* the governess, and thus to behave like Mrs. Grose, or *not to believe the governess*, and thus to behave precisely *like the governess*. Since it is the governess who, within the text, plays the role of the suspicious reader, occupies the *place* of the interpreter, to *suspect* that place and that position is, thereby, *to take it*. To demystify the governess is only possible on one condition: the condition of *repeating* the governess's very gesture" ("Turning the Screw of Interpretation," p. 190). Thus, for example, "it is precisely by proclaiming that the governess is mad that [Edmund] Wilson inadvertently imitates the very madness he denounces, unwittingly *participates in it*" (p. 196).

According to the psychoanalytic account of transference and countertransference, the structures of the unconscious are revealed not by the interpretive statements of the analyst's metalinguistic discourse but by the effects perceived in the roles analysts find themselves playing in their encounters with the patient's discourse. "Le transfert," says Lacan, "est la mise en acte de la réalité de l'inconscient" [Transference is the enactment of the reality of the unconscious] (*Les Quatre Concepts fondamentaux de la psychanalyse*, pp. 133, 137). The truth of the unconscious emerges in the transference and the countertransference, as the analyst gets caught up in a repetition of key structures of the patient's unconscious. If transference is a structure of repetition linking analyst and the analyzed discourse—the patient's or the text's—we have something comparable in the situation Felman describes: the interpreter replays a pattern in the text; reading is a displaced repetition of the structure it seeks to analyze. In that case, the prior readings an interpreter confronts are not errors to be discarded, nor partial truths to be complemented by contrary truths, but revealing repetitions of textual structures. The value of these readings emerges when a later critic—here Felman—transferentially anticipating a transferential relation between critic and text, reads *The Turn of the Screw* as anticipating and dramatizing the quarrels and interpretive moves of earlier critics.

Analysis of what Barbara Johnson calls "the transferential structure of all reading" has become an important aspect of deconstructive criticism. In "Melville's Fist" Johnson finds that the contrast between Billy and Claggart is also an opposition between two models of interpretation, and that the tradition of interpretations for this story is a displaced reenactment of the story. The conflicting interpretations, relying on the conflicting assumptions that produce the confrontation between Billy and Claggart, come to blows over the blow, which not only destroys Claggart and condemns Billy but also strikes the two critical positions since, as we saw, the *way* it means for each interpretation contradicts *what* it means for each interpretation. Further interpretive moves also repeat positions inscribed in the story, as when critics attempt—like Vere—to adjudicate the question of innocence or guilt or when they try to achieve a detached, ironic vision, in a replaying of the Dansker's role. The reading of this text in the context of its interpretations permits the analyst to discover certain regular effects of the sort that Johnson describes in a spectacular discussion of a nested series of readings: Derrida on Lacan on Poe. Detailing Derrida's repetition of the moves he analyzes and criticizes in Lacan, Johnson brings out what she calls "the transfer of the repetition compulsion from the original *text* to the scene of its *reading*" ("The Frame of Reference," p. 154). The transferential structure of reading, as deconstructive criticism has come to analyze it, involves a compulsion to repeat independent of the psychology of individual critics, based on a curious complicity of reading and writing.

The most complex relation to prior readings, however, emerges in the writings of Paul de Man. Readers have been struck by the way his essays turn against readings they have convincingly expounded, with phrases such as "Before yielding to this very persuasive scheme, we must . . ." (*Allegories of Reading*, p. 147). This formulation suggests that we will necessarily or inevitably yield to this scheme but that to yield is still an error. We are not dealing here, it would seem, with the tense coexistence of partial truths but with a combination of error and necessity that is difficult to describe. In de Man's earliest writings, the errors of prior readings were seen as insightful and productive. "Les Exégèses de Hölderlin par Martin Heidegger" praises the insight of Heidegger's reading, despite the fact that Heidegger got Hölderlin precisely backwards, finding in his poems a naming of Being instead of the repeated failure to capture Being. "Hölderlin says exactly the opposite of what Heidegger makes him say." But "at this level of reflection," de Man remarks, "it is difficult to distinguish between a proposition and what constitutes its opposite. To say the opposite is still to talk about the same thing, though in the opposite way, and it is already quite something in a dialogue of this order when two speakers succeed in speaking of the same thing." The great merit of Heidegger's readings of Hölderlin "is to have identified with precision the central concern of his *oeuvre*" (p. 809). What permits this insight is "the blind and violent passion with which Heidegger treats texts" (p. 817), and though de Man's essay may suggest that Heidegger's error can be dialectically reversed into truth, the solidarity of blindness and insight is clearly indicated. De Man's praise of Heidegger's "erroneous" reading is explicable only if the error is in some way necessary to the insight.

The dependency of insight on error is more extensively discussed in *Blindness and Insight*, where de Man analyzes readings by a number of critics—Lukács, Blanchot, Poulet, certain New Critics—and concludes that in each case "the insight seems . . . to have been gained from a negative movement that animates the critic's thought, an unstated principle that leads his language away from its asserted stand, perverting and dissolving his stated commitment to the point where it becomes emptied of substance, as if the very possibility of assertion had been put into question. Yet it is this negative, apparently destructive labor that led to what could legitimately be called insight" (p. 103). The stated commitment, asserted stand, or methodological principle plays a crucial role in producing the negative movement of insight that undermines it. It is because the New Critics were committed to a Coleridgian notion of organic form, with its celebration of the poem as an autonomous harmonization of contraries, that they were able to arrive at a description of literary language as inescapably ironic and ambiguous—an insight which "annihilated the premises that led up to it" (p. 104). "All these critics," de Man concludes,

seem curiously doomed to say something quite different from what they meant to say. Their critical stance—Lukács's propheticism, Poulet's belief in the power of an original *cogito*, Blanchot's claim of meta-Mallarmean impersonality—is defeated by their own critical results. A penetrating but difficult insight into the nature of literary language ensues. It seems, however, that this insight could only be gained because the critics were in the grip of this peculiar blindness: their language could grope towards a certain degree of insight only because their method remained oblivious to the perception of this insight. The insight exists only for a reader in the privileged position of being able to observe the blindness as a phenomenon in its own right—the question of his own blindness being one which he is by definition incompetent to ask—and so being able to distinguish between statement and meaning. He has to undo the explicit results of a vision that is able to move toward the light only because, being already blind, it does not have to fear the power of this light. But the vision is unable to report correctly what it has perceived in the course of its journey. To write critically about critics thus becomes a way to reflect on the paradoxical effectiveness of a blinded vision that has to be rectified by means of insights that it unwittingly provides. [Pp. 105–6]

The reference to "rectifying" the blinded vision by means of the insights it provides may seem to suggest that the superior critic—here de Man—can have the insights without the blindness, correcting error into truth, but when he extends this pattern to Derrida's reading of Rousseau, de Man makes it clear that the pattern of blindness and insight should be conceived as applying to the most careful and astute readings, even those that decisively rectify the blindness of previous readings. "Rousseau's best modern interpreter," de Man writes, "had to go out of his way *not* to understand him" (p. 135). The brilliant insights of Derrida's reading of Rousseau are made possible by his erroneous identification of Rousseau with a *period* in the history of Western thought and thus with the metaphysics of that period. "He postulates within Rousseau a metaphysics of presence which can then be shown not to operate, or to be dependent upon the implicit power of a language which disrupts it and tears it away from its foundation" (p. 119). Derrida's reading of Rousseau is, in the end, comparable to Heidegger's reading of Hölderlin: "Derrida's version of this misunderstanding comes closer than any previous version to Rousseau's actual statement because it singles out as the point of maximum blindness the area of greatest lucidity: the theory of rhetoric and its inevitable consequences" (p. 136).

There are several important features to de Man's account of prior readings. First, it is striking in its emphasis on truth and error; there is no question of trying to stand above or outside the play of truth and falsity and pluralistically allow each competing view a validity of sorts, as in Miller's account of competing positions capaciously contained within the Western tradition. Such attempts to avoid truth and falsity are misguided, "for no reading is conceivable in which the question of its truth or falsehood is not primarily involved" ("Foreword," p. xi). Where Derrida is cagey and oblique, de Man writes in a more traditional critical role, didactically asserting what he claims is true, confidently advising us of what texts truly say, while knowing, as critics have always known in their hope that it might be otherwise, that the temporality of reading and understanding makes each statement subject to rereading and exposure as error. Critics who find de Man's lordly assurance irritating and argue that his recognition of blindness should bring modesty to his own assertions have failed to understand that critical assertions will still claim to speak the truth, however hedged about they may be with qualifications and modest disclaimers.

Second, while implicitly claiming to present the insights others have reached through error, de Man identifies the structure into which his own discourse fits. As Derrida's reading of Rousseau makes it possible for de Man to use Rousseau to identify Derrida's misreadings, so de Man's account will enable later critics to use Derrida and Rousseau against de Man. This is a complicated situation that is not well understood. We are often inclined to deny that any reading has a special status authorizing it to judge another: the reading that claims to rectify a prior interpretation is only another reading. But at other times we want to claim that a particular reading does have a privileged status and can identify the successes and failures of other readings. Both these views assume an atemporal framework—a reading either is or is not in a position of logical superiority with respect to other readings. But the fact is, as we show when we are ourselves so engaged, interpretation occurs in historical situations created in part by prior readings and it works by framing or situating those readings, whose blindness and insights it may thus be able to judge. Resourceful readings frequently prove able to use the text to show where prior interpretations went wrong and thus to make claims about the limitations of their methods or the relation between their theory and their practice. As de Man notes in an introduction to Hans Robert Jauss's criticism, "the horizon of Jauss's methodology, like all methodologies, has limitations that are not accessible to its own analytical tools." In general, one should notice that the distinctions between truth and falsity, blindness and insight, or reading and misreading remain crucial, but they are not grounded in ways that might permit one definitively to establish the truth or insight of one's own reading.

Third, de Man's account of the relation between readings and prior readings enables him to continue participating in one of the traditional activities of literary criticism, that of celebrating the insights and achievements of great writings of the past. "The more ambivalent the original utterance," de Man writes, "the more uniform and universal the pattern of consistent error in the followers and commentators" (*Blindness and Insight*, p. 111). In the reading of the greatest works there is a transference of blindness from author to readers. "The existence of a particularly rich aberrant tradition in the case of the writers who can legitimately be called the most enlightened, is therefore no accident but a constitutive part of all literature, the basis, in fact, of literary history" (p. 141). The greater the text, the more it can be used to undo the unavoidable aberrations of prior readings, and in treating such works the critic is in "the most favorable of all critical positions: . . . dealing with an author as clear-sighted as language lets him be who, for that very reason, is being systematically misread; the author's own works, newly interpreted, can then be played off against the most talented of his deluded interpreters or followers" (p. 139). Nietzsche, Rousseau, Shelley, Wordsworth, Baudelaire, and Hölderlin are celebrated for the truths—albeit negative—that their writings tell.

Fourth, de Man's account represents the irreducible iterability of the critical process. Just as Julie cannot avoid repeating the tropological moves she has so lucidly denounced, so the critic skilled in detecting the blindness of prior readings (including, at times, his own prior readings) will produce similar errors in turn. Discussing in *Allegories of Reading* the traditional readings of Rousseau's political and autobiographical writings, de Man notes that "the rhetorical reading leaves these fallacies behind by accounting, at least to some degree, for their predictable occurrence" (p. 258), but such predictability extends, to some degree, to the analysis that exposes prior fallacies. "Needless to say, this new interpretation will, in its turn, be caught in its own form of blindness"—that is the argument of *Blindness and Insight* (p. 139).

But *Allegories of Reading* goes further in describing how a deconstructive reading that identifies the errors of the tradition and shows the text exposing its own founding concepts as tropological aberrations is itself put in question by the further moments in which the text adumbrates an allegory of unreadability. In this account the terms "blindness" and "insight," with their references to acts and failures of perception, no longer appear, for what is involved here are aspects of language and properties of discourse which insure that critical writings, like other texts, will end up doing what they maintain cannot be done, exceeding or falling short of what they assert by the very act of asserting it. In discussing Rousseau, de Man stresses the mechanical and inexorable processes of grammar and discursive organization in remarks that also apply to critical attempts to master Rousseau's writings. *The Social Contract*, for example, discredits *promises*, yet it promises a great deal.

> The reintroduction of the promise, despite the fact that its impossibility has been established, does not occur at the discretion of the writer. . . . The redoubtable efficacy of the text is due to the rhetorical model of which it is a version. This model is a fact of language over which Rousseau himself has no control. Just as any other reader, he is bound to misread his text as a promise of political change. The error is not within the reader; language itself dissociates the cognition from the act. *Die Sprache verspricht* (*sich*) [Language promises]; to the extent that it is necessarily misleading, language just as necessarily conveys the promise of its own truth." [Pp. 276–77]

Misreading here is a repeated result of the problematical relation between the performative and constative functioning of language.

The uncomfortable situation we have been describing, where misreading is both an error to be exposed and the unavoidable fate of reading, emerges most dramatically in the conclusion of "Shelley Disfigured," where de Man is both using the text to characterize other readings as errors and indicating the way in which his own text must inevitably figure among the objects so denounced. There is no more striking way to end our discussion of deconstructive criticism than with this passage which repeatedly includes itself in the inevitable aberrations it denounces.

De Man has been discussing the way in which our readings of romantic literature aestheticize fragments and representations of death, transforming the dead into historical and aesthetic monuments. "Such monumentalization is by no means necessarily a naive or evasive gesture, and it is certainly not a gesture that anyone can pretend to avoid making." Whether it fails or succeeds, this gesture becomes a

> challenge to understanding that always again demands to be read. And to read is to understand, to question, to know, to forget, to erase, to deface, to repeat—that is to say, the endless prosopopoeia by which the dead are made to have a face and a voice which tells the allegory of their demise and allows us to apostrophize them in our turn. No degree of knowledge can ever stop this madness, for it is the madness of words. What *would* be naive is to believe that this strategy, which is not *our* strategy as subjects, since we are its product rather than its agent, can be a source of value and has to be celebrated or denounced accordingly.
>
> Whenever this belief occurs—and it occurs all the time—it leads to a misreading that can and should be discarded, unlike the coercive "forgetting" that Shelley's poem analytically thematizes and that stands beyond good and evil. It would be of little use to enumerate and categorize the various forms and names which this belief takes on in our present critical and literary scene. It functions along monotonously predictable lines, by the historicization and the aesthetification of texts, as well as by their use, as in this essay, for the assertion of methodological claims made all the more pious by their denial of piety. Attempts to define, to understand, or to circumscribe romanticism in relation to ourselves and in relation to other literary movements are all part of this naive belief. *The Triumph of Life* warns us that nothing, whether deed, word, thought, or text, ever happens in relation, positive or negative, to anything that precedes, follows, or exists elsewhere, but only as a random event whose power, like the power of death, is due to the randomness of its occurrence. It also warns us why and how these events then have to be reintegrated in a historical and aesthetic system of recuperation that repeats itself regardless of the exposure of its fallacy. ["Shelley Disfigured," pp. 68–69]

If nothing else, passages such as this would indicate that those critics who write of "the pleasure-oriented formalism of the Yale critics" are caught up in a pattern of systematic misreading.[7] It is difficult to imagine a critic more obsessively con-

---

[7]Frank Lentricchia, *After the New Criticism*, p. 176. Lentricchia also speaks of a "new hedonism" suggested "pervasively" in the work of Hartman, Miller, and de Man, whom he believes to form a school (p. 169).

cerned with truth and knowledge, in the face of structures that would make the denial of truth and knowledge a tempting alternative. But this passage also illustrates one of the most problematical aspects of deconstructive criticism: the identification of what texts say about language, texts, articulation, order, and power as truths about language, texts, articulation, order, and power. If *The Triumph of Life* does in fact warn us that nothing ever happens in any relation to anything else, what reason have we for thinking this true? The deconstructive critic is frequently accused of treating the text being analyzed as an entirely self-referential play of forms with no cognitive, ethical, or referential value, but this might be one more illustration of the way in which, as de Man says, a truly modern writer will be "compulsively misinterpreted and oversimplified and made to say the opposite of what he actually said" (*Blindness and Insight*, p. 186). For in fact, deconstructive readings draw far-reaching lessons from the texts they study. *Allegories of Reading* reads Rousseau's texts as telling us the truth about a wide range of matters.

> What the *Discourse on Inequality* tells us, and what the classical interpretation of Rousseau has stubbornly refused to hear, is that the political destiny of man is structured like and derived from a linguistic model that exists independently of nature and independently of the subject: it coincides with the blind metaphorization called "passion," and this metaphorization is not an intentional act. . . . If society and government derive from a tension between man and his language, then they are not natural (depending on a relationship between man and things), nor ethical (depending on a relationship among men), nor theological, since language is not conceived as a transcendental principle but as the possibility of contingent error. The political thus becomes a burden for man rather than an opportunity. . . . [pp. 156–57]

Conclusions about knowledge, speech acts, guilt, and the self are presented in much the same way in other essays: as truths stated, suggested, or enacted by Rousseau's writings. And deconstructive readings are inclined to find statements not about what may happen or often happens but about what must happen. *Billy Budd* does not show us how authority *might* work; "Melville shows in *Billy Budd* that authority consists precisely in the impossibility of containing the effects of its own application" (Johnson, *The Critical Difference*, p. 108). And indeed, for Johnson *Billy Budd*'s authority extends so far that its insights are stated as necessities: "the legal order, which attempts to submit 'brute force' to 'forms, measured forms,' *can only* eliminate violence by transforming violence into the final authority. And cognition, which perhaps begins as a power play against the play of power, *can only* increase, through its own elaboration, the range of what it tries to dominate" (pp. 108–9, my italics).

In numerous cases critic and work argue well for the truths derived from the work; they sometimes explain the nature of the necessity that makes the truth hold for all language, all speech acts, all passions, all cognitions. In other cases, as in de Man's account of the warning of *The Triumph of Life*, one cannot even imagine how the critic might argue for the truth in question, such as the claim that nothing ever happens in any relation to anything that precedes, follows, or exists elsewhere; and one is led to suspect that a certain faith in the text and the truth of its most fundamental and surprising implications is the blindness that makes possible the insights of deconstructive criticism, or the methodological necessity that cannot be justified but is tolerated for the power of its results. The strategic role of this commitment to the truth of the text when exhaustively read doubtless helps to explain why American deconstructive criticism has concentrated on major authors of the canon: if such analysis requires the presumption that truth will emerge from a resourceful, high-pressured reading, one will feel less need to defend that presumption when one reads Wordsworth, Rousseau, Melville, or Mallarmé than when one reads noncanonical authors. Rumors that deconstructive criticism denigrates literature, celebrates the free associations of readers, and eliminates meaning and referentiality, seem comically aberrant when one examines a few of the many examples of deconstructive criticism. Perhaps these rumors are best understood as defenses against the claims about language and the world that these critics reveal in the works they explicate.

BIBLIOGRAPHY

Abraham, Nicolas, and Maria Torok. *Cryptonymie: Le Verbier de l'homme aux loups*. Paris: Aubier-Flammarion, 1976. On the Wolfman's multilingual signifying chains, with a preface by Derrida.

——. *L'Ecorce et le noyau*. Paris: Aubier-Flammarion, 1978. English trans. of pp. 203–26: "The Shell and the Kernel." *Diacritics*, 9:1 (1979), 16–28. Psychoanalytic essays.

Abrams, M. H. "The Deconstructive Angel." *Critical Inquiry*, 3 (1977), 425–38. A critique of deconstruction in a debate with J. Hillis Miller.

——. "How to Do Things with Texts." *Partisan Review*, 46 (1979), 566–88. On the new modes of reading by Derrida, Fish, and Bloom.

——. *The Mirror and the Lamp: Romantic Theory and the Critical Tradition*. New York: Oxford University Press, 1953.

Adams, Maurianne. "*Jane Eyre*: Woman's Estate." In *The Authority of Experience*, ed. Lee Edwards and Arlyn Diamond. Amherst: University of Massachusetts Press, 1977, pp. 137–59.

Agacinski, Sylviane. *Aparté: Conceptions et morts de Søren Kierkegaard*. Paris: Aubier-Flammarion, 1977. A Derridean analysis.

Altieri, Charles. *Act and Quality: A Theory of Literary Meaning and Humanistic Understanding*. Amherst: University of Massachusetts Press, 1981. Based on work in the philosophy of language.

——. "Wittgenstein on Consciousness and Language: A Challenge to Derridean Literary Theory." *Modern Language Notes*, 91 (1976) 1397–1423.

Arac, Jonathan, et al. *The Yale Critics: Deconstruction in America*. Minneapolis: University of Minnesota Press, forthcoming. Essays emphasizing the early work of de Man, Hartman, Miller, and Bloom.

Argyros, Alexander. "Daughters of the Desert." *Diacritics*, 10:3 (1980), 27–35. On Derrida's *Eperons*.

Austin, J. L. *How to Do Things with Words*. Cambridge: Harvard University Press, 1975.

——. *Philosophical Papers*. London: Oxford University Press, 1970.

Bahti, Timothy. "Figures of Interpretation; The Interpretation of Figures: A Reading of Wordsworth's 'Dream of the Arab.'" *Studies in Romanticism*, 18 (1979), 601–28.

Barthes, Roland. "Analyse textuelle d'un conte d'Edgar Poe." In *Sémiotique narrative et textuelle*, ed. Claude Chabrol. Paris: Larousse, 1973, pp. 29–54. English trans.: "Textual Analysis of Poe's 'Valdemar.'" In *Untying the Text*, ed. Robert Young. London: Routledge & Kegan Paul, 1981, pp. 133–61. Continues the analysis of codes begun in S/Z.

——. *Critique et vérité*. Paris: Seuil, 1966. Part II defines a structuralist poetics.

——. *Essais critiques*. Paris: Seuil, 1964. English trans.: *Critical Essays*. Evanston: Northwestern University Press, 1972.

——. *Image, Music, Text*. New York: Hill & Wang, 1977. Includes some classic essays not collected in French.

——. "Introduction à l'analyse structurale des récits." *Communications*, 8 (1966) 1–27. English trans.: "Introduction to the Structural Analysis of Narratives." In *Image, Music, Text*, pp. 74–124. A program for narratology.

——. *Le Plaisir du texte*. Paris: Seuil, 1973. English trans.: *The Pleasure of the Text*. New York: Hill & Wang, 1974. Fragments on reading, pleasure, and the text.

——. *S/Z*. Paris: Seuil, 1970. English trans.: New York: Hill and Wang, 1974. Systematic analysis of Balzac's "Sarrasine."

——. *Système de la mode*. Paris: Seuil, 1967. On the semiotic system of fashion.

——. "Texte, théorie du." *Encyclopaedia Universalis*. Paris: 1968–75. Vol. 15, pp. 1013–17.

Beauvoir, Simone de. *The Second Sex*. New York: Knopf, 1953. A classic of women's liberation and feminist criticism.

Bleich, David. *Readings and Feelings*. Urbana, Ill.: National Council of Teachers of English,1975.

——. *Subjective Criticism*. Baltimore: Johns Hopkins University Press, 1978. A critical theory stressing the value of readers' personal responses.

Bloom, Harold. *The Anxiety of Influence: A Theory of Poetry*. New York: Oxford University Press, 1973.

——. *Kabbalah and Criticism*. New York: Seabury, 1975. Brings kabbalistic categories to bear on his theory of poetic production.

——. *A Map of Misreading*. New York: Oxford University Press, 1975. Elaboration of the interpretive implications of the anxiety of influence.

——. *Wallace Stevens: The Poems of Our Climate*. Ithaca: Cornell University Press, 1977. Full deployment of Bloom's theory of poetry.

——, et al. *Deconstruction and Criticism*. New York: Seabury, 1979. Essays, mostly on Shelley, by five members of the "Yale School": Bloom, Hartman, de Man, Miller, Derrida.

Booth, Stephen. *An Essay on Shakespeare's Sonnets*. New Haven: Yale University Press, 1969. Interpretations based on a reader's line-by-line experience.

——. "On the Value of *Hamlet*." In *Literary Criticism: Idea and Act*, ed. W. K. Wimsatt. Berkeley: University of California Press, 1974, pp. 284–310. Treats the play as a series of actions upon the understanding of an audience.

Booth, Wayne. *Critical Understanding: The Powers and Limits of Pluralism*. Chicago: University of Chicago Press, 1979.

Bové, Paul. *Destructive Poetics: Heidegger and Modern American Poetry*. New York: Columbia University Press, 1980. A Heideggerian indictment of recent criticism and a reading of Whitman, Stevens, and Olson.

Brenkman, John. *Culture and Domination*. Ithaca: Cornell University Press, forthcoming. Essays on literature providing a Marxist critique of psychoanalytic interpretation and a psychoanalytic critique of Marxist interpretation.

——. "Narcissus in the Text." *Georgia Review*, 30 (1976), 293–327. A classic deconstructive reading.

Brooks, Cleanth. *A Shaping Joy: Studies in the Writer's Craft*. London: Methuen, 1971.

——. *The Well Wrought Urn*. New York: Harcourt Brace, 1947.

Brooks, Peter. "Fictions of the Wolfman: Freud and Narrative Understanding." *Diacritics*, 9:1 (1979), 72–83.

Brutting, Richard. *"Ecriture" und "Texte": Die französische Literaturtheorie "nach dem Strukturalismus."* Bonn: Bouvier Verlag Herbert Grundmann, 1976.

Burt, Ellen. "Rousseau the Scribe." *Studies in Romanticism*, 18 (1979), 629–67. Detailed analysis of the problems of autobiography.

Cain, William E. "Deconstruction in America: The Recent Literary Criticism of J. Hillis Miller." *College English*, 41 (1979), 367–82.

Carroll, David. "Freud and the Myth of Origins." *New Literary History*, 6 (1975), 511–28.

Cave, Terence. *The Cornucopian Text: Problems of Writing in the French Renaissance*. Oxford: Clarendon Press, 1979.

Charles, Michel. *Rhétorique de la lecture*. Paris: Seuil, 1977. Analyzes possible and impossible roles of the reader in various French works.

Chase, Cynthia. "The Accidents of Disfiguration: Limits to Literal and Rhetorical Reading in Book V of *The Prelude*." *Studies in Romanticism*, 18 (1979), 547–66. Problems of rhetoric and reflexivity.

——. "The Decomposition of the Elephants: Double-Reading *Daniel Deronda*." *PMLA*, 93 (1978), 215–27. A deconstructive analysis of narrative.

——. "Oedipal Textuality: Reading Freud's Reading of *Oedipus*." *Diacritics*, 9:1 (1979), 54–68.

——. "Paragon, Parergon: Baudelaire Translates Rousseau." *Diacritics*, 11:2 (1981), 42–51. Discusses intertextual incorporation.

Cixous, Hélène. "La Fiction et ses fantômes." *Poétique*, 10 (1972) 199–216. English trans. in *New Literary History*, 7 (1976), 525–48. On Freud's "Das Unheimliche."

——. "Le Rire de la Méduse." *L'Arc*, 61 (1975), 3–54. English trans.: "The Laugh of the Medusa." *Signs*, 1 (1976), 875–93. A manifesto for women's writing.

——. "Sorties." In Cixous and Catherine Clément. *La Jeune Née*. Paris: Union générale d'éditions, 1979, pp. 114–275. Critique of the opposition man/woman.

Coste, Didier. "Trois Conceptions du lecteur." *Poétique*, 43 (1980), 354–71.

Coward, Rosalind, and John Ellis. *Language and Materialism: Developments in Semiology and the Theory of the Subject*. London: Routledge & Kegan Paul, 1977. A Marxist critique and development of semiotics and psychoanalysis.

Crews, Frederick. "Reductionism and Its Discontents." *Critical Inquiry*, 1 (1975), 543–58. The problem of reductionism in psychoanalytic criticism.

Culler, Jonathan. *Barthes*. London: Fontana, and New York: Oxford University Press, 1983.

——. *Ferdinand de Saussure*. London: Fontana, 1976; New York: Penguin, 1977.

——. *Flaubert: The Uses of Uncertainty*. Ithaca: Cornell University Press, and London: Elek, 1974.

——. *The Pursuit of Signs: Semiotics, Literature, Deconstruction*. Ithaca: Cornell University Press, and London: Routledge & Kegan Paul, 1981.

——. *Structuralist Poetics: Structuralism, Linguistics, and the Study of Literature*. Ithaca: Cornell University Press, and London: Routledge & Kegan Paul, 1975.

Davis, Walter. *The Act of Interpretation: A Critique of Literary Reason*. Chicago: University of Chicago Press, 1978. A metacritical exploration of three ways of unifying Faulkner's *The Bear*.

De Man, Paul. *Allegories of Reading: Figural Language in Rousseau,*

Nietzsche, Rilke, and Proust. New Haven: Yale University Press, 1979.

——. "Autobiography as De-facement." *MLN*, 94 (1979), 919–30. On Wordsworth, epitaphs, and prosopopoeia.

——. *Blindness and Insight: Essays in the Rhetoric of Contemporary Criticism.* New York: Oxford University Press, 1971. On Derrida, Blanchot, the New Critics, and others.

——. "The Epistemology of Metaphor." *Critical Inquiry*, 5 (1978), 13–30.

——. "Les Exégèses de Hölderlin par Martin Heidegger." *Critique*, 11 (1955), 800–819.

——. "Foreword." *The Dissimulating Harmony*, by Carol Jacobs. Baltimore: John Hopkins University Press, 1978, pp. vii–xiii. A statement on critical reading.

——. "Hypogram and Inscription: Michael Riffaterre's Poetics of Reading." *Diacritics*, 11:4 (1981), 17–35.

——. "Introduction." *Studies in Romanticism*, 18 (1979), 495–99. Comments on the contributions to this issue on "The Rhetoric of Romanticism."

——. "Introduction." *Towards an Aesthetics of Reception*, by Hans Robert Jauss. Minneapolis: University of Minnesota Press, 1982. Identifies the limitations of Jauss's method.

——. "Literature and Language: A Commentary." *New Literary History*, 4 (1972), 181–92.

——. "Pascal's Allegory of Persuasion." *Allegory and Representation*, ed. Stephen Greenblatt. Baltimore: Johns Hopkins University Press, 1981, pp. 1–25.

——. "The Resistance to Literary Theory." *Yale French Studies*, 63 (1982), 3–20. A broad statement about theory and its prospects.

——. "The Rhetoric of Temporality." In *Interpretation: Theory and Practice*, ed. Charles Singleton. Baltimore: Johns Hopkins University Press, 1969, pp. 173–209. An influential essay on symbol and allegory in romanticism.

——. "Shelley Disfigured." In Bloom et al., *Deconstruction and Criticism*. New York: Seabury, 1979, pp. 39–74.

——. "Sign and Symbol in Hegel's Aesthetics." *Critical Inquiry*, 8 (1982).

Derrida, Jacques. "L'Age de Hegel." In GREPH, *Qui a peur de la philosophie?* Paris: Flammarion, 1977, pp. 73–107. Discussion of Hegel's discussion of the teaching of philosophy.

——. "L'Archéologie du frivole." Introduction to Condillac, *Essai sur l'origine de la connaissance humaine.* Paris: Galilée, 1973. Published separately by Gonthier, 1976. English trans.: *The Archeology of the Frivolous: Reading Condillac.* Pittsburgh: Duquesne University Press, 1981.

——. "Avoir l'oreille de la philosophie." In Lucette Finas, et al.,

Ecarts: Quatre essais à propos de Jacques Derrida. Paris: Fayard, 1973, pp. 301–12. A lucid general interview.

——. *La Carte postale: De Socrate à Freud et au-delà.* Paris: Flammarion, 1980. English translations: "The Purveyor of Truth," *Yale French Studies*, 52 (1975), 31–114; "Speculating—On Freud" (extracts from pp. 277–311), *Oxford Literary Review*, 3 (1978), 78–97; "Coming into One's Own" (extracts from pp. 315–57), *Psychoanalysis and the Question of the Text*, ed. Geoffrey Hartman, Baltimore: Johns Hopkins University Press, 1978, pp. 114–48. Complete English trans.: *The Post Card.* Chicago: University of Chicago Press, forthcoming. Fictional love letters discussing a range of subjects and two substantial essays on psychoanalysis.

——. "The Conflict of Faculties." In *Languages of Knowledge and of Inquiry*, ed. Michael Riffaterre. New York: Columbia University Press, 1982. On Kant's essay on the distribution of authority among university faculties.

——. *De la grammatologie.* Paris: Minuit, 1967. English trans.: *Of Grammatology.* Baltimore: Johns Hopkins University Press, 1976. Speech and writing in Saussure, Lévi-Strauss, and Rousseau.

——. *La Dissémination.* Paris, Seuil, 1972. English trans.: *Dissemination.* Chicago: University of Chicago Press, 1982. Essays on Plato, Mallarmé, and Sollers.

——. "D'un ton apocalyptique adopté naguère en philosophie." In *Les Fins de l'homme: A partir du travail de Jacques Derrida*, ed. Philippe Lacoue-Labarthe and Jean-Luc Nancy. Paris: Galilée, 1981, pp. 445–79. On Kant, tone, and problems of the mystical. This volume also contains numerous remarks by Derrida during the discussions of this colloquium.

——. "Economimesis." In S. Agacinski et al., *Mimesis des articulations.* Paris: Flammarion, 1975, pp. 55–93. English trans. in *Diacritics*, 11:2 (1981), 3–25. The economy of and economy in Kant's aesthetic theory.

——. *L'Ecriture et la différence.* Paris: Seuil, 1967. English trans.: *Writing and Difference.* Chicago: University of Chicago Press, 1978. Essays on Lévi-Strauss, Artaud, Bataille, Freud, Foucault, and others.

——. "Entre crochets." *Digraphe*, 8 (1976), 97–114. An interview.

——. *Eperons: Les styles de Nietzsche.* Venice: Corbo & Fiore, 1976. Paris: Flammarion, 1978. English trans.: *Spurs.* Chicago: University of Chicago Press, 1979. On "woman" and "style" in Nietzsche.

——. "Fors: Les mots anglés de N. Abraham et M. Torok." Preface to Abraham and Torok, *Cryptonymie: Le Verbier de l'homme aux loups.* Paris: Flammarion, 1976, pp. 7–73. English trans.: "Fors." *The Georgia Review*, 31 (1977), 64–116.

——. *Glas.* Paris: Galilée, 1974. On Hegel and Genet.

——. "Ja, ou le faux bond." *Digraphe*, 11 (1977), 84–121. An interview.

——. *Limited Inc.* Supplement to *Glyph* 2. Baltimore: Johns Hopkins University Press, 1977. English trans. in *Glyph*, 2 (1977), 162–254. A response to Searle's critique in *Glyph* 1.

——. "Living On: Border Lines." In Bloom et al., *Deconstruction and Criticism*. New York: Seabury, 1979, pp. 75–175. French version, "Survivre," unpublished. On Blanchot and Shelley.

——. "La Loi du genre." *Glyph*, 7 (1980), 176–201. English trans.: "The Law of Genre." Ibid, pp. 202–29. On Blanchot, the *récit*, and genre.

——. *Marges de la philosophie.* Paris: Minuit, 1972. English trans.: "Differance" and "Form and Meaning: A Note on the Phenomenology of Language," in Derrida, *Speech and Phenomena*, Evanston: Northwestern University Press, 1973, pp. 107–60. "Ousia and Grammè," in *Phenomenology in Perspective*, ed. F. J. Smith. The Hague: Nijhoff, 1970, pp. 54–93. "The Ends of Man," *Philosophical and Phenomenological Research*, 30 (1969), 31–57. "The Supplement of Copula," *The Georgia Review*, 30 (1976), 527–64. "White Mythology," *New Literary History*, 6 (1974), 5–74. "Signature Event Context," *Glyph*, 1 (1977), 172–97. Complete English trans.: *Margins of Philosophy*. Chicago: University of Chicago Press, forthcoming.

——. "Les Morts de Roland Barthes." *Poétique*, 47 (1981), 269–292. A tribute to Barthes, focused on *La Chambre claire*.

——. "Me—Psychoanalysis." *Diacritics*, 9:1 (1979), 4–12. French original: "Moi, la psychanalyse . . ." forthcoming in *Confrontations*, (1982). Introduction to the work of Abraham and Torok.

——. *L'Origine de la géometrie*, by Edmund Husserl. Translated with an introduction. Paris: Presses Universitaire de France, 1962. English trans.: *The Origin of Geometry*. New York: Nicolas Hays, 1977. Brighton: Harvester, 1978. A lengthy introduction, on writing in Husserl's theory of ideal objects.

——. "Où commence et comment finit un corps enseignant." In *Politiques de la philosophie*, ed. Dominique Grisoni. Paris: Grasset, 1976, pp. 55–97. On deconstruction as a struggle to transform the theory and practice of philosophical education.

——. "Pas." *Gramma*, 3/4 (1976), 111–215. On Blanchot.

——. "La Philosophie et ses classes." In GREPH, *Qui a peur de la philosophie?* Paris: Flammarion, 1977, pp. 445–50. On the problems concerning a defense of philosophy in the school system.

——. *Positions.* Paris: Minuit, 1972. English trans.: Chicago: University of Chicago Press, 1981. Three lucid interviews, the last on Marxism, psychoanalysis, and deconstruction.

——. "Le Retrait de la métaphore." *Po&sie*, 6 (1979), 103–26. English trans.: "The Retrait of Metaphor." *Enclitic*, 2:2 (1978), 5–34. A sequel to "La Mythologie blanche" in *Marges*.

——. "Scribble (pouvoir/écrire)." Introduction to W. Warburton. *L'Essai sur les hiéroglyphes*. Paris: Flammarion, 1978. English trans.: "Scribble (writing-power)." *Yale French Studies*, 58 (1979), 116–47. An introduction concerned with relations between writing and power.

——. "Signéponge." Part I in *Francis Ponge: Colloque de Cérisy*. Paris: Union générale d'éditions, 1977, pp. 115–51. Part II, *Digraphe*, 8 (1976), 17–39. On Ponge, things, and signatures.

——. "Titre (à préciser)." *Nuova Corrente*, 28 (1981), 7–32. English trans. forthcoming in *Sub-stance*.

——. *La Vérité en peinture*. Paris: Flammarion, 1978. English trans. of "Le Parergon," part II: "The Parergon." *October*, 9 (1979), 3–40. Essays on art: Kant's aesthetics, Adami, Titus-Carmel, and Van Gogh (as discussed by Heidegger and Shapiro).

——. *La Voix et le phénomène*. Paris: Presses Universitaires de France, 1967. English trans.: *Speech and Phenomena*. Evanston: Northwestern University Press, 1973. A critique of Husserl's theory of signs.

Descombes, Vincent. *L'Inconscient malgré lui*. Paris: Minuit, 1977. Constructs Lacanian psychoanalytic theory in the terms of analytical philosophy.

——. *Le Même et l'autre: Quarante-cinq ans de philosophie française*. Paris: Minuit, 1979. English trans.: *Modern French Philosophy*. London: Cambridge University Press, 1980. A brilliant account of fundamental issues in recent French philosophy.

Dinnerstein, Dorothy. *The Mermaid and the Minotaur: Sexual Arrangements and Human Malaise*. New York: Harper, 1976. The psychological effects of nurturing arrangements.

Donato, Eugenio. "'Here, Now'/'Always, Already': Incidental Remarks on Some Recent Characterizations of the Text." *Diacritics*, 6:3 (1976), 24–29. On Derrida and Edward Said.

——. "The Idioms of the *Text*: Notes on the Language of Philosophy and the Fictions of Literature." *Glyph*, 2 (1977), 1–13.

Donoghue, Denis. "Deconstructing Deconstruction." *New York Review of Books*, 12 June 1980, pp. 37–41. Review of *Deconstruction and Criticism* and *Allegories of Reading*.

——. *Ferocious Alphabets*. Boston: Little, Brown, 1981. On critics who look for "voice" and critics who look for "writing."

Douglas, Ann. *The Feminization of American Culture*. New York: Knopf, 1977.

Eagleton, Terry. *Marxism and Literary Criticism*. London: Methuen, 1976.

Eco, Umberto. *L'Opera aperta*. Milan: Bompiani, 1962. A pioneering study of the "open" work.

——. *The Role of the Reader: Explorations in the Semiotics of Texts.* Bloomington: Indiana University Press, 1979.

——. *A Theory of Semiotics.* Bloomington: Indiana University Press, 1976.

Edwards, Lee, and Arlyn Diamond. *The Authority of Experience: Essays in Feminist Criticism.* Amherst: University of Massachusetts Press, 1977.

Eisenstein, Hester, and Alice Jardine, eds. *The Future of Difference.* Boston: G. K. Hall, 1980. An excellent anthology on literary, linguistic, and theoretical aspects of sexual difference.

Ellmann, Mary. *Thinking about Women.* New York: Harcourt Brace, 1968. An early exposure of phallic criticism.

Felman, Shoshana. *La Folie et la chose littéraire.* Paris: Seuil, 1978. English trans. forthcoming from Cornell University Press. A wide-ranging collection of essays by a member of the "école de Yale."

——. "Rereading Femininity." *Yale French Studies*, 62 (1981), 19–44. On Balzac's *La Fille aux yeux d'or.*

——. *Le Scandale du corps parlant: Don Juan avec Austin ou La séduction en deux langues.* Paris: Seuil, 1980. English trans. forthcoming from Cornell University Press. An Austinian reading of Molière and a Lacanian reading of Austin.

——. "Turning the Screw of Interpretation." *Yale French Studies*, 55/56 (1977), 94–207. A remarkable analysis of the text and readings of *The Turn of the Screw.*

——. "Women and Madness: The Critical Phallacy." *Diacritics*, 5:4 (1975), 2–10. A feminist reading of Balzac.

Ferguson, Frances. "Reading Heidegger: Jacques Derrida and Paul de Man." *Boundary 2*, 4 (1976), 593–610.

——. *Wordsworth: Language as Counter-Spirit.* New Haven: Yale University Press, 1977.

Fetterly, Judith. *The Resisting Reader: A Feminist Approach to American Fiction.* Bloomington: Indiana University Press, 1978. A critique of major novels and a call to resistance.

Fiedler, Leslie. *Love and Death in the American Novel.* New York: Criterion, 1960.

Finas, Lucette. "Le Coup de D. e(s)t judas." In Finas et al., *Ecarts: Quatre essais à propos de Jacques Derrida.* Paris: Fayard, 1973, 9–105. A heterogeneous discussion of Derrida.

Fish, Stanley. *Is There a Text in This Class?* Cambridge: Harvard University Press, 1980. Important essays displaying the growth of a critic's mind.

——. *Self-Consuming Artifacts: The Experience of Seventeenth-Century Literature.* Berkeley: University of California Press, 1972.

——. *Surprised by Sin: The Reader in Paradise Lost.* Berkeley: University of California Press, 1967. An early work of reader-response criticism.

——. "Why No One's Afraid of Wolfgang Iser." *Diacritics*, 11:1 (1981), 2–13. A critique of Iser's theory of reading.

Fokkema, D. W., and Elrud Kunne-Ibsch. *Theories of Literature in the Twentieth Century: Structuralism, Marxism, Aesthetics of Reception, Semiotics*. New York: St. Martin, 1977. A useful overview.

Forrest-Thomson, Veronica. *Poetic Artifice: A Theory of Twentieth-Century Poetry*. Manchester: University of Manchester Press, 1978. On the radical formalism of poetic language.

Frank, Manfred. *Das Sagbare und das Unsagbare: Studien zur neuesten französischen Hermeneutik und Texttheorie*. Frankfurt: Suhrkamp, 1980. Takes Schleiermacher as the point of departure for discussions of Sartre, Lacan, and Derrida.

Freud, Sigmund. *Complete Psychological Works*, ed. James Strachey. London: Hogarth, 1953–74. 24 vols.

Fynsk, Christopher. "A Decelebration of Philosophy." *Diacritics*, 8:2 (1978), 80–90. A fine review of *Qui a peur de la philosophie?*

Gasché, Rodolphe. "Deconstruction as Criticism." *Glyph*, 6 (1979), 177–216. Attributes to deconstructive critics a misunderstanding of Derrida.

——. "The Scene of Writing: A Deferred Outset." *Glyph*, 1 (1977), 150–71. On *Moby-Dick*.

——. "'Setzung' and 'Ubersetzung': Notes on Paul de Man." *Diacritics*, 11:4 (1981), 36–57. On *Allegories of Reading*.

——. "La Sorcière métapsychologique." *Digraphe*, 3 (1974), 83–122. On Freud's puzzling relation to metapsychological speculation.

Gilbert, Sandra M., and Susan Gubar. *The Madwoman in the Attic: The Woman Writer and the Nineteenth Century Literary Imagination*. New Haven: Yale University Press, 1979.

Girard, René. Interview. *Diacritics*, 8:1 (1978), 31–54.

——. *Mensonge romantique et vérité romanesque*. Paris: Grasset, 1961. English trans.: *Deceit, Desire, and the Novel: The Self and Other in Literary Structure*. Baltimore: Johns Hopkins University Press, 1965. A theory of the novel based on mimetic desire.

——. *"To Double Business Bound": Essays in Literature, Mimesis, and Anthropology*. Baltimore: Johns Hopkins University Press, 1978.

——. *La Violence et le sacré*. Paris: Grasset, 1972. English trans.: *Violence and the Sacred*. Baltimore: Johns Hopkins University Press, 1977. Discussions of the scapegoat and the origins of culture.

Gouldner, Alvin, W. *The Dialectic of Ideology and Technology*. New York: Seabury, 1976.

Graff, Gerald. *Literature against Itself: Literary Ideas in Modern Society*. Chicago: University of Chicago Press, 1977. Attacks contemporary criticism as a continuation of the New Criticism adapted to the postindustrial capitalism it pretends to oppose.

Hamon, Philippe. "Texte littéraire et métalangage." *Poétique*, 31 (1977), 261–84. On metalinguistic functions within the work.

Harari, Josué, ed. *Textual Strategies: Perspectives in Post-Structuralist Criticism*. Ithaca: Cornell University Press, 1979. A critical miscellany.

——. *Structuralists and Structuralisms*. Ithaca: Diacritics, 1971. A bibliography.

Hartman, Geoffrey. *Criticism in the Wilderness*. New Haven: Yale University Press, 1980. Essays on the possibilities of criticism.

——. *The Fate of Reading and Other Essays*. Chicago: University of Chicago Press, 1975.

——. *Saving the Text: Literature/Derrida/Philosophy*. Baltimore: Johns Hopkins University Press, 1981. On *Glas* and the possibilities of commentary.

Heidegger, Martin. "The Question Concerning Technology." *Basic Writings*, ed. D. F. Krell. New York: Harper, 1977, pp. 283–318. On "Enframing."

Heilbrun, Carolyn. "Millett's *Sexual Politics*: A Year Later." *Aphra*, 2 (1971), 38–47.

Hertz, Neil. "Freud and the Sandman." In *Textual Strategies*, ed. J. Harari. Ithaca: Cornell University Press, 1979, pp. 296–321.

——. "The Notion of Blockage in the Literature of the Sublime." In *Psychoanalysis and the Question of the Text*, ed. Geoffrey Hartman. Baltimore: Johns Hopkins University Press, 1978, pp. 62–85. The functioning of the scenario of the Sublime in a wide range of situations.

——. "Recognizing Casaubon." *Glyph*, 6 (1979), 24–41. On author-surrogates and *Middlemarch*.

Hirsch, E. D. *The Aims of Interpretation*. Chicago: University of Chicago Press, 1976. A defense of his version of hermeneutics.

Hofstader, Douglas. *Gödel, Escher, Bach: An Eternal Golden Braid*. New York: Basic, 1979. Explorations of self-referentiality.

Hohendahl, Peter Uwe. *The Institution of Criticism*. Ithaca: Cornell University Press, 1982. A social history of German criticism and reflection on criticism as an institution in the modern age.

Holland, Norman. *5 Readers Reading*. New Haven: Yale University Press, 1975. Discussion of their personalities and responses.

——. "Unity Identity Text Self." *PMLA*, 90 (1975), 813–22. A summary of his theory of reading.

Horton, Susan. *Interpreting Interpreting: Interpreting Dickens' "Dombey."* Baltimore: Johns Hopkins University Press, 1979. A metacritical inquiry.

Hoy, David Couzins. *The Critical Circle: Literature and History in Con-*

temporary Hermeneutics. Berkeley: University of California Press, 1978. Hirsch, Gadamer, and modern critical theory.

Ingarden, Roman. *The Cognition of the Literary Work of Art*. Evanston: Northwestern University Press, 1973. A phenomenological study.

——. *The Literary Work of Art*. Evanston: Northwestern University Press, 1973. A translation of the 1931 classic which defines the strata of the work of art.

Irigaray, Luce. *Ce Sexe qui n'en est pas un*. Paris: Minuit, 1977. Feminist essays on psychoanalysis and writing.

——. *Speculum, de l'autre femme*. Paris: Minuit, 1974. Primarily a critique of Freud's theory of sexuality. English trans. forthcoming from Cornell University Press.

Iser, Wolfgang. *The Act of Reading: A Theory of Aesthetic Response*. Baltimore: Johns Hopkins University Press, 1978.

——. *The Implied Reader: Patterns of Communication in Prose Fiction from Bunyan to Beckett*. Baltimore: Johns Hopkins University Press, 1974.

——. Interview. *Diacritics*, 10:2 (1980), 57–74.

——. "Talk like Whales." *Diacritics*, 11:3 (1981), 82–7. Response to Fish.

Jacobs, Carol. *The Dissimulating Harmony: The Image of Interpretation in Nietzsche, Rilke, Artaud, and Benjamin*. Baltimore: Johns Hopkins University Press, 1978.

——. "The (too) Good Soldier: 'a real story.'" *Glyph* 3 (1978), 32–51. On Ford Madox Ford.

Jacobus, Mary. "Sue the Obscure." *Essays in Criticism*, 25 (1975), 304–28. A response to Millett.

——, ed. *Women Writing and Writing about Women*. London: Croom Helm, 1979. Essays on women writers and feminist criticism.

James, Henry. *Selected Literary Criticism*, ed. Morris Shapira. New York: Horizon, 1964.

Jameson, Fredric. "Ideology of the Text." *Salmagundi*, 31 (1975–6), 204–46. A critique of recent theory.

——. *The Political Unconscious: Narrative as a Socially Symbolic Act*. Ithaca: Cornell University Press, 1980. A major work of Marxist criticism.

Jardine, Alice. "Pre-Texts for the Transatlantic Feminist." *Yale French Studies*, 62 (1981), 220–36. Introduces French feminist theory.

Jauss, Hans Robert. *Aesthetische Erfahrung und literarische Hermeneutik*. I. *Versuche im Feld der aesthetischen Erfahrung*. Munich: Fink, 1977. Work on a theory of aesthetic affect or experience.

——. *Literaturgeschichte als Provokation*. Frankfurt: Suhrkamp, 1970. Partial English trans.: "Literary History as a Challenge to Literary Theory." In *New Directions in Literary History*, ed. Ralph Cohen. Baltimore: Johns Hopkins University Press, 1974, pp. 11–41. On the aesthetics of reception.

Johnson, Barbara. *The Critical Difference: Essays in the Contemporary Rhetoric of Reading*. Baltimore: Johns Hopkins University Press, 1980. Deconstructive readings of Baudelaire, Barthes, Mallarmé, Melville, and Lacan/Derrida/Poe.

———. *Défigurations du langage poétique*. Paris: Flammarion, 1979. On Baudelaire's and Mallarmé's prose poems.

———. "The Frame of Reference: Poe, Lacan, Derrida." In *Psychoanalysis and the Question of the Text*. ed. Geoffrey Hartman. Baltimore: John Hopkins University Press, 1978, pp. 149–71. A shortened version of the essay in *The Critical Difference* but with some new and valuable formulations.

———. "Nothing Fails like Success." *SCE Reports*, 8 (1980), 7–16. On criticisms of deconstruction and its future strategies.

Kamuf, Peggy. "Writing like a Woman." In *Women and Language in Literature and Society*, ed. S. McConnell-Ginet et al. New York: Praeger, 1980, pp. 284–99. A feminist essay focused on *Les Lettres portugaises*.

Kant, Immanuel. *Critique of Judgment*. Oxford: Oxford University Press, 1952.

Klein, Richard. "The Blindness of Hyperboles; the Ellipses of Insight." *Diacritics*, 3:2 (1973), 33–44. On de Man.

———. "Kant's Sunshine." *Diacritics*, 11:2 (1981), 26–41. The "heliopoetics" of Kant's aesthetics.

Kofman, Sarah. *Aberrations: Le devenir-femme d'Auguste Comte*. Paris: Flammarion, 1978. A resourceful reading of Comte's life and works.

———. *L'Enfance de l'art: Une interprétation de l'esthétique freudienne*. Paris: Payot, 1972.

———. *L'Enigme de la femme: La femme dans les textes de Freud*. Paris: Galilée, 1980. English trans. (of pp. 60–80): "The Narcissistic Woman: Freud and Girard." *Diacritics*, 10:3 (1980), 36–45. (of pp. 83–97): "Freud's Suspension of the Mother." *Enclitic*, 4:2 (1980), 17–28. Complete English trans. forthcoming from Cornell University Press. A deconstructive reading.

———. *Nerval: Le Charme de la répétition*. Lausanne: L'Age d'homme, 1979.

———. *Nietzsche et la métaphore*. Paris: Payot, 1972. An early study emphasizing rhetoric.

———. *Nietzsche et la scène philosophique*. Paris: Union générale d'éditions, 1979 Lucid readings of numerous texts.

———. "Un philosophe 'unheimlich.'" In L. Finas et al., *Ecarts: Quartre essais à propos de Jacques Derrida*. Paris: Fayard, 1973, pp. 107–204. On Derrida.

——. *Quatre Romans analytiques*. Paris: Galilée, 1974. Studies of four Freudian analyses.

——. *Le Respect des femmes*. Paris: Galilée, 1982. On women in Kant and Rousseau.

——. "Vautour rouge: Le double dans *Les Elixirs du diable* d'Hoffmann." In S. Agacinski et al., *Mimesis des articulations*. Paris: Flammarion, 1976, pp. 95–164.

Kolodny, Annette. "Reply to Commentaries: Women Writers, Literary Historians, and Martian Readers." *New Literary History*, 11 (1980), 587–92. A defense of feminist views on literary history and literary value.

——. "Some Notes on Defining a 'Feminist Literary Criticism.'" *Critical Inquiry*, 2 (1975), 75–92.

Krieger, Murray, and Larry Dembo, ed. *Directions for Criticism: Structuralism and Its Alternatives*. Madison: University of Wisconsin Press, 1977. Essays critical of directions taken by recent theory.

——. *Theory of Criticism: A Tradition and Its System*. Baltimore: Johns Hopkins University Press, 1976.

Kristeva, Julia. *Desire in Language*. New York: Columbia University Press, 1980. Essays from *Semiotike* and *Polylogue*.

——. "La Femme, ce n'est jamais ça." *Tel Quel*, 59 (1974), 19–24. Partial English trans.: "Woman Cannot Be Defined." In *New French Feminisms*, ed. Elaine Marks and Isabelle de Courtivron. Amherst: University of Massachusetts Press, 1980, pp. 137–41. An interview.

——, ed. *Folle Vérité*. Paris: Seuil, 1979. Papers on truth in psychotic discourse.

——. *Polylogue*. Paris: Seuil, 1977. Includes theoretical essays on art, the novel, and the subject.

Lacan, Jacques. *Ecrits*. Paris: Seuil, 1966. Partial English trans.: *Ecrits: A Selection*. London: Tavistock, 1977.

——. *Les Quatre Concepts fondamentaux de la psychanalyse*. (Le Séminaire, livre xi). Paris: Seuil, 1973. English trans.: *The Four Fundamental Concepts of Psycho-analysis*. London: Tavistock, 1977.

Lacoue-Labarthe, Philippe. "Note sur Freud et la représentation." *Digraphe*, 3 (1974), 70–81. English trans.: "*Theatrum Analyticum*." *Glyph*, 2 (1977), pp. 122–43. On Freud's "Psychopathic Characters on the Stage."

——. "Typographie." In S. Agacinski et al., *Mimesis des articulations*. Paris: Flammarion, 1976, pp. 165–270. Partial English trans.: "Mimesis and Truth." *Diacritics*, 8:1 (1978), 10–23. On Plato, Nietzsche, Heidegger, and Girard.

——, and Jean-Luc Nancy. *L'Absolu littéraire*. Paris: Seuil, 1978. Texts and discussion of the literary theory of German romanticism.

———, eds. *Les Fins de l'homme: A partir du travail de Jacques Derrida.* Paris: Galilée, 1981. A 700-page record of the Colloque de Cérisy centered on Derrida. A very rich collection of papers and synopses of the discussions.

———. *Le Titre de la lettre.* Paris: Galilée, 1973. On Lacan.

Lander, Dawn. "Eve among the Indians." In *The Authority of Experience,* ed. Lee Edwards and Arlyn Diamond. Amherst: University of Massachusetts Press, 1977, pp. 194–211. On the image and the reality of frontier women.

Laplanche, Jean. *Vie et mort en psychanalyse.* Paris: Flammarion, 1970. English trans.: *Life and Death in Psychoanalysis.* Baltimore: Johns Hopkins University Press, 1976. A lucid Lacanian reading of Freud.

———, and Serge Leclaire. "The Unconscious: A Psychoanalytic Study." *Yale French Studies,* 48 (1972), 118–75.

Laporte, Roger. "Une Double Stratégie." In L. Finas et al., *Ecarts: Quatre essais à propos de Jacques Derrida,* Paris: Fayard, 1973, pp. 205–63.

Leitch, Vincent B. "The Lateral Dance: The Deconstructive Criticism of J. Hillis Miller." *Critical Inquiry,* 6 (1980), 593–607.

Lentricchia, Frank. *After the New Criticism.* Chicago: University of Chicago Press, 1980. Discussion of recent critical theory and of four "exemplary" theorists.

Lenz, Carolyn, et al., eds. *The Woman's Part: Feminist Criticism of Shakespeare.* Urbana: University of Illinois Press, 1980.

Lévesque, Claude. *L'Etrangeté du texte: Essai sur Nietzsche, Freud, Blanchot, et Derrida.* Paris: Union générale d'éditions, 1978.

Lewis, Philip E. "The Post-Structuralist Condition." *Diacritics,* 12:1 (1982), 1–24. A critical evaluation of this problematic concept.

Lyons, John. *Semantics.* Cambridge: Cambridge University Press, 1977. 2 vols.

Lyotard, Jean-François. *La Condition post-moderne.* Paris: Minuit, 1979. On the distribution of communicational roles and techniques of legitimation.

MacCannell, Dean. *The Tourist.* New York: Schocken, 1976. A theory of "modernity," studying its structures of meaning and authenticity through tourism.

MacCannell, Juliet Flower. "Nature and Self-Love: A Reinterpretation of Rousseau's 'passion primitive.'" *PMLA,* 92 (1978), 890–902.

———. "Phallacious Theories of the Subject." *Semiotica,* 30 (1980), 359–74.

Macksey, Richard, and Eugenio Donato, eds. *The Structuralist Controversy: The Languages of Criticism and the Sciences of Man.* Baltimore: Johns Hopkins University Press, 1970. Proceedings of an important colloquium.

Mailer, Norman. *The Prisoner of Sex*. Boston: Little, Brown, 1971. A defense of sexism.

Mailloux, Steven. *Interpretive Conventions: The Reader in the Study of American Fiction*. Ithaca: Cornell University Press, 1982. An account of reader-response criticism and the relevance of the study of response to various critical projects.

———. "Learning to Read: Interpretation and Reader-Response Criticism." *Studies in the Literary Imagination*, 12 (1979), 93–107. On the uses of response in interpretation.

Marin, Louis. *La Critique du discours: Etudes sur la "Logique de Port-Royal" et les "Pensées" de Pascal*. Paris: Minuit, 1975. Pascal's writing as a deconstruction of Cartesian logic.

———. *Le Récit est un piège*. Paris: Minuit, 1978. On the power of narrativity.

Markiewicz, Henryk. "Places of Indeterminacy in a Literary Work." In *Roman Ingarden and Contemporary Polish Aesthetics*, ed. Piotr Graff and Slaw Krzemien-Ojak. Warsaw: Polish Scientific Publishers, 1975, pp. 159–72.

Marks, Elaine. "Women and Literature in France." *Signs*, 3 (1978), 832–42.

———, and Isabelle de Courtivron, eds. *New French Feminisms*. Amherst: University of Massachusetts Press, 1980.

Martin, Wallace. "Literary Critics and Their Discontents: A Response to Geoffrey Hartman." *Critical Inquiry*, 4 (1977), 397–406. A gentle critique of Hartman's position.

McDonald, Christie V. "Jacques Derrida's Reading of Rousseau." *The Eighteenth Century*, 20 (1970), 82–95.

Mehlman, Jeffrey. *Cataract: A Study of Diderot*. Middletown: Wesleyan University Press, 1979. Establishes surprising connections through *cataracts* of all sorts.

———. "How to Read Freud on Jokes: The Critic as Schadchen." *New Literary History*, 4 (1975), 439–61.

———. "On Tear-Work: *L'ar de Valéry*." *Yale French Studies*, 52 (1975). 152–73. Reveals an important signifying complex in Valéry's poetry.

———. *Revolution and Repetition: Marx/Hugo/Balzac*. Berkeley: University of California Press, 1977. An intertextual reading.

———. "Trimethylamin: Notes on Freud's Specimen Dream." *Diacritics*, 6:1 (1976), 42–45.

Michaels, Walter Benn. "The Interpreter's Self: Peirce on the Cartesian 'Subject.'" *Georgia Review*, 31 (1977), 383–402. Argues that "subjectivity" in interpretation is a false problem.

———. "'Saving the Text': Reference and Belief." *MLN*, 93 (1978), 771–93. On the role of beliefs in interpretation.

——. "*Walden*'s False Bottoms." *Glyph*, 1 (1977), 132–49. Analysis of its contradictions.

Miller, J. Hillis. "Ariachne's Broken Woof." *Georgia Review*, 31 (1977), 44–60. Contradiction in *Troilus and Cressida*.

——. "Ariadne's Thread: Repetition and the Narrative Line." *Critical Inquiry*, 3 (1976), 57–78.

——. "A 'Buchstäbliches' Reading of *The Elective Affinities*." *Glyph*, 6 (1979), 1–23.

——. "The Critic as Host." *Critical Inquiry*, 3 (1977), 439–47. On criticism and parasitism. Expanded version in Bloom et al., *Deconstruction and Criticism*. New York: Seabury, 1979, pp. 217–253.

——. "Deconstructing the Deconstructors." *Diacritics*, 5:2 (1975), 24–31. Review of Riddel, *The Inverted Bell*.

——. *Fiction and Repetition: Seven English Novels*. Cambridge: Harvard University Press, 1982. Analyzes their resistance to their own totalizing forces.

——. "Narrative and History." *ELH*, 41 (1974), 455–73. How narratives undo their historical claims.

——. "Stevens' Rock and Criticism as Cure." *Georgia Review*, 30 (1976), 5–33 (part I) and 330–48 (part II). A reading of Stevens, followed by a discussion of "canny" and "uncanny" criticism.

Millett, Kate. *Sexual Politics*. New York: Doubleday, 1970. A critique of domination in sexual relations and in their literary representations.

Mitchell, Juliet. *Psychoanalysis and Feminism*. New York: Random House, 1975. A pioneering study.

Nancy, Jean-Luc. *Le Discours de la syncope*, I: *Logodaedalus*. Paris: Flammarion, 1976. On Kant.

——. *Ego Sum*. Paris: Flammarion, 1979. Partial English trans.: "Larvatus Pro Deo." *Glyph*, 2 (1977), 14–36. Deconstructive investigations of Cartesian problems.

——. *La Remarque spéculative*. Paris: Galilée, 1973. On Hegel.

——. "Le Ventriloque." In S. Agacinski et al., *Mimesis des articulations*. Paris: Flammarion, 1975, pp. 271–38. On Plato.

Nelson, Cary. "The Psychology of Criticism, or What Can Be Said." In *Psychoanalysis and the Question of the Text*, ed. G. Hartman. Baltimore: Johns Hopkins University Press, 1978, pp. 86–114. On conventions governing the critic's self-exposure.

Nietzsche, Friedrich. *Werke*. Ed. Karl Schlechta, Munich: Hanser, 1966. 3 vols.

Parker, Andrew. "Of Politics and Limits: Derrida Re-Marx." *SCE Reports*, 8 (1980), 83–104. A valuable discussion of deconstruction and Marxism.

——. "Taking Sides (On History): Derrida Re-Marx." *Diacritics*, 11:3 (1981), 57–73. Review of Lentricchia, *After the New Criticism*.

Pautrat, Bernard. "Politique en scène: Brecht." In Agacinski et al., *Mimesis des articulations*. Paris: Flammarion, 1976, pp. 339–52.

——. *Versions du soleil: Figures et système de Nietzsche*. Paris: Seuil, 1971.

Peirce, Charles Sanders. *Collected Papers*. Ed. Charles Hartshorne and Paul Weiss. Cambridge: Harvard University Press, 1931–58. 8 vols.

Phillips, William. "The State of Criticism: New Criticism to Structuralism." *Partisan Review*, 47 (1980), 372–85.

Prince, Gerald. "Introduction à l'étude du narrataire." *Poétique*, 14 (1973), 178–96. English trans.: "Introduction to the Study of the Narratee." In *Reader-Response Criticism*, ed. Jane Tompkins. Baltimore: Johns Hopkins University Press, 1980, pp. 7–25. Introduces the structural counterpart of the narrator.

Rabinowitz, Peter. "Truth in Fiction: A Reexamination of Audiences." *Critical Inquiry*, 4 (1977), 121–42. Distinguishes the different audiences presupposed by literary works.

Rand, Nicolas. "'Vous joyeuse melodie—nourrie de crasse': A propos d'une transposition des *Fleurs du Mal* par Stephan George." *Poétique* (1982). Intertextual translation as incorporation.

Rand, Richard. "Geraldine." *Glyph*, 3 (1978), 74–97. A deconstructive reading of Coleridge.

Reichert, John. *Making Sense of Literature*. Chicago: University of Chicago Press, 1977. Defends a "common sense" approach involving few special procedures or conventions.

Rey, Jean-Michel. *L'Enjeu des signes: Lecture de Nietzsche*. Paris: Seuil, 1965.

——. "Note en marge sur un texte en cours." In Lucette Finas et al., *Ecarts: Quatre Essais à propos de Jacques Derrida*. Paris: Fayard, 1973, pp. 265–95.

——. *Parcours de Freud: Economie et discours*. Paris: Galilée, 1974.

Riddel, Joseph. "Decentering the Image: The 'Project' of 'American' Poetics?" In *Textual Strategies*, ed. J. Harari. Ithaca: Cornell University Press, 1979, pp. 322–58.

——. *The Inverted Bell: Modernism and the Counter Poetics of William Carlos Williams*. Baton Rouge: Louisiana State University Press, 1974. Draws extensively upon Heidegger and Derrida.

——. "'Keep Your Pecker Up'—*Paterson Five* and the Question of Metapoetry." *Glyph*, 8 (1981), 203–31.

——. "A Miller's Tale." *Diacritics*, 5:3 (1975), 56–65. A response to Miller's critique.

Riffaterre, Michael. *La Production du texte*. Paris: Seuil, 1979. Essays on a range of poetic devices and their intertextual relations.

——. *Semiotics of Poetry*. Bloomington: Indiana University Press, 1978. A theory of reading and interpretation of nineteenth- and twentieth-century French poems.

——. "Syllepsis." *Critical Inquiry*, 6 (1980), 625–38. A reading of the conclusion of *Glas*.

Rorty, Richard. "Freud, Morality, Hermeneutics." *New Literary History*, 12 (1980), 177–86. On the difficulties of assimilating Freud's radical redescriptions.

——. *Philosophy and the Mirror of Nature*. Princeton: Princeton University Press, 1980. A critique of philosophy as a foundational discipline.

——. "Philosophy as a Kind of Writing: An Essay on Derrida." *New Literary History*, 10 (1978), 141–60.

——. "Professionalized Philosophy and Transcendentalist Culture." *Georgia Review*, 30 (1976), 757–71. On philosophy's relinquishment of its cultural role.

Ryan, Michael. *Marxism and Deconstruction*. Baltimore: Johns Hopkins University Press, 1982. Proposes political uses of deconstruction.

——. "The Question of Autobiography in Cardinal Newman's *Apologia pro vita sua*." *Georgia Review*, 31 (1977), 672–99. A deconstructive reading.

——. "Self-Evidence." *Diacritics*, 10:2 (1980), 2–16. A critique of reflexivity in theories of autobiography.

Said, Edward. *Beginnings: Intention and Method*. New York: Basic, 1975. Influential discussions of fictional and nonfictional writings.

——. "The Problem of Textuality: Two Exemplary Positions." *Critical Inquiry*, 4 (1978), 673–714. Compares Derrida and Foucault and prefers the latter.

Sartre, Jean-Paul. *Qu'est-ce que la littérature?* Paris: Gallimard, 1948. English trans.: *What Is Literature?* London: Methuen, 1950. Contains a remarkable capsule history of French literature based on the audience for which writers wrote.

Saussure, Ferdinand de. *Cours de linguistique générale*. Paris: Payot, 1973. English trans.: *Course in General Linguistics*. London: Peter Owen, 1960.

Schor, Naomi. "Female Paranoia: The Case of Psychoanalytic Feminist Criticism." *Yale French Studies*, 62 (1981), 204–19.

Searle, John. "Reiterating the Differences: A Reply to Derrida." *Glyph*, 1 (1977), 198–208. A critique of Derrida's "Signature événement contexte."

——. *Speech Acts: An Essay in the Philosophy of Language.* Cambridge: Cambridge University Press, 1969.

Serres, Michel. *Hermes.* Paris: Minuit, 1968–77. 4 vols. Original essays on a wide range of literary and nonliterary writings.

——. *Le Parasite.* Paris: Grasset, 1980. A study that brings together various sorts of parasitism.

Showalter, Elaine. "Feminist Criticism in the Wilderness." *Critical Inquiry,* 8 (1981), 179–206. A stock-taking.

——. "Towards a Feminist Poetics." In *Women Writing and Writing About Women,* ed. M. Jacobs. London: Croom Helm, 1979, pp. 22–41.

——. "The Unmanning of the Mayor of Casterbridge." In *Critical Approaches to the Fiction of Thomas Hardy,* ed. Dale Kramer. London: Macmillan, 1979, pp. 99–115. A feminist reading of the novel.

——. "Women and the Literary Curriculum." *College English,* 32 (1971), 855–62.

Slatoff, Walter. *With Respect to Readers: Dimensions of Literary Response.* Ithaca: Cornell University Press, 1970. One of the first works to emphasize readers.

Smith, Barbara Herrnstein. "Narrative Versions, Narrative Theories." *Critical Inquiry,* 7 (1980), 213–36. An incisive critique of theories of narrative.

——. *On the Margins of Discourse: The Relation of Literature to Language.* Chicago: University of Chicago Press, 1979.

Sosnoski, James. "Reading Acts and Reading Warrants: Some Implications of Reader's Responding to Joyce's Portrait of Stephen." *James Joyce Quarterly,* 16 (1978/79), 42–63. Attempts to account for varying interpretations.

Spivak, Gayatri Chakravorty. "Draupadi," by Mahasveta Devi. Translated with a Foreword by Gayatri Spivak. *Critical Inquiry,* 8 (1981), 381–402. Critical commentary on a story by a Bengali feminist writer.

——. "Finding Feminist Readings: Dante-Yeats." *Social Text,* 3 (1980), 73–87.

——. "French Feminism in an International Frame." *Yale French Studies,* 62 (1981), 154–84. How can French feminism relate to Third World feminism?

——. "Revolutions That as Yet Have No Model: Derrida's *Limited Inc.*" *Diacritics,* 10:4 (1980), 29–49.

Sprinker, Michael. "Criticism as Reaction." *Diacritics,* 10:3 (1980), 2–14. On Graff's *Literature against Itself.*

——. "Textual Politics: Foucault and Derrida." *Boundary 2,* 8 (1980), 75–98. A Foucauldian critique.

Stewart, Susan. *Nonsense: Aspects of Intertextuality in Folklore and Literature.* Baltimore: Johns Hopkins University Press, 1979. On techniques of nonsense, including self-reference and repetition.

——. "The Pickpocket: A Study in Tradition and Allusion." *MLN*, 95 (1980), 1127–54.

Strickland, Geoffrey. *Structuralism or Criticism: Some Thoughts on How We Read.* Cambridge: Cambridge University Press, 1981. Defends authorial meaning against an ill-defined structuralism.

Suleiman, Susan, and Inge Crosman, eds. *The Reader in the Text: Essays on Audience and Interpretation.* Princeton: Princeton University Press, 1980.

Sussman, Henry. *Franz Kafka: Geometrician of Metaphor.* Madison: Coda Press, 1979. A deconstructive reading.

——. "The Deconstructor as Politician: Melville's *Confidence-Man*." *Glyph*, 4 (1978), 32–56.

Thompson, Michael. *Rubbish Theory: The Creation and Destruction of Value.* Oxford: Oxford University Press, 1979. A theory of value based on the marginal.

Tompkins, Jane. "Sentimental Power: *Uncle Tom's Cabin* and the Politics of Literary History." *Glyph*, 8 (1981), 79–102. A feminist critique of the ideology of literary history and a new perspective on "sentimental" fiction.

——. "The Reader in History: The Changing Shape of Literary Response." In *Reader-Response Criticism*, ed. Tompkins. Baltimore: Johns Hopkins University Press, 1980, pp. 201–32. On changing notions of response in criticism from classical to modern times. Included in an excellent anthology of modern response theory.

Trilling, Lionel. *The Opposing Self.* New York: Viking, 1955.

Turkle, Sherry. *Psychoanalytic Politics: Freud's French Revolution.* New York: Basic Books, 1978. An informative history of Lacanian movements.

Ulmer, Gregory. "The Post-Age." *Diacritics*, 11:3 (1981), 39–56. An authoritative review of Derrida's *La Carte postale*.

Vance, Eugene. "Mervelous Signals: Poetics, Sign Theory, and Politics in Chaucer's *Troilus*." *New Literary History*, 10 (1979), 293–337.

Warminski, Andrzej. "Pre-positional By-play." *Glyph*, 3 (1978), 98–117. On *Beispiel* in Hegel.

——. "Reading for Example: Sense-Certainty in Hegel's *Phenomenology of Spirit*." *Diacritics*, 11:2 (1981), 83–94.

Warning, Rainer. "Rezeptionsästhetik als literaturwissenschaftliche Pragmatik." In *Rezeptionsästhetik*, ed. R. Warning. Munich: Fink, 1975, pp. 9–41. A good theoretical explanation in an excellent anthology, primarily of material from the Konstanz School.

Weber, Samuel. "Closure and Exclusion." *Diacritics*, 10:2 (1980), 35–46. On Peirce.

——. "The Divaricator: Remarks on Freud's *Witz*." *Glyph*, 1 (1977), 1–27.

——. *Freud-Legende: Drei Studien zum psychoanalitischen Denken.* Olten and Freiburg: Walter Verlag, 1979.

——. "It." *Glyph*, 4(1978), 1–29. On iterability in Derrida and repetition in Freud.

——. "Saussure and the Apparition of Language." *MLN*, 91 (1976), 913–38.

——. "The Sideshow, or: Remarks on a Canny Moment." *MLN*, 88 (1973), 1102–33.

——. "The Struggle for Control: Wolfgang Iser's Third Dimension." University of Strasbourg. Unpublished m/s. The dependency of Iser's theory on the ultimate authority of the author.

Wellek, René, and Austin Warren. *Theory of Literature.* New York: Harcourt Brace, 1956.

White, Hayden. *Tropics of Discourse: Essays in Cultural Criticism.* Baltimore: Johns Hopkins University Press, 1978. On rhetoric, history, and critical theory.

Wilden, Anthony. *System and Structure: Essays on Communication and Exchange.* London: Tavistock, 1972. Structuralist and psychoanalytic studies of a wide range of texts and problems.

Wittgenstein, Ludwig. *Lectures and Conversations on Aesthetics, Psychology and Religious Belief.* Oxford: Blackwell, 1966.

——. *On Certainty.* Oxford: Blackwell, 1969.

Woolf, Virginia. *Collected Essays.* London: Hogarth, 1966. 4 vols.

INDEX

References to works are indexed under their authors.

Abraham, Nicolas, 190–191, 209–210
Abrams, M. H., 130n, 177, 200, 222, 269
Adams, Maurianne, 44
Aesthetic judgment, 193–199
Allegory, 185, 214, 257–259
Altieri, Charles, 130n
Ambiguity, 81, 234, 240
Anasemia, 209–212
Aporia, 23, 96, 109, 134, 155, 221, 259
Aristotle, 35–36, 147
Artaud, Antonin, 184
Austin, J. L., 110–125, 128, 153, 214, 216, 261

Balzac, Honoré de, 62–63, 174
Barth, John, 34
Barthes, Roland, 25–26, 31–35, 38–39, 70, 222–223, 241
Baudelaire, Charles, 261
Beauvoir, Simone de, 46–47
Bercovitch, Sacvan, 56
Blanchot, Maurice, 137, 205, 273
Bleich, David, 64–65
Blindness, and insight, 80–81, 272–278
Bloom, Harold, 29, 60n, 79–80, 175, 179
Booth, Stephen, 35, 69
Booth, Wayne, 7–8, 132n, 177
Boulez, Pierre, 37
Brenkman, John, 19, 252–257

Bronte, Charlotte, 44
Brooks, Cleanth, 36, 201–205, 218, 234
Brooks, Peter, 160n
Burke, Kenneth, 177
Burt, Ellen, 248n

Canny and uncanny criticism, 23–28
Carroll, David, 160n
Causality, deconstruction of, 86–88
Cérisy, Colloque de, 228n
Chase, Cynthia, 160n, 191n, 248n
Cixous, Hélène, 160n, 165, 173
Close reading, 220, 242–259
Codes, 32–34
Constative utterances, 112–113, 133–134, 157
Context, 121–125, 128–130, 133, 215–216
Convention, 26, 32–35, 37–38, 74, 78, 79n, 153; and meaning, 111, 114–116, 119–125, 128

Davis, Walter, 31
De Man, Paul, 227–229, 240, 242–251, 257–259, 272–280; on reading and misreading, 80–81, 178, 199, 214, 217; on rhetoric, 134, 148, 183–85
Derrida, Jacques: "L'Age de Hegel," 221; "Avoir l'oreille de la philosophie," 130, 146, 172; La Carte postale, 27n, 137–139, 169; "The Conflict

Derrida, Jacques (*cont.*)
of Faculties," 156–157; *De la grammatologie*, 92–93, 95, 97–109, 158,
166, 183, 184, 189, 208, 212, 214,
217–218, 274; "Différance," 95,
129, 162–163; *La Dissémination*, 88–
89, 134, 142–149, 185–187, 207,
209–212, 218–219; "La Double Séance," 134, 144–149, 185–187,
209–212; "Economimesis," 135,
186, 200; *L'Ecriture et la différence*,
92, 131–134, 140, 164, 184–185,
206; "Entre crochets," 158; *Eperons*,
61n, 167n; "Le Facteur de la vérité," 27n, 139; "Fors," 190–191;
"Freud et la scène de l'écriture," 140,
164; *Glas*, 135–141, 189–192, 210,
221; "Ja, ou le faux bond," 247;
Limited Inc., 93, 117–128, 131, 133;
"Living On," 123, 137, 139; "La Loi
du genre," 196, 205; *Marges*, 86,
95, 111–129, 136, 139, 141, 147–
148, 162–163, 181–184, 216; "La
Mythologie blanche," 147–148;
"Où commence et comment finit
un corps enseignant," 159; "Parergon," 140, 193–199; "La Pharmacie
de Platon," 88–89, 142–149, 218–
219; *Positions*, 85–86, 96–97, 99,
129, 135, 165–166, 173, 179, 188;
"Qual Quelle," 181–184; "Signature
événement contexte," 86, 111–128,
141, 216; "Signéponge," 192; "Spé-
culer—Sur 'Freud,'" 137–139, 169;
"La Structure, le signe et le jeu,"
92, 131–134; "Tympan," 136; *La
Vérité en peinture*, 140–142, 193–199
Descartes, René, 94, 140, 151, 161
Descombes, Vincent, 18, 127
Deutsch, Helene, 262–263
Dewey, John, 152
Diacritics, 227
Différance, 95, 97, 129, 142, 146, 162,
164
Dinnerstein, Dorothy, 53–54, 58, 60
Donato, Eugenio, 25
Donne, John, 201–205
Donoghue, Denis, 228n
Double bind, 80–81, 136, 234, 241
Douglas, Ann, 56

Eagleton, Terry, 207
Eco, Umberto, 37, 70–71, 114

Eliot, George, 249, 259
Eliot, T. S., 36
Ellmann, Mary, 54
Emerson, R. W., 229
Existentialism, 206
Experience, of the reader, 35–36,
39–51, 54, 58, 63–69, 82, 132; of
speech, 107, 109

Felman, Shoshana, 49, 62–63, 116n,
118n, 171, 174, 261, 270–271
Feminist criticism, 30, 42–64, 172–
175, 207; as analysis of male mis-
readings, 54–58; as critique of logo-
centrism, 43–49; and the hypothesis
of a woman reader, 49–56; as a
response of women readers, 43–49
Ferguson, Frances, 248n
Fetterly, Judith, 51–55
Fiedler, Leslie, 51–52
Figurative language, 146–150, 185,
249–250, 256–259, 265–268; *see
also* Metaphor; Metonymy; *and*
Rhetorical reading
Finas, Lucette, 172
Fish, Stanley, 35, 39–41, 65–75, 79
Flaubert, Gustave, 79n
Forrest-Thomson, Veronica, 38–39
Foucault, Michel, 25, 140, 223
Frame, 193–199
Frederick the Great, 261
Freud, Sigmund, 9, 137–138, 140,
159–174, 191, 201, 209–210, 214;
on jokes, 72–73; on patriarchy,
59–60; on "The Sandman," 261–
268; on women, 165–174
Fynsk, Christopher, 157

Gadamer, Hans Georg, 9
Gasché, Rodolphe, 85n, 160n, 205,
228n
General text, 130–131, 157
Genet, Jean, 47, 136, 210–211
Genette, Gérard, 20, 25
Gilbert, Sandra, 50n, 60n, 167n
Gilman, Charlotte, 45
Girard, René, 21, 25, 29–30
Glyph, 227
Gödel, Kurt, 133
Goethe, J. W. von, 269–270
Goffman, Erving, 9
Gouldner, Alvin, 11
GREPH, 157–158
Gynocriticism, 50n

Harari, Josué, 25
Hardy, Thomas, 43–44, 48
Hartman, Geoffrey, 19, 28, 44, 132n, 137n, 191n
Hegel, G. W. F., 85n, 88, 136, 145, 221
Heidegger, Martin, 85n, 88, 139, 148, 198, 272
Heilbrun, Carolyn, 48–49
Hertz, Neil, 18n, 160n, 261–268
Hierarchies, deconstruction of, 85–86, 93, 95, 100–101, 106–108, 113–114, 140–141, 150–151, 159–179, 181–187, 213, 232–234
Hirsch, E. D., 31, 76–77
Historical reality, 105–106
History, and deconstruction, 128–130, 221, 248–249
Hoffmann, E. T. A., 261–268
Hofstader, Douglas, 9, 201n
Hölderlin, Friedrich, 272
Holland, Norman, 64–65, 69–70
Howe, Irving, 43–44
Hugo, Victor, 260–261
Hume, David, 87
Husserl, Edmund, 85n, 88

Illocutionary force, 111–115, 121–128
Indeterminacy, 133–134, 189, 222
Ingarden, Roman, 37
Inside/outside, 107, 143, 192–205
Intention, 111, 115–116, 120n, 122–128, 216–219
Interpretation, as goal of criticism, 20–21, 220–222, 260
Interpretive community, 68
Intertextuality, 32–33, 130–131, 135–136, 157, 182, 199, 266–268
Invagination, 198–199, 205, 223, 241
Irigaray, Luce, 58, 167–169, 173
Irving, Washington, 51–52
Iser, Wolfgang, 34–35, 37, 75–79

Jabès, Edmond, 206
Jacobs, Carol, 242
Jacobus, Mary, 48n
James, Henry, 36, 45, 54–55, 270–271
Jauss, Hans Robert, 275
Johnson, Barbara, 27n, 139, 178, 213, 235–242, 261, 268, 271–272, 280
Joyce, James, 37

Kamuf, Peggy, 57–58, 64
Kant, Immanuel, 135, 156–157, 261; on aesthetic framing, 193–200; on

metaphor, 148; on the sublime, 17, 266
Katz, Jerrold, 116n
Kierkegaard, Søren, 259
Klein, Richard, 261
Kofman, Sarah, 87n, 159n, 169–174
Kolodny, Annette, 45, 51
Kristeva, Julia, 19, 173–175
Kuhn, Thomas, 77

Lacan, Jacques, 9, 26–27, 139, 160n, 167, 172, 261, 271–272
Lacoue-Labarthe, Philippe, 30n, 160n, 182
Lander, Dawn, 45
Language, theory of, 95–103, 107–125, 130–135, 187–192
Laplanche, Jean, 160n, 162n, 163
Lawrence, D. H., 47
Leiris, Michel, 136
Lentricchia, Frank, 12, 22, 42n, 229, 278n
Lévi-Strauss, Claude, 25, 88
Lewis, Philip, 25
Linguistics, 21–23, 96–101, 113, 187–190, 222–224
Literal/figurative, 81, 147–148, 150, 233–234, 246, 249–251
Literary criticism, goals of, 7–8, 219–225
Literary history, 248–249
Literature, notion of, 10–11, 181–185
Logocentrism, 92–94, 99–111, 126, 151–155, 165, 172, 186–187, 216, 269
Lukács, Georg, 273
Lyons, John, 113

MacCannell, Dean, 9
Mailer, Norman, 47–48, 54
Mailloux, Steven, 79n
Mallarmé, Stéphane, 144–146, 209–212
Marginal, 139–141, 154, 215–216, 222–223; see also Supplement
Marks, Elaine, 61n
Marx, Karl, 9, 260–261
Marxism, 221
Marxist criticism, 206–207
Meaning, 76–77, 95–96, 110–134, 189–192, 208–210, 222–224; determinacy or indeterminacy of, 130–134, 189

Mehlman, Jeffrey, 160n, 260–261
Melville, Herman, 235–242, 257, 271, 279–280
Metalanguage, 124–125, 199, 235, 243–247
Metaphor, 60, 146–148, 185, 243–246, 257–258
Metonymy, 60, 87, 243–246
Michaels, Walter, 229–235
Miller, Henry, 47–48
Miller, J. Hillis, 22–24, 27–29, 219, 249, 251, 269–270
Millett, Kate, 47–48
Milton, John, 40, 41, 66–67
Mimesis, 185–187, 190, 200
Misreading, 80–81, 175–180, 184, 214, 220, 272–279
Misunderstanding: *see* Misreading
Mitchell, Juliet, 170
Modernism, 36
Molière, 261
Motivation, of signs, 189–192

Nabokov, Vladimir, 34
Nachträglichkeit, 162–164, 187
Nancy, J.-L., 182, 186
Narcissus, 252–257
Narratee, 34
Narrative structure, 251–259
New Criticism, 8, 19–21, 36–37, 200–205, 218, 220, 224, 229, 273
Newsweek, 227
New York Review of Books, 227–228n
Nietzsche, Friedrich, 23, 86–88, 131, 149, 241, 245
Nouveau roman, 26, 38, 222

Onomatopoeia, 189–190
Open works, 37, 70–71
Organicism, 200–201, 248–249, 273
Ovid, 252–257

Paleonymy, 140–141, 175, 178, 208, 212
Paradox, 81, 94–97, 155, 201–202
Parergon, 137, 193–199, 212
Parker, Andrew, 42n, 192
Pater, Walter, 71
Patriarchy, 58–62
Peirce, C. S., 188
Performative utterance, 80, 112–126, 133–134, 157, 240, 277

Phallogocentrism, 61, 165–167, 172–177; and feminist criticism, 58–62
Pharmakon, 142–144, 218–219
Phillips, William, 18
Philosophy, 8–11, 85–95, 106–109, 142–155; and art, 186–187, 193–202; and literature, 144–150, 181–185; and writing, 88–92, 140, 184
Phonocentrism, 92, 98–103, 106–110
Plato, 58, 88, 100, 142–144, 166, 185–187, 193, 218–219
Poe, E. A., 139
Political strategies, 52–53, 63, 156–159, 172–175, 238–241
Ponge, Francis, 192
Post-structuralism, 22–30, 219–225
Poulet, Georges, 273
Pragmatism, 152–155
Presence, 82, 92–96, 103–109, 115–116, 125–126, 129–131, 161–164, 200–205, 274
Prince, Gerald, 34
Proust, Marcel, 243–245, 257
Psychoanalytic criticism, 139, 206–207, 237, 261–268, 271
Pun, 91–92, 144–149, 190–192, 240

Rabinowitz, Peter, 34
Rand, Nicolas, 191n
Realism, 62
Referentiality, 81, 249–251, 279–280
Reichert, John, 31–32, 67n
Repetition compulsion, 261–268, 270–272
Representation, philosophy as a theory of, 151–153
Rey, Jean-Michel, 160n
Rhetoric, 81, 86–88, 183–184, 242–247
Rhetorical reading, 242–251
Richard, Jean-Pierre, 209
Riffaterre, Michael, 33, 35, 69, 78, 137n, 229
Romanticism, 182, 185, 248–249, 277–278
Rorty, Richard, 8–10, 77–78, 89–90, 144, 151–153, 179
Rousseau: de Man on, 80–81, 183–184, 248–251, 257–259, 274–277; Derrida on, 102–106, 140, 183–184, 217–218
Russell, Bertrand, 201–202

Salomé, Lou-Andreas, 262–263
Sartre, Jean-Paul, 76
Saussure, Ferdinand de, 28, 96–101, 110–111, 115, 187–190, 223–224
Scientific ambitions, 21–28, 219–224
Searle, John, 110–111, 117–120, 124, 153
Self, 253–257, 266–268
Self-deconstruction, 98, 109, 155, 166, 169–172, 200, 245–247, 256–259
Self-referentiality, 137–139, 200–205, 214–215, 240, 243–247
Semiotics, 22–25, 32–34, 98, 114
Serious/nonserious, 115–123, 181
Serres, Michel, 18
Shakespeare, 46
Shelley, Percy Bysshe, 137, 269, 277–279
Showalter, Elaine, 43–44, 50–51
Sign, 98–102, 136, 187–192, 209–210
Signature, 125–128, 192, 194, 210–211
Signifier/signified, 91–92, 96, 108–109, 188–192
Slatoff, Walter, 41–42
Speech act theory, 111–128, 134–135, 153, 157, 261
Spivak, Gayatri, 49, 85n, 224–225
Stowe, Harriet Beecher, 56–57
Strickland, Geoffrey, 31
Structuralism, 18–30, 32–35, 37–39, 98–100, 110–111, 219–225
Structure and event, 95–97, 110–111, 114
Sublime, 17, 266–267
Suleiman, Susan, 32
Supplement, 102–106, 113, 116n, 126, 135, 140, 164, 166–170, 187, 193–199, 212, 217–218
Swift, Jonathan, 34–35
Symbol, 185

Tausk, Victor, 262–267
Text: determinacy of, 73–78; in stories of reading, 70–73, 82
Thematic criticism, 46–48, 206–212
Theory, status of, 7–11, 19, 128, 133, 219–225
Thompson, Michael, 9
Thoreau, Henry, 229–235
Todorov, Tzvetan, 20, 25
Tompkins, Jane, 36n, 39–40, 56–57
Torok, Maria, 190–191, 209–210
Trace, 94–96, 99
Transference, 27, 139, 204–205, 207, 214–215, 270–272
Trilling, Lionel, 45
Truth, 108, 152–154, 178, 186, 257, 274, 279–280

Uncanny, 24, 261–268
Unconscious, 124, 127, 161–164, 271
Undecidability, 80–81, 96, 145, 202, 234, 246–247
Unity, 33, 78, 199–200, 220–221, 234–235, 246–247, 251–256
Unreadability, 80–81, 257–259, 276–278

Valéry, Paul, 181–183

Warner, William, 149n
Weber, Samuel, 72–73, 75, 160n
Weinberg, Bernard, 36
Wellek, René, 20, 198
Wimsatt, W. K., 39
Wittgenstein, Ludwig, 124, 130–131
Wolfman, the, 163, 190–191
Woman, 42–64, 165–175
Woolf, Virginia, 45, 50
Wordsworth, William, 18, 36, 248
Writing, 88–110, 142–143, 150, 166, 173, 208, 255–256

"Yale School," 29, 278n
Yeats, W. B., 246–247

Zeno, 94–95